THE
BEST
BUSINESS
WRITING
2015

Edited by

Dean Starkman,

Martha M. Hamilton,

and Ryan Chittum

Columbia University Press   New York

Columbia University Press
Publishers Since 1893
New York   Chichester, West Sussex
cup.columbia.edu
Copyright © 2015 Columbia University Press
All rights reserved

ISBN 978-0-231-17017-8

Columbia University Press books are printed on permanent and durable acid-free paper.
This book is printed on paper with recycled content.
Printed in the United States of America

p 10 9 8 7 6 5 4 3 2 1

COVER DESIGN: NOAH ARLOW

References to websites (URLs) were accurate at the time of writing. Neither the author nor Columbia University Press is responsible for URLs that may have expired or changed since the manuscript was prepared.

Contents

Part IV. Business Accountability

Part V. Financial Follies

Introduction
Dean Starkman

This collection of brilliant journalism, the fourth in a series, is a testament to business journalism's resilience in an age of extreme disruption in its own business—media—and to the fact that the business-news ocean is vast and full of unexpected discoveries. It is a particularly rich collection this year; readers will find an astonishing range of topics across an equally astonishing range of outlets. Marcus Stern and Sebastian Jones tell of how the combination of volatile crude oil moving across aging railroad infrastructure has put towns across the continent in danger of disasters like one that happened in Lac-Mégantic, Quebec, not long ago. That piece represents the joint efforts of relatively new players on the business-investigative scene, InsideClimate News and the Weather Channel. Alexis Madrigal in *The Atlantic* uses Google's ambitious, and unnerving, drone-development problem to explore how the search giant really thinks and where it's going. Jordan Weissmann offers a delicious take on the surprising economics of Katz's, the legendary New York deli, for *Slate*, which by now is a digital-news elder statesman.

It's also true that one prominent and important new outlet, the International Consortium of Investigative Journalists, is not represented here—despite publishing some of the most remarkable business journalism of recent years, including 2014's devastating exposé of the British Swiss banking giant, HSBC. Based on a trove of 60,000 leaked files with details on more than 100,000 HSBC clients, a team of journalists from more than 50 countries unearthed secret bank accounts maintained for criminals, traffickers, tax dodgers, and others, including prominent politicians and celebrities. The series, which evoked a clear mea culpa and promise of change from a humbled HSBC, doesn't appear here only because two of the three editors of this volume were deeply involved in producing the series for ICIJ (hint: I wasn't one of them). Their argument that the conflict of interest was too great to include in *Best Business Writing 2015* won out over my strenuous objections, but at least readers should be aware of ICIJ's presence as a new force in journalism.

But it is also true that so-called legacy news organizations are well represented in this volume. The estimable Gretchen Morgenson of the *New York Times* argues trenchantly that the overweening size of the financial sector not only puts taxpayers at risk of "too big to fail" bank collapses but also imposes insidious costs on the real economy by allocating capital not to its highest use but to bubble-prone sectors like real estate. The *Wall Street Journal*'s highly regarded veterans Mark Maremont and Leslie Scism deliver a scintillating read on the fall of a young insurance magnate whose investments included a Caravaggio. Let's not forget Franklin Foer's trenchant explanation of why the Amazon monopoly is bad for the republic, published in the century-old *New Republic* (from which Foer has since resigned over disagreement about its direction). And Bloomberg, founded in the early 1980s, emerged as a global journalism force last year with several enormously interesting stories, led by Zach Mider's exploration of how the richest among us pay so little in taxes. It is correctly headlined, "The Greatest Tax Story Ever Told," and is certainly the only one that includes a tax loophole set to an operetta.

But let's not kid ourselves. Earlier exultations about a flowering of journalism in the age of the Internet have given way to more sober assessments about the difficulties of supporting a full-fledged newsroom on the meager returns from digital sources. A Pew study last year ran the numbers and found that the thirty largest all-digital operations—*Vice, Buzzfeed, Vox, Huffington Post, Business Insider,* and other famous names—account for only 3,000 journalism jobs combined. That is a fifth of what has been lost in the newspaper industry, which still remains backbone of American newsgathering—even in its shrunken, desiccated infirmity. Newspaper advertising is now at the lowest levels on record, considering inflation. And newspapers continue to struggle with declining print revenues and no growth engine to offset the losses. Newspaper subscription revenue fell 3 percent last year, Pew says, throwing cold water on hopes that digital paywalls and other reader-pay devices would provide a floor under revenue declines.

Disruption remains the order of the day. A much-heralded accountability-journalism enterprise founded in 2013 by the eBay billionaire Pierre Omidyar was forced to significantly scale back its ambitions two years later and then hit more bumps when its star writer, Matt Taibbi, walked and a much anticipated financial magazine was scraped. Not long after Foer published his exposé, he was gone from *TNR,* along with a huge chunk of the staff in a mass resignation, after a Facebook billionaire took over and turned the place inside-out, not in a good way. Meanwhile, the former *Columbia Journalism Review* executive editor Michael Massing, in a lengthy meditation on the digital news landscape in the *New York Review of Books,* has found the output of the digital entrants, while laudable in some particulars, wholly inadequate overall to inform a republic as sprawling and complex as ours.

And he is right. The main losses have been felt in city halls and state houses and at the once-great regional papers in Providence, Baltimore, Des Moines, and Louisville, where coverage of local government has essentially evaporated. The loss to civil society and public knowledge is beyond calculation. Meanwhile, it's a great time for grafters and crooks and special interests.

Business news has fared better, but there are worrisome signs everywhere. The *Wall Street Journal* announced layoffs, having previously dramatically reduced the amount of long-form journalism it produced after its 2007 purchase by Rupert Murdoch. *Forbes* was sold to Chinese investors and long ago drifted from its tradition of quirky and often biting long-form investigations. In the wake of the financial crisis, *Fortune* cut back its number of issues to eighteen from twenty-five, and that's where it remains. No one thinks the *New York Times* is thriving, and the paper has already lost some of its top business-investigative reporters. The *Financial Times* just was sold from its cozy spot inside a British education giant, Pearson PLC, to a Japanese media company, where the future may hold culture clashes. Bloomberg, which mints money in its financial-data business, is in turmoil as it struggles to figure out its media model.

And that's because, so far, there isn't one. And that signals danger.

Does anyone think that the world of business, markets, and economics isn't taking up an increasingly large space in the public sphere? Does anyone really believe that Wall Street is less powerful now than before the crisis? That Silicon Valley—the Googles, Facebooks, and Amazons—has less of a direct role to play in each of our personal lives? That Washington is less beholden to corporate lobbying? That the world of business is less complex and influential and in need of exploration and explanation than it was a few years ago? I don't think so.

So, reader, when you pick up this book and scan the rich array of powerful business journalism (and do *not* miss Francesca Mara's dissection of class issues in the personal assistant economy), I sincerely hope you enjoy it.

Just don't take it for granted.

Acknowledgments

Dean Starkman thanks Alex and Julian.
Ryan Chittum thanks Anna, Clara, Nina, and Molly.
Martha Hamilton thanks Alec, Felix and Josh.

THE

BEST

BUSINESS

WRITING

2015

Part I

Business Unusual

Bloomberg

The dispute between the Russian billionaire Dmitry Rybolovlev and the Swiss art dealer Yves Bouvier over Mark Rothko's *No. 6 (Violet, Green, and Red)* was all about the green. The dispute centered on whether the art dealer misled the forty-eight-year-old billionaire into paying $186 million, the highest amount ever paid for a work by the American painter. And it opens the door to the world of private sales of high-priced art and freeports—bonded warehouses where the superrich can store paintings, wine, and antiques tax-free. It's the type of murky, unregulated market that lends itself to price manipulation and money laundering. Bloomberg's Stephanie Baker and Hugo Miller provide a fascinating glimpse into this rarified world.

Stephanie Baker and
Hugo Miller

1. The Billionaire, the Dealer, and the $186 Million Rothko

On a sunny morning in late February, Yves Bouvier, a Swiss art dealer, flew into Nice and drove twenty miles along the French Riviera to Monaco to meet his top client, the Russian billionaire Dmitry Rybolovlev. Bouvier had come to work out the final payment for Mark Rothko's *No. 6 (Violet, Green, and Red)*, which Rybolovlev had agreed to buy for €140 million back in August. Bouvier, fifty-one, entered the lobby of the cream-colored, belle époque mansion where Rybolovlev's penthouse apartment overlooks Monte Carlo's yacht-filled marina.

Assuming business as usual, Bouvier approached a man he thought was one of Rybolovlev's bodyguards. He was wrong, *Bloomberg Markets* magazine will report in its June 2015 issue. The man turned out to be one of eight Monaco police officers who were there to arrest him. Bouvier didn't know that six weeks earlier, Rybolovlev had filed a complaint against him for fraud, alleging Bouvier had misled him about the prices of artworks he was buying.

That evening, while Bouvier sat in a Monte Carlo police station, Rybolovlev, majority owner of AS Monaco Football Club, was celebrating with Prince Albert II at London's Emirates Stadium: His team beat perennial English powerhouse Arsenal, 3–1.

The dispute between Bouvier and Rybolovlev has turned into one of the biggest cases of alleged fraud to ever hit the art market, pitting one of Russia's richest men against a little-known Swiss art merchant. Rybolovlev, a forty-eight-year-old cardiologist-turned-businessman from the Urals region, made most of his $10 billion fortune through the sale of his fertilizer company, Uralkali, in 2010. Using a series of offshore companies during the past decade, he's spent more than $2 billion buying almost forty works of art through Bouvier, amassing a dream collection of works by Picasso, Leonardo da Vinci, Rothko, Gauguin, Matisse, and Rodin.

Bouvier owns an art-shipping company along with stakes in a network of freeports—bonded warehouses where the superrich can store paintings, wine, and antiques tax-free. In the past five years, he's exported the freeport concept from Geneva to Singapore and Luxembourg. All the while, operating below the radar, he's quietly become one of the biggest art dealers in the business.

After three days of questioning, Monaco's Public Prosecution Department indicted Bouvier on criminal charges of fraud and complicity in money laundering and released him on €10 million ($11 million) bail. As part of the alleged fraud, the indictment cites the sale of the Rothko—one of his best-known works, its bold rectangular blotches bleeding into one another.

The Monaco complaint alleges Bouvier fraudulently inflated invoices for some of the artwork Rybolovlev bought and may have "secretly withheld part of the sale price." The prosecutor charged Tania Rappo, Rybolovlev's translator and godmother to his second child, with money laundering in connection with the commissions Bouvier paid her as an intermediary. Frank Michel, Rappo's lawyer, says her commissions were "perfectly legal and justified." Bouvier denies he was complicit in any money laundering and says commissions paid to those who introduce a buyer to a vendor, as Rappo did, are normal in the art world. If convicted, Bouvier could face up to five years in prison for fraud and ten years for complicity in money laundering. He denies the charges.

.   .   .

The showdown in Monaco has blown the lid off an opaque area of the art market: private sales, in which the most sought-after pieces often change hands through well-connected dealers, avoiding a public bidding war. Of the record €51 billion in art sold last year, 52 percent of the transactions were private deals, says Clare McAndrew, founder of research and consulting firm Art Economics.

In this arena, billionaires often bid against one another without even knowing it, frequently through offshore companies. Rather than flaunting art on their villa walls, investors are increasingly stashing it in freeports, where it can appreciate tax-free before being sold again, tax-free. The value of the works is often hard to assess, determined mostly by what a buyer's willing to pay. What Rybolovlev paid for *No. 6* was a record for a Rothko, whose large canvases have soared in value. In February, Qatar Museums, according to widespread reports, bought Paul Gauguin's *When Will You Marry?* for $300 million, the highest price ever paid for a work of art. (Qatar Museums did not respond to calls for comment.)

Nouriel Roubini, an economist at New York University and an art collector, said on his personal blog earlier this year that the art market is prone to money laundering and price manipulation and badly needs regulation. "There are a number of serious distortions in the art market that suggest that there is some shady behavior going on," he wrote in February, adding later, "Price opacity in the art market leads to insider information, which makes insider trading in art far more likely."

.   .   .

At its heart, the Bouvier-Rybolovlev feud centers on a decade-long arrangement that was never spelled out on paper. Rybolovlev, who declined to be interviewed for this story, considered Bouvier his broker, negotiating prices from third-party sellers, says Tetiana Bersheda, a lawyer representing Rybolovlev. "He made us believe that we were acquiring the paintings directly from the owners and paying him a commission," she says. "In reality, he would charge the highest price to my client while making us believe this was the lowest price he could get from the seller."

Bouvier says he never had any formal contract with Rybolovlev. He says he was merely a seller, not a broker, adding that 80 percent of the bills he issued to Rybolovlev's companies listed him as the seller. "He chose to pay those prices," Bouvier says during a two-hour interview at his lawyer's office in Geneva in March. "He is not a naïve man. He knows very well how the market works for such masterpieces."

Complicating the picture is a protracted divorce between Rybolovlev and his ex-wife, Elena Rybolovleva, which began in 2008 and has yet to be resolved. She was awarded 4 billion Swiss francs ($4.2 billion) by a Geneva court in May 2014, a decision that Rybolovlev is appealing. Rybolovleva's lawyers have sought unsuccessfully to enforce a Swiss order to freeze fourteen works acquired by a Rybolovlev trust while they were still married. Since 2010, according to his Monaco complaint, Rybolovlev has bought paintings through Accent Delight International, a British Virgin Islands–based company held by a Cyprus trust he set up to benefit, among others, his eldest daughter, Ekaterina—a move that has bedeviled the divvying up of assets in the divorce.

·   ·   ·

Bouvier's relationship with Rybolovlev might have continued but for a chance encounter on the Caribbean island of St. Barts in the run-up to New Year's Eve last year. Rybolovlev was lunching with friends at Jean-Georges Vongerichten's restaurant at the Eden Rock hotel. As they chatted overlooking the turquoise waters of St. Jean Bay, a mutual friend introduced Rybolovlev to

Sandy Heller, art adviser to hedge-fund billionaire and noted collector Steven A. Cohen.

They began talking about the art market, according to people familiar with the conversation. The discussion moved on to Amedeo Modigliani's *Reclining Nude with Blue Cushion*, which Cohen had sold in 2012 to a mystery buyer. What unfolded next was a surprise to both men. With Cohen's blessing, Heller disclosed that he'd received $93.5 million for the Modigliani.

Rybolovlev was shocked, the people say. He'd paid $118 million for the painting—more than $24 million above what Cohen got—in a deal arranged by Bouvier, whom he considered a trusted adviser. Now, Rybolovlev told Heller, he was worried Bouvier might have been milking him on other paintings over the years. Could Heller have a look at other deals? Heller did and concurred, saying the prices Rybolovlev had paid for some works appeared wide of the mark. Less than two weeks after meeting Heller, Rybolovlev sprang into action and filed a fraud complaint against Bouvier in Monaco, where the two had met at least five times to hash out deals.

In March, at the Russian billionaire's instigation, the High Court in Singapore, where Bouvier is a resident, froze up to $500 million of his assets pending the outcome of the Monaco investigation. Three weeks later, the court ordered Rybolovlev to post a $20 million deposit in the event damages are awarded to Bouvier.

•　　　•　　　•

Bouvier's position as the owner of an art shipping and storage business gave him not only a Rolodex of top collectors around the world but also a privileged perspective on what artworks are in play. To keep track of his empire, he says he typically travels 300 days a year. Bouvier displays a meticulous approach to detail; he wears hand-tailored shirts monogrammed with his initials as well as the year and season in which he acquired them.

Bouvier's high-flying lifestyle is far from what he says was an ordinary childhood in Geneva, where his father owned a general shipping and storage company called Natural Le Coultre. Bouvier began studies at the University of Geneva before dropping out to work for his dad in between spells as a snowboarding instructor in the Alps.

In 1989, Bouvier and his father began specializing in art shipping for galleries, auction houses, and museums. Natural Le Coultre rents space from Geneva Freeport, a 125-year-old bonded warehouse that once stored mainly grain, tobacco, and wine. Historically, freeports have existed to allow exporters and importers to store goods free of customs duties before they reach their final destination, where taxes are paid. Today, Geneva Freeport holds tens of billions of dollars' worth of fine art, according to Robert Read, head of fine art at the London insurer Hiscox. Bouvier says his holding company, Euroasia Investment, owns less than 5 percent of the freeport, alongside the Canton of Geneva, which owns 86 percent.

Even in Bouvier's hometown, his role as a dealer was something of a secret. Philippe Davet of the Geneva-based gallery and art consultants Blondeau & Cie. says it was news to him. "He was known as a transporter, very reliable, very discreet," he says. "There were rumors that he was a dealer, but it was a surprise to me." Bouvier says bigger dealers knew of him as a buyer of major works.

Bouvier first met Rybolovlev by chance in 2003 at Geneva Freeport, where the Russian was viewing a painting by Marc Chagall that he wanted to buy from another dealer. Rybolovlev speaks little English or French so he brought along Rappo to translate. According to court documents, Bouvier later contacted Rappo with a message to pass on: If Rybolovlev wanted to continue investing in art, Bouvier could help—and the Russian was keen.

As Rybolovlev began buying, according to his Monaco complaint, he rarely signed a sales contract with either a third-party seller or with Bouvier. Bouvier issued an invoice for the sale price, and the painting was transferred as soon as the money hit his bank account. "Bouvier said we needed to keep things confidential," the lawyer Bersheda says. "He said he would be able to get a better price if people didn't know the acquisition was being made by a trust related to a Russian billionaire."

Bersheda says Bouvier charged a 2 percent commission on most transactions. Bouvier says the charge was not a broker's commission but rather a fee to cover administrative costs, including insurance, transport, and condition reports and, in some cases, escrow accounts between down payment and final payment. Some art experts and dealers say it's unusual for a seller to be charging for administrative costs, which rarely amount to 2 percent of the sale price.

In the wake of the financial crisis, Bouvier's freeport business took off as investors began shifting some of their assets out of stocks and bonds. "After the banks lost everything, there was a feeling that people should diversify into property and art," he says. "There was a surge in demand for a place to store that art. We became a hub."

In 2010, Bouvier opened a 30,000-square-meter (323,000-square-foot) high-tech freeport warehouse on the grounds of Singapore's Changi Airport. Christie's leased a whole floor at the storage facility, which is majority owned by Bouvier and also houses wine, jewelry, antiques, and vintage cars.

The deal that sparked his feud with Rybolovlev began in late 2011, when Bouvier started negotiating to buy Modigliani's *Reclining Nude*. On December 23, he e-mailed Mikhail Sazonov, a financial adviser to Rybolovlev, according to the Monaco complaint. The owner of a "very important painting" might put it on the market, Bouvier wrote. "For financial and tax reasons, I think he's going to sell."

Unknown to Rybolovlev, the owner was Cohen, who had consigned the painting's sale to now-defunct New York art dealer Giraud Pissarro Ségalot. The dealer sold it to Bouvier for $93.5 million, plus a commission of about $2.5 million, according to an affidavit filed by Sazonov in Singapore. In January 2012, Bouvier's Hong Kong–based company, MEI Invest, presented Rybolovlev's trust with an invoice for $118 million, leaving Bouvier with $22 million after the New York dealer's commission.

The blockbuster deals kept coming. In early 2013, Bouvier told Sazonov that Leonardo da Vinci's recently discovered, masterful oil-on-walnut painting of Christ, *Salvator Mundi*, was up for sale. In May of that year, a Rybolovlev trust agreed to pay $127.5 million for the painting. Rybolovlev questioned the price he'd paid after reading a *New York Times* article—citing unnamed dealers—that said the da Vinci was sold by a consortium for $75 million to $80 million, according to the Monaco complaint. Bouvier declined to discuss the details, citing the investigation.

•   •   •

With his freeport hat on, Bouvier last September opened a €52 million facility in Luxembourg that looks more like London's Tate Modern than a warehouse. Bouvier owns 60 percent of the freeport, which has private art showrooms and can store 750,000 bottles of wine.

In the summer of 2014, as he was gearing up for the Luxembourg opening, Bouvier presented Rybolovlev with an opportunity to buy a work by one of America's most important postwar artists: Mark Rothko. Christie's had sold his *Orange, Red, Yellow* at auction for a record $87 million in 2012. Bouvier had found a private collector who wanted to sell *No. 6 (Violet, Green, and Red)*, one of the abstract impressionist's most famous works. He began negotiating with Rybolovlev on the price.

After some back and forth, the two men settled on €140 million, making it one of the most expensive paintings ever sold. Rybolovlev agreed to sell a Modigliani sculpture, *Tête*—which he'd bought via Bouvier in 2012—for €60 million as a partial payment for the Rothko. "I convinced the seller of the importance of *Tête* by Modigliani, and he agrees to take it in part exchange for 60m euros," Bouvier wrote to Sazonov on August 4, 2014, the complaint says.

Unknown to Rybolovlev, the seller of the Rothko was Cherise Moueix, the wife of Christian Moueix, a French winemaker who oversees Château Pétrus. She declined to comment. Bouvier told the Monaco prosecutor that he bought the Rothko from Moueix through an intermediary for $80 million plus an unspecified commission—roughly €80 million less than the Russian agreed to pay at the time.

The Singapore court, meanwhile, has put *No. 6* under judicial supervision; its exact whereabouts haven't been disclosed. Bouvier says Rybolovlev still owes him about $40 million for the painting, based on the agreed price. Rybolovlev has refused to pay the balance, saying he's already shelled out more than the $80 million Bouvier paid.

Bouvier says no one forced Rybolovlev to pay the prices he did. "No matter the price, he wanted it, and he was ready to pay the agreed price," says Bouvier. "That Rothko is the most beautiful painting in the world. Everybody wanted to buy that piece." David Bitton, Bouvier's lawyer, says the dispute is just a pawn in Rybolovlev's fierce divorce battle. Marc Bonnant, the lawyer for Rybolovlev's ex-wife, says Rybolovlev may even be trying to get a court to endorse the notion that his art collection is overvalued to help reduce his divorce bill. "He won't succeed," says Bonnant. Bersheda, the lawyer for Rybolovlev, says the divorce proceedings have nothing to do with her client's complaint against Bouvier. She says it was the St. Barts encounter that prompted Rybolovlev to lodge his complaint in Monaco—eight months after the $4.2 billion divorce ruling. "Their argument makes no sense," she says.

Bouvier—sitting in his lawyer's office in Geneva in March, juggling two buzzing phones, red eyed from lack of sleep—says the accusation that he ripped off a man as smart as Rybolovlev is ridiculous. "How could a Russian who's become a billionaire, achieved all he did, and is so clearly bright, be taken advantage of by me?" he asks.

New York

Awash in venture capital, tech's young geniuses are aiming to disrupt even the most quotidian industries—washing clothes, for instance. Enter Washio, a startup that aims to be the "Uber of laundry." It's a low-margin business, but Washio still must fend off a horde of like-minded competitors—which is where the cookies and the hunky drivers come in. Jessica Pressler's eye for the absurd makes this long read about laundry one of the year's great stories.

Jessica Pressler

2. "Let's, Like, Demolish Laundry"

There was a problem with the cookies.

When Jordan Metzner and Juan Dulanto launched Washio, it had already distinguished itself from other laundry and dry-cleaning services. There was no storefront, no rotating rack, no little pieces of paper to keep track of. Customers ordered their clothing picked up via the website or a mobile app, and it was returned to them not in a tangle of WE ♥ OUR CUSTOMERS hangers but in sleek black bags marked with the Washio logo, an understated silhouette of a shirt collar. The company called the drivers who completed these deliveries, usually in twenty-four hours' time, "ninjas." Still, the founders wanted to make sure their business stood out from the competition—that Washio established itself as the washing and dry-cleaning service by and for the convenience-loving, whimsy-embracing millennials of the New Tech Boom. "So we came up with the cookies," says Metzner.

Inspired by Silicon Valley guru Paul Graham's seminal essay to "do things that don't scale," they sourced cookies from bakeries in their three markets—snickerdoodles in San Francisco, frosted red velvet in L.A., classic chocolate chip in Washington, D.C.—which the ninja delivered, wrapped, along with the freshly laundered clothing. The gesture added another logistical wrinkle to an already complicated business, but it was worth it. "In the beginning, people loved it," says Metzner. "Our social media went crazy, like, 'Oh my God, Washio is the best!'"

That was in the beginning.

One Wednesday morning this spring, after staff at Washio had gathered for their daily "stand-up" meeting—a ritual suggested in the *Manifesto for Agile Software Development*, a 2001 work-processes manual that advocates keeping employees on their toes by having them give status updates literally on their feet—operations manager Sam Nadler broke some bad news. "Actually," he said, "we're starting to get a lot of requests for healthy treats instead of cookies."

Ha, well, of course they were. Entitlement is a straight line pointing heavenward, and it should come as no surprise to Washio, where business is based on human beings' ever-increasing desires, that their customers were upping the ante yet again.

Remember the scrub board? One imagines people were thrilled when that came along and they could stop beating garments on rocks, but then someone went ahead and invented the washing machine, and everyone had to have that, followed by the *electric* washing machine, and then the services came along where, if you had enough money, you could pay someone to wash your clothes *for* you, and eventually even this started to seem like a burden—all that picking up and dropping off—and the places offering delivery, well, you had to *call* them, and sometimes they had *accents*, and *are we not living in the modern world?* "We had this crazy idea," says Metzner, "that someone should press a button on their phone and someone will come and pick up their laundry."

So Washio made it thus. For a while, this was pleasing. But in the hubs and coastal cities of Los Angeles and Washington, D.C., and San Francisco—*especially* San Francisco—new innovations are dying from the day they are born, and laundry delivered with a fresh-baked cookie is no longer quite enough. There's a term for this. It's called the hedonic treadmill.

Fortunately, the employees of Washio are on their toes. "What if we did bananas?" Nadler suggested. Everyone laughed.

Metzner held up a small brown bag featuring a silhouette of a flower and a clean lowercase font. "I've been talking to the CEO of NatureBox," he said. "It's like a Birchbox for healthy treats. Every month they send you nuts and . . ."

"Banana chips?" said Brittany Barrett, whose job as Washio's community manager includes cookie selection. Everyone laughed, again.

Metzner looked down at the bag. "Flax crostini," he said. "I think it's a much better value proposition than a cookie." He looked at the bag again. "What *is* a flax crostini?"

We are living in a time of Great Change and also a time of Not-So-Great Change. The tidal wave of innovation that has swept out from Silicon Valley, transforming the way we communicate, read, shop, and travel, has carried along with it an epic shit-ton of digital flotsam. Looking around at the newly minted billionaires behind the enjoyable but wholly unnecessary Facebook and WhatsApp, Uber and Nest, the brightest minds of a generation, the high test-scorers and mathematically inclined, have taken the knowledge acquired at our most august institutions and applied themselves to solving increasingly minor First World problems. The marketplace of ideas has become one long late-night infomercial. Want a blazer embedded with GPS technology? A Bluetooth-controlled necklace? A hair dryer big enough for your entire body? *They can be yours!* In the rush to disrupt everything we have ever known, not even the humble crostini has been spared.

This was the atmosphere Metzner, Dulanto, and Nadler found when they arrived back in the United States in 2010 from Buenos Aires, where they'd settled after college and remained while America slumped into the recession. For kids in their early twenties, they had done impressively little screwing around. Dulanto, a Florida State graduate, had opened a juice bar, which is where he met Metzner and Nadler, friends from Indiana University who were opening a place called California Burrito next door. Two years later, Dulanto had opened a second juice bar, and California Burrito was a chain of fourteen.

But these accomplishments seemed meager when the friends returned to visit their home country. Things were very different from how they'd left them, and, like time travelers, they regarded the changes with awe. "Everyone had a Prius and everyone had an iPhone and everyone had Direct TV, and I was just like, *Whoa*," Metzner says one afternoon this spring, sitting in the Washio break room, a sunny space in Santa Monica with an array of snacks and a fridge full of beer. "And I'm not, like, very materialistic at all," he continues. "Like, I'm not a person who can't live without my iPhone. But I'm thinking to myself, like, *Wow, there's a lot of life I'm sacrificing to live in this country.*" At the time, Argentina's wet noodle of an economy was foundering. Every day, California Burrito had to readjust prices to keep up with inflation. The conveniences his friends at home took for granted were a far-off dream. "iPhones were like $2,000. We were paying ourselves like $1,200 a month. And I realized that I was missing out on the great luxuries of the American lifestyle."

Metzner flicks his brown bangs out of his eyes. At thirty, he looks exactly like the now-grown-up actor who played the kid brother on *Growing Pains*, and, in fact, he was a child actor of the same era, having starred in commercials and an episode of *Tales From the Crypt* before realizing that his innate showmanship was better suited to business.

Metzner and Nadler sold California Burrito and moved back home for good. Nadler enrolled in an MBA. program at MIT; Metzner went to L.A. and immersed himself in the culture of what a group of young entrepreneurs were calling Silicon Beach. He acquired a Prius, an iPhone, and a day job at a company that handles payments for video games; meanwhile, he went looking for opportunities in the tech space. It all went back to the iPhone, he realized. He may have been able to live without it before, but it was about to become indispensable.

"This thing, it's alive," he says now, holding up his phone. "It knows the weather, it knows what you like to eat, it knows your location, it knows what you like to buy." He was particularly fascinated with the on-demand car service Uber, which was quickly building an empire on the back of smart phones. "We're just going to see more and more businesses that we never would have seen before that exist on the premise that everyone has one of these in their pocket," he says. "It's like [Marc] Andreessen said. Software is eating the world."

The question was, what areas of commerce remained undigested?

Metzner scoured TaskRabbit, the website on which the broke and eager underbid one another for the chance to do tasks for the moneyed and lazy, to see what services were most in demand. A lot of people, it turned out, wanted someone to do their laundry. "That spoke to me," says Metzner, whose father sells discount clothing to retailers like T. J. Maxx and bestows on him a great deal of overflow, a luxury that inevitably becomes a burden. "I hate doing laundry," Metzner says. "It's my worst."

That was one thing Argentina had over the United States, he told Dulanto, who had sold his juice bars and was crashing on Metzner's couch. The *lavanderias*. "These women would just stay there all day and do laundry, and your clothes smell incredible, they fold them perfectly, they package them perfectly."

What if, Metzner proposed to Dulanto, they started a service where people could order their laundry picked up and delivered on their smart phones? Kind of like, he said, *"the Uber of laundry?"*

Of course, they wouldn't have to actually do the washing. That they would outsource: to wholesalers, maybe, the types of cleaners used by hotels. They'd charge $1.60 a pound, and though they'd lose part of the margin, they could avoid the costs of rent and expensive machinery. And if they hired drivers on the Uber model—people who used their own cars and their own phones—there would be no need to buy and maintain vehicles. They'd just be the middleman, organizing the transaction and taking a slice of the profit—which, admittedly, was not huge with wash-and-fold. But once they had the laundry, the dry-cleaning would follow. Profits are higher on dry-cleaning, because who knows what dark alchemy is required to remove stains? No one, and everyone is willing to pay a premium to stay uninformed. The trick was to think big: "That's where the numbers become exciting," Metzner says. "Let's do it in fifty, sixty cities," he told Dulanto. "Let's literally go into every market."

The competition, as they saw it, was negligible. "We kind of thought it was low-hanging fruit," Dulanto recalls. Sure, plenty of people had their own laundry machines. But you know what *people* are like.

"It's really kind of amazing the amount of anxiety laundry causes," says Nadler, who came back from MIT to join Washio full-time and is completing his coursework remotely. "Like, it's Sunday, and they just want to hang out on the couch, and they are looking at this big pile of laundry they have to tackle or else they aren't going to have any clothes. I was talking to a classmate who said he and his wife were fighting because someone had to go to the dingy basement, and he felt bad because he didn't want to send *her* to the dingy basement, but he was tired, and then someone needs to get quarters, and it just was a whole *thing*."

In urban centers like New York and Chicago, many places offer delivery already. But: "The laundry and dry-cleaning industry, it's all, like, old people," says Dulanto in the nose-wrinkling manner of someone for whom aging is still an abstract concept. "They're not tech savvy, and they still put up those really ugly stickers with that nineties clip art."

Convinced they were the only members of their demographic who had discovered this particular market inefficiency, they started to imagine a future of wealth and power. Maybe one day Washio would get bought by a larger company like Amazon or Uber itself. Maybe they would strike out on their own. Go public. Use their delivery infrastructure to offer other products— maybe even overtake the Amazons and Ubers of the world. "But first," Metzner said, "let's, like, *demolish* laundry."

The biannual clean show, formally known as the World Educational Congress for Laundering and Drycleaning, does not usually draw the young and overeducated. But this past June at the New Orleans Memorial Convention Center, a handful of flinty-eyed millennials in Bonobos lurked among the suits picked off the unclaimed-garment racks. Metzner was there. So were David Salama and Eric Small, the founder and head of technology of a fledgling New York–based dry-cleaning-and-laundry start-up called FlyCleaners, who had come to see if the industry was as technologically backward as they suspected. So far, the featured performance by viral sensation the Washing Machine Drummer Boy was the only thing they'd seen that placed them in this century. "There were only two technology-based things there," recalls Salama, "and they were pushed off to the side." As he paced the floor, Salama got a text from Small, who had ducked into a seminar called "Marketing Your Coin-Operated Laundry Business." "He's like, 'David, all they keep saying is that the next big thing in marketing is having a *website*.' And they were like, 'If you really, *really* want to be advanced, you should have a Facebook page.' That's basically where these people are."

Salama did a small inner fist pump. This was just the kind of inefficiency he'd sought to exploit as a trader at SAC Capital, the notoriously hypercompetitive Greenwich hedge fund where he'd worked after college. He'd left the job in 2008 after the market crashed and the atmosphere took a turn for the worse. "When times are good, it's semi-poisonous," says Salama, now thirty-one. "When times are bad, it's just outright hostile." But just as he can't shake his Brooklyn accent, he retains a certain amount of SAC muscle memory. "You're trying to beat a market," he says. "So you realize the importance of trying to think in ways other people are not."

This had clicked last February, after Salama's friend Seth Berkowitz had spent a good portion of the Knicks-Warriors game complaining about dry cleaners—no matter which one he went to, it was always a process; they were never open at convenient times; they took forever; and had he seen the *Curb Your Enthusiasm* where Larry David asked a senator for federal oversight of dry-cleaning? The entire industry needed to be disrupted. What they really needed, he said, was an Uber for laundry.

If it had been anyone else talking, Salama might have told him to shut up and watch the game. But Berkowitz's offhand ideas had a history of working out. As an undergrad at the University of Pennsylvania, he'd started his own company, Insomnia Cookies, to fulfill the theretofore-unrealized desires of college students to have warm cookies delivered at two in the morning. It now has fifty outposts. And a few weeks after the Knicks game, Salama had quit his job to become the CEO of a company that would provide laundry and dry-cleaning on demand, by smart phone.

Ever since then, Salama had that unsure feeling in the pit of his stomach, the one he knew so well from SAC. "It's always a little scary," he says, "because often you're swimming alone, but you have to retain confidence." The Clean Show made him feel like he was swimming in the right direction. He called Berkowitz from the convention center's floor. "This has got to be one of the few conventions left in America where technology is pushed off to the fringes and nobody is interested in it," he told him.

Of course, this was not at all true. In reality, when people in a privileged society look deep within themselves to find what is missing, a streamlined clothes-cleaning experience comes up a lot. More often than not, the people who come up with ways of lessening this burden on mankind are dudes, or duos of dudes, who have only recently experienced the crushing realization that their laundry is now their own responsibility, forever. Paradoxically, many of these dudes start companies that make laundry the central focus of their lives.

Back in 2005, a San Francisco techie named Arik Levy founded Laundry Locker, which aimed to "change the way the world does laundry" by creating dedicated lockers where customers could drop off and pick up their clothes. "I'd tried to use the laundry-delivery services," he says now. "But it was a *nightmare.* I'd have to pick a time slot, and then I'd have to wait . . ." In the past nine years, Levy has licensed the company's "locker technology" to a host of other businesses, including Pressbox in Chicago and DashLocker in New York, which was founded two years ago by another SAC alum. Still, travel to a locker requires an effort some are not willing to make, particularly people who work in Manhattan office buildings and have acclimated to the luxury of restaurant-delivery websites like Seamless Web. Thus, in the winter of 2012, two rival laundry sites in the mold of Seamless launched simultaneously in New York. One was Brinkmat, founded by two Goldman Sachs software engineers. ("Like, 'brink' like 'on the brink,'" explains founder Tim O'Malley, "and 'mat' like laundromat." Awkward pause. "Names are hard," his partner adds.) The other was SpotlessCity, the brainchild of the corporate lawyer Hissan Bajwa, whose presentation at the 2012 TechCrunch: Disrupt conference was spirited but unconvincing. "Are you really solving a problem, or making it a simpler process?" one judge asked skeptically. "Well," explained Bajwa, wearing a blue shirt with the company logo of a silhouetted iron, "the idea is you don't want to pick up the phone, or lug around your stuff . . ."

One year later in L.A., Metzner, who is by his own account a "master schmoozer," was cold-calling venture capitalists and getting the same kind of response. "This is a terrible idea," one told him point-blank. It was a few months before the Clean Show, and Washio had launched, sort of. The founders were doing all the driving, although they still drew the line at doing any laundry themselves. ("Ugh, no," says Metzner.) They were considering throwing in the towel—figuratively—when they got a break. "I think you need about $500K, and I think I know the people that can give it to you," said a voice on the phone, as Metzner frantically Googled to figure out who he was speaking with. "Give me a couple of days."

The voice belonged to Haroon Mokhtarzada, an early Internet prodigy who had sold his build-your-own-website website, Webs.com, for $118 million in 2011. Mokhtarzada *got* Washio. He understood the indignities the company was trying to prevent. "You have to put your clothes in a car and drive them somewhere," he says. "You have to take them out in *public*."

Mokhtarzada had friends in the right places. He was tight with Shervin Pishevar, an early Uber investor and celebrity magnet *Forbes* had labeled a "superconnector." When he got involved, "it was a game-changer," says Dulanto. "We went from being the dork in high school to the hot girl."

All of a sudden, Washio had $1.3 million—enough to afford a nice office in Santa Monica, spitting distance from shaving-industry disrupter Dollar Shave Club, dating-site disrupter Tinder, and Zuckerberg-disrupter Snapchat, with whom it started a soccer league. Washio did some hiring: engineers, an assistant for Metzner, and drivers.

Since these were the main people interacting with customers, Metzner was adamant about being choosy. "I'm positive that we could go on Craigslist and post an ad for a delivery driver, and find plenty of people with crappy cars who would work for minimum wage," he says, grabbing his laptop and flopping onto a couch in the Washio break room. "But I mean, you are going to get crappy people who don't want to put their best effort forward and have a shitty vehicle that looks not nice. We decided to go a different route, where we can have premium people doing premium work." He presses play on a promotional video of a pretty brunette in a Washio T-shirt, leaning against her black Mercedes.

In Los Angeles, a lot of the drivers are actors, and their headshots are tacked on a bulletin board at the office. "That guy," he says of one hunky blond we see picking up a bag of laundry to take out, "he could be in *Twilight* or something." They chose the name ninjas in part to signify the company's relationship to Silicon Valley, where the title is handed out freely. "It stems from Disney, which called everyone a cast member," explains Metzner, in his stonery-didactic way. "All of these nameifications, or whatever, is basically to get everyone to think they're not doing what they are actually doing, right? No one wants to be the trash guy at Disneyland. 'No, I'm a *cast member.*' At Trader Joe's, they're all associates. What does that mean? It means nothing, but I would rather be an associate than a cashier. It helps people elevate themselves and think they are doing something for a greater good."

Washio does its part to sustain this delusion by pretending not to be a job. Every month, it throws a party for the ninjas, an open bar or a barbecue or bowling. "So they feel part of a community," Metzner says.

Like the other enlightened start-ups it has modeled itself on, Washio would like to think of itself as making the world a better place, not just making a naked grab for market share. To that end, once a month the company brings clothing collected from customers by ninjas to a clothing drive organized by a nonprofit called Laundry Love.

"It's really good," says Nadler as we are driving back from a visit to the vast building where Washio gets its laundry done, largely by immigrants who are not invited to the open bars or barbecues. "It's a bonding event for Washio-as-culture," he goes on. "It's good press. And it's useful because it makes it easier for our customers. You know, because people always have things they want to donate to Goodwill, but then you have to go, and you have to organize it, and you have this bag sitting around forever—" He catches himself and laughs. "Actually, it's not really *that* big a deal."

Washio's halcyon days came to a halt in July 2013, when Y Combinator, the country's premier tech incubator, announced the launch of Prim, an on-demand laundry start-up by two Stanford graduates. To Metzner and Dulanto, it felt like a personal slight: They had applied to the incubator and been rejected. To add injury to insult, Prim was offering pickup and delivery for a mere twenty-five dollars a bag—about half the price of Washio. And its logo? A silhouette of a bow tie on a blue background. Washio's investors were nervous. "YC companies get a lot of attention," warned Mokhtarzada.

The company needed to make a move, one that showed the tech community who the alpha laundry company was. In early October, Washio opened up shop in San Francisco. Not surprisingly, the area around Silicon Valley was already awash in laundry disrupters. In addition to Prim, there was Laundry Locker, along with three other locker-technology-enabled businesses: Sudzee, Drop Locker, and Bizzie Box. There was Sfwash, which offered ecofriendly cleaning on top of pickup and delivery. There was even, briefly, a service called Your Hero Delivery, whose driver-founders dressed like superheroes. ("At the end of the day, did we really want to spend our whole lives schlepping dirty laundry?" one of them told PandoDaily of their decision to fold. "No.") Another upstart was about to launch: Rinse, whose founders described their business to a Dartmouth alumni newsletter as "an 'Uber' for dry cleaning and laundry."

Metzner knew someone in common with the founders of Rinse, so he decided to give its CEO, Ajay Prakash, a call. Just to let him know his company was coming to San Francisco. And so forth. "It was, you know, a perfectly civil conversation," says Prakash, which may have been what Alan Arkin termed a "business lie."

"It's *really* competitive," says Minh Dang, a former Laundry Locker employee who saw the laundry boom coming and opened his own wholesaler, Wash Then Fold, to service all of the new businesses. "It's man-eat-man."

The companies weren't just competing against each other and the existing infrastructure for customers; they were competing for vendors like Dang—the people who would clean the clothes. And here, the young men from Dartmouth were outmatched: "I had to tell them no," says Dang. "I didn't want to get into some kind of turf battle, man," he says. "I didn't want to fight over laundry."

Just before the holidays came more unwelcome news for Washio. An article in *TechCrunch* announced that FlyCleaners, the New York City–based start-up, had raised $2 million from investors. Unlike its competitors, who required that customers pick a time slot—basically the old model, app-ified—FlyCleaners was offering its customers "true on-demand" service, Salama told the site. With the click of a button, they could summon one of FlyCleaners's trucks to their location within minutes.

Reading about the West Coast's boom in laundry disruption had sent Salama into Sun Tzu mode. "Once we identified the competition, it was a matter of learning about them and understanding their strengths and weaknesses," he says. He had to admit that his competitors' logos were, well, cleaner than FlyCleaners's, which featured a stopwatch filled with bubbles on a dark-blue background and looked vaguely like a snowman caught in a spin cycle. "Everybody says that," he says.

Although they call their drivers FlyGuys and keep the office stocked with snacks, they're more concerned with being seen as a business rather than a start-up. "We've done this in a New York way," Salama says. "We have really gone at the technology, and we're super-serious about it. It's not like fun and games and slides in the office."

While their competitors were elbowing one another in Silicon Valley, FlyCleaners had been scouring Silicon Alley for a team as tough and experienced as the founders themselves. Among its recruits was Brian Tiemann, a software engineer from Bridgewater Capital, the world's largest hedge fund. "You were expecting laundry machines," Tiemann intones from behind the *Star Trek*–like array of screens, when I enter FlyCleaners's Flatiron offices on a recent visit. Blond and bespectacled, Tiemann is that rare breed of tech nerd who took a job at a hedge fund not for the money but because of the technological opportunities it afforded. From the looks of him, he doesn't know from fabric softener, but he enjoys the logistics of getting laundry and dry-cleaning all the places it needs to go. Squinting at the screen, Tiemann types in a command, enabling a driver to avoid a traffic jam on North Sixth Street in Williamsburg.

In New York, hiring drivers on Washio's Uber-inspired model wasn't an option. FlyCleaners had to use trucks, and because of the traffic and narrow streets, the trucks had to be efficient. They built racks for laundry bags, and Tiemann, whose hobby is pimping out cars for the Bullrun, the annual race in which billionaires in souped-up vehicles race one another cross-country, outfitted each one with a tablet that provides drivers with order details, alternate traffic routes, selective streaming from accident-mapping services, and direct communication with headquarters. With guys like this at the controls, mom-and-pops don't stand a chance. "That's the idea," Tiemann says grimly, sinking back into his screens.

Team Washio was intent on staying in first place. Mokhtarzada began mobilizing the troops, and over the next few weeks, Metzner would be in his office, leading the stand-up meeting or evaluating the skills of a ninja interviewee, when he'd feel a ping in his pocket signifying an e-mail from Shervin Pishevar, CC-ing him on a pitch to Jerry Yang, or Scooter Braun, or Nas. "The craziest one on the e-mail chain," Metzner recalls, "was Kanye."

The next thing he knew, Metzner was at Ashton Kutcher's house, presenting him with the idea of an Uber for laundry. "Mila

[Kunis] was there," he says. "She made snacks." Kutcher's investment through A Grade, his partnership with Ron Burkle, helped bring Washio's total funding to $3.6 million. ("We were most impressed with Jordan as a founder," the *Two and a Half Men* star said in a statement e-mailed by a representative. "With trends and consumers all leaning towards a [*sic*] increased level of connivence [*sic*] Jordan has targeted a new vertical that we believe in.")

In Silicon Valley, where The Work of creating The Future is sacrosanct, the suggestion that there might be something not entirely normal about this—that it might be a little weird that investors are sinking millions of dollars into a laundry company they had been introduced to over e-mail *that doesn't even do laundry*; that maybe you don't really need engineers to do what is essentially a minor household chore—would be taken as blasphemy. Outside mecca, though, there are still moments of lucidity.

Sitting in an upscale pizza restaurant in Santa Monica, the kind of place where the cuisine has been disrupted so many times it has pretty much reverted to its original state, Metzner takes a breath. "It's always easy to say in hindsight?" he says. "But in the middle of it, you can't really tell if you are in a bubble or if you are just in a successful time. Because, like, Facebook went out and paid $19 billion for WhatsApp. That actually *happened*."

The waitress brings him a beer. "People with money are going to figure out ways to invest their money to make more money," he says. "If you look at finance, like when credit-default swaps were huge, right, everyone was investing in that. And when subprime was huge, people were investing in that. Now, it's Silicon Valley." He looks up at the television above the bar, which is showing the Lakers game across town. A shot of Ashton and Mila, sitting courtside, appears onscreen. The chyron informs us they are engaged. Metzner tips his beer toward them in congratulations. He's not worried. "It's like Vegas," he says. "The excitement of winning far exceeds the downside of losing."

A few months after Washio landed in San Francisco, Prim, the Y Combinator start-up, folded. In an interview, the founders gave several reasons, among them increased competition for and with vendors.

Asked if he thinks Washio had anything to do with its demise, Metzner smirks.

"That's one down," Mokhtarzada told him.

And on my last morning in the Washio offices, Metzner is still feeling confident. "I think we have established ourselves as the clear market leader," he says, draping his arm casually over the sofa. Washio's Washington, D.C., launch had gone well. The company had brought on a Ph.D. in mathematics to work on its routing systems, and a group of Harvard undergrads was helping refine the ninja-hiring system. More excitingly, Kutcher had gone on *Jimmy Kimmel Live* and talked up the company. "It was surreal," Metzner says.

Not long ago, a friend of Nadler's brought back a flier from South Africa advertising a company with a logo similar to Washio's. And the previous night, Nadler had pulled him aside to show him the app for Dryv, Chicago's Uber of Laundry. Their logo: a hanger, in silhouette. "It's survival of the fittest," says Metzner. "Eventually, these guys who think they can mimic will get frustrated, and they will go away."

But these are times of great change. The hedonic treadmill keeps its steady pace, creating new desires, new niches, new competitors. In the coming weeks, the Laundry Chute, a Palm Beach–based start-up catering to college students, will raise $100,000 in seed funding. An on-demand laundry app called Cleanly, launched in New York last year, will expand operations, and one called MintLocker, which offers its customers cupcakes, will start up in Vegas. "Every day you see another one," says Arik Levy of Laundry Locker, which itself has embraced delivery and is partnering with Deliv to provide a service similar to Washio's. "Although," he adds, "ours is about 25 percent cheaper." He'll have to contend with Brinkmat, the victor of the first laundry wars, which was acquired by Delivery.com and is now doing business under the much simpler laundry.delivery.com. Even the fogies are innovating: Zips, a discount dry-cleaner franchise, is developing an app that lets you watch your garment get cleaned using high-resolution cameras.

In Santa Monica, it's time for lunch. Metzner flicks his bangs and goes to look for his assistant. As he leaves, I notice the screen on someone's computer is opened to a website featuring a gigantic picture of a chocolate-chip cookie. Not an ordinary chocolate-chip cookie. It's a chocolate-chip cookie shaped like a shot glass and filled with milk, the latest creation of noted baked-goods disrupter Dominique Ansel. "The best dessert *ever*," the website, Sploid, enthuses in the headline. For now.

Mary Pilon

3. Monopoly's Inventor

The Progressive Who Didn't Pass "Go"

For generations, the story of Monopoly's Depression-era origins delighted fans almost as much as the board game itself.

The tale, repeated for decades and often tucked into the game's box along with the Community Chest and Chance cards, was that an unemployed man named Charles Darrow dreamed up Monopoly in the 1930s. He sold it and became a millionaire, his inventiveness saving him—and Parker Brothers, the beloved New England board-game maker—from the brink of destruction.

This month, fans of the game learned that Hasbro, which has owned the brand since 1991, would tuck real money into a handful of Monopoly sets as part of the game's eightieth "anniversary" celebration.

The trouble is, that origin story isn't exactly true.

It turns out that Monopoly's origins begin not with Darrow eighty years ago but decades before with a bold, progressive woman named Elizabeth Magie, who until recently has largely been lost to history, and in some cases deliberately written out of it.

Magie lived a highly unusual life. Unlike most women of her era, she supported herself and didn't marry until the advanced age of forty-four. In addition to working as a stenographer and a secretary, she wrote poetry and short stories and did comedic routines onstage. She also spent her leisure time creating a board game that was an expression of her strongly held political beliefs.

Magie filed a legal claim for her Landlord's Game in 1903, more than three decades before Parker Brothers began manufacturing Monopoly. She actually designed the game as a protest against the big monopolists of her time—people like Andrew Carnegie and John D. Rockefeller.

She created two sets of rules for her game: an antimonopolist set in which all were rewarded when wealth was created, and a monopolist set in which the goal was to create monopolies and crush opponents. Her dualistic approach was a teaching tool meant to demonstrate that the first set of rules was morally superior.

And yet it was the monopolist version of the game that caught on, with Darrow claiming a version of it as his own and selling it to Parker Brothers. While Darrow made millions and struck an agreement that ensured he would receive royalties, Magie's income for her creation was reported to be a mere $500.

Amid the press surrounding Darrow and the nationwide Monopoly craze, Magie lashed out. In 1936 interviews with the *Washington Post* and the *Evening Star* she expressed anger at Darrow's appropriation of her idea. Then elderly, her gray hair tied back in a bun, she hoisted her own game boards before a photographer's lens to prove that she was the game's true creator.

"Probably, if one counts lawyer's, printer's and Patent Office fees used up in developing it," the *Evening Star* said, "the game has cost her more than she made from it."

In 1948, Magie died in relative obscurity, a widow without children. Neither her headstone nor her obituary mentions her role in the creation of Monopoly.

A Born Provocateur

Elizabeth Magie was born in Macomb, Ill., in 1866, the year after the Civil War ended and Abraham Lincoln was assassinated. Her father, James Magie, was a newspaper publisher and an abolitionist who accompanied Lincoln as he traveled around Illinois in the late 1850s debating politics with Stephen Douglas.

James Magie gained a reputation as a rousing stump speaker. "I have often been called a 'chip off the old block,'" Elizabeth said of her relationship with her father, "which I consider quite a compliment, for I am proud of my father for being the kind of an 'old block' that he is."

Because of her father's part ownership of the *Canton Register*, Elizabeth was exposed to journalism at an early age. She also watched and listened as, shortly after the Civil War, her father clerked in the Illinois legislature and ran for office on an antimonopoly ticket—an election that he lost.

The seeds of the Monopoly game were planted when James Magie shared with his daughter a copy of Henry George's bestselling book, *Progress and Poverty*, written in 1879.

As an antimonopolist, James Magie drew from the theories of George, a charismatic politician and economist who believed that individuals should own 100 percent of what they made or created but that everything found in nature, particularly land, should belong to everyone. George was a proponent of the "land value tax," also known as the "single tax." The general idea was to tax land, and only land, shifting the tax burden to wealthy landlords. His message resonated with many Americans in the late 1800s, when poverty and squalor were on full display in the country's urban centers.

The antimonopoly movement also served as a staging area for women's rights advocates, attracting followers like James and Elizabeth Magie.

In the early 1880s, Elizabeth Magie worked as a stenographer. At the time, stenography was a growing profession, one that opened up to women as the Civil War removed many men from the work force. The typewriter was gaining commercial popularity, leaving many to ponder a strange new world in which typists sat at desks, hands fixed to keys, memorizing seemingly illogical arrangements of letters on the new qwerty keyboards.

When she wasn't working, Magie, known to her friends as Lizzie, struggled to be heard creatively. In the evenings, she pursued her literary ambitions, and as a player in Washington's nascent theater scene, performed on the stage, where she earned praise for her comedic roles. Though small-framed, she had a presence—an audience at the Masonic Hall exploded with laughter at her comical rendition of a simpering old woman.

She also spent her time drawing and redrawing, thinking and rethinking the game that she wanted to be based on the theories of George, who died in 1897.

When she applied for a patent for her game in 1903, Magie was in her thirties. She represented the less than 1 percent of all patent applicants at the time who were women. (Magie also dabbled in engineering; in her twenties, she invented a gadget that allowed paper to pass through typewriter rollers with more ease.)

Unusually, Magie was the head of her household. She had saved up for and bought her home near Washington, along with several acres of property.

It hadn't been easy. Several years after she obtained the patent for her game, and finding it difficult to support herself on the ten dollars a week she was earning as a stenographer, Magie staged an audacious stunt mocking marriage as the only option for women; it made national headlines. Purchasing an advertisement, she offered herself for sale as a "young woman American slave" to the highest bidder. Her ad said that she was "not beautiful, but very attractive," and that she had "features full of character and strength, yet truly feminine."

The ad quickly became the subject of news stories and gossip columns in newspapers around the country. The goal of the stunt, Magie told reporters, was to make a statement about the dismal position of women. "We are not machines," Magie said. "Girls have minds, desires, hopes and ambition."

If Magie's goal had been to gain an audience for her ideas, she succeeded. In the fall of 1906 she took a job as a newspaper reporter. Four years later, she married a businessman, Albert Phillips, who, at fifty-four, was ten years Lizzie's senior. The union was an unusual one—a woman in the forties embarking on a first marriage, and a man marrying a woman who had publicly expressed her skepticism of marriage as an institution.

Cult Hit to Best-Seller

It was a time of shifting attitudes and behaviors. At the turn of the twentieth century, board games were becoming increasingly commonplace for middle-class families. Changing workplaces gave rise to more leisure time. Electric lighting was becoming common in American homes, reinventing the daily schedule: Games could now be played more safely and enjoyably, and for longer hours, than had been possible during the gaslight era.

Magie's game featured a path that allowed players to circle the board, in contrast to the linear-path design used by many games at the time. In one corner were the Poor House and the Public Park, and across the board was the Jail. Another corner contained an image of the globe and an homage to Henry George: "Labor Upon Mother Earth Produces Wages." Also included on the board were three words that have endured for more than a century after Lizzie scrawled them there: "Go to Jail."

"It is a practical demonstration of the present system of land-grabbing with all its usual outcomes and consequences," Magie said of her game in a 1902 issue of *The Single Tax Review*. "It might well have been called the 'Game of Life,' as it contains all the elements of success and failure in the real world, and the object is the same as the human race in general seem to have, i.e., the accumulation of wealth."

On some level, Lizzie understood that the game provided a context—it was just a game, after all—in which players could lash out at friends and family in a way that they often couldn't in daily life. She understood the power of drama and the potency of assuming roles outside of one's everyday identity. Her game spread, becoming a folk favorite among left-wing intellectuals, particularly in the Northeast. It was played at several college campuses, including what was then called the Wharton School of Finance and Economy, Harvard University, and Columbia University. Quakers who had established a community in Atlantic City embraced the game and added their neighborhood properties to the board.

It was a version of this game that Charles Darrow was taught by a friend, played, and eventually sold to Parker Brothers. The version of that game had the core of Magie's game but also modifications added by the Quakers to make the game easier to play. In addition to properties named after Atlantic City streets, fixed prices were added to the board. In its efforts to seize total control of Monopoly and other related games, the company struck a deal with Magie to purchase her Landlord's Game patent and two more of her game ideas not long after it made its deal with Darrow.

In a letter to George Parker, Magie expressed high hopes for the future of her Landlord's Game at Parker Brothers and the prospect of having two more games published with the company. Yet there's no evidence that Parker Brothers shared this optimism, nor could the company—or Darrow—have known that Monopoly wouldn't be a mere hit, but a perennial best-seller for generations.

Representatives for Hasbro did not respond to a request for comment.

Magie's identity as Monopoly's inventor was uncovered by accident. In 1973, Ralph Anspach, an economics professor, began a decade-long legal battle against Parker Brothers over the creation of his Anti-Monopoly game. In researching his case, he uncovered Magie's patents and Monopoly's folk-game roots. He became consumed with telling the truth of what he calls "the Monopoly lie."

In a deposition for that case, Robert Barton, the Parker Brothers president who oversaw the Monopoly deal, called Magie's game "completely worthless" and said that Parker Brothers had published a small run of her games "merely to make her happy."

Mr. Anspach's legal battle lasted a decade and ended at the Supreme Court. But he won the right to produce his Anti-Monopoly games, and his research into Magie and the game's origins was confirmed.

Roughly forty years have passed since the truth about Monopoly began to appear publicly, yet the Darrow myth persists as an inspirational parable of American innovation. It's hard not to wonder how many other buried histories are still out there—stories belonging to lost Lizzie Magies who quietly chip away at creating pieces of the world, their contributions so seamless that few of us ever stop to think about the person or people behind the idea.

Who should get credit for an invention and how? The Monopoly game raises that question in a particularly compelling way. "Success has many fathers," goes the adage—to say nothing of the mothers.

Slate

Anyone wondering why there aren't so many delis anymore should read this fascinating (and appetizing) look behind the steam counter of one of America's most famous restaurants, Katz's, on Manhattan's Lower East Side. Think that the deli's profits are powered by its famous pastrami sandwich at a twenty dollars a pop? Think again. In Jordan Weissmann's telling, iconic dishes turn out to be loss leaders and nonfood items (location, location, location) are the difference makers.

Jordan Weissmann

4. The Ur-Deli

When I sit down with Jake Dell, the twenty-seven-year-old heir to Katz's Delicatessen, at a table toward the back of his family's storied restaurant, he's staring distractedly into his phone. His expression reads one part bewilderment, two parts resignation.

"Did you know there was a *Beef* magazine? Or a *Cattle Network*?" he asks. "I'm head first in cattle pricing—more than I've ever been."

Katz's is New York's oldest surviving delicatessen. It is also, of course, the restaurant where Meg Ryan faked an orgasm in *When Harry Met Sally* (and has a sign inside to remind you). But far more importantly, it is the ur-deli, a place that, for a certain kind of American Jew, might trump the Western Wall in the hierarchy of Hebraic cultural heritage sites. While the current location, with its schmutzy wood paneling and walls covered with photos of celebrity diners, merely dates back to 1949, the restaurant has operated on the Lower East Side since 1888, serving up heaping, hand-sliced portions of its smoky, peppery, and unctuously fatty pastrami, along with house-cured corned beef, bocce-sized matzo balls, and other classics of the deli canon. To step inside its front door, under the pink neon signage and past the curtain of salamis hanging in its window, is to be enveloped by the thick, meaty aroma of history (as well as a throng of tourists, especially if you show up on a weekend).

But with a throwback menu comes a throwback business model, the downsides of which are especially apparent in these days of astronomical beef prices. That's one reason why Dell—whose grandfather purchased Katz's in 1988 and who in recent years has taken over most day-to-day oversight from his father and uncle—is fretting. If you want to fully appreciate why a place like Katz's is special, you have to appreciate its odd economics, which pretty much ensure there will never be another deli quite like it.

The fundamental problem facing every remaining deli, Katz's included, is that the gargantuan sandwiches for which they are known aren't very profitable. Rather, they're a legacy of the early twentieth century, when brisket (used in corned beef) and navel plate (the fattier, bovine belly meat Katz's uses for pastrami) were considered cheap trash cuts and hundreds of Jewish restaurants could compete for immigrant clientele with rock-bottom prices. But the days of inexpensive navel and brisket are long gone—thanks in part to the national love affair with Texas-style barbecue—and delis can only raise their prices so high before turning off customers. As a result, the margins on a pastrami or corned beef on rye are perilously thin. In his 2009 book *Save the Deli* (an indispensable read for lovers of Jewish comfort food), David Sax writes that "most New York delis are breaking even or losing money on their namesake item." Profitable sandwiches, he reports, make margins somewhere between 5 and 15 percent.

To put that in perspective, keep in mind that after subtracting food and labor costs, the median sit-down restaurant has a margin of roughly 35 percent (the exact number varies with average check size). "If all I did was sell sandwiches, I couldn't pay the staff," Dell tells me.

All of this might sound a bit suspect to someone who casually glances at Katz's menu, which currently charges a hefty $19.75 for a pastrami on rye. But stop and consider it for a moment, and it's easy to see how a nearly $20 sandwich might not actually be much of a moneymaker. Preparing a proper pastrami is a painstaking, labor-intensive process. At Katz's, the raw navels are wet-cured for weeks before being coated in a dry rub of salt and spices, then smoked at a low temperature for about three days. Afterward, they're steamed to soften up the meat, before the deli's famous countermen—who are unionized, with health benefits—hand-slice it on the spot for customers. Cutting thinner slices with a machine would probably be more efficient and lead to less waste, but would leave the sandwich's texture and character unrecognizably altered. In the end, it probably takes somewhere around a pound and a half of raw meat to yield a single, three-quarter-pound Katz's sandwich.

"It's a terrible catch-22," Dell says of the art of pastrami. "Because the thing that makes us loved is also the thing that makes it hardest from an economic standpoint."

The economics have gotten markedly worse of late. Thanks to years of drought in Texas, the U.S. cattle herd is the smallest it's been in more than sixty years, which has led to a sharp rise in beef prices and left Dell scouring *Beef* magazine for ideas about controlling costs.

Despite all this, Katz's remains a healthy, profitable business. But according to Dell, it makes most of its actual profits on side orders. Much as McDonald's is really in the business of selling french fries and Coca-Cola for high markups—meanwhile using extremely cheap burgers to lure in customers—Katz's keeps the lights on thanks to latkes, coleslaw, Matzo ball soup, potato salad, and Dr. Brown's cream sodas. To pull this off, it needs a massive volume of business, bulked up by those droves of tourists (though, thankfully, it's probably less of a tourist trap than its fellow survivor uptown, the Carnegie Deli). That foot traffic is possible in part because there simply isn't much competition anymore. In other words, Katz's lives on precisely because it's among the last of its breed.

The newer generation of artisanal delicatessens that have risen up in recent years—restaurants like Brooklyn's Mile End Deli and Washington, D.C.'s, DGS Delicatessen—are fundamentally different. They serve their own excellent, obsessively sourced variations of house-cured and smoked pastrami (or Montreal-style "smoked meat," in Mile End's case). But volume isn't really part of their equation. Instead, they emphasize profitable alcohol sales and have more varied menus with higher-margin main dishes. And, crucially, they can pack less meat onto the plate, which would be anathema at an old-school deli like Katz's.

"Katz's is super-special. It's the only thing of its kind in the entire world," Mile End's founder, Noah Bernamoff, tells me.

The reason Katz's was able to live on while its competitors disappeared largely boils down to real estate. As Sax writes in *Save the Deli*, New York's delicatessens can basically be divided into two groups: those that rent their buildings and those that own. Famous renters, like the Stage Deli and Second Avenue Deli, have closed in the face of rent hikes. Famous owners, like Carnegie and Katz's, have lived on. (And when Second Avenue Deli reopened, it bought a building . . . on New York's Third Avenue). If Katz's had to deal with a landlord, it would likely have disappeared or moved long ago.

Instead, it seems set to stay put indefinitely. Recently, news broke that Katz's had sold the air rights over its iconic building. While Dell says he can't share details of the agreement, including the buyer—it's widely presumed to be a developer who bought adjacent lots on the block to build luxury condos—he does offer a list of things that won't happen. Nothing is being built on top of Katz's. Nobody is going to cantilever a building from next door. And Katz's won't be closing, even temporarily.

"We're here, and that's it, and we're here to stay," he says. But that doesn't mean he can stop worrying about cattle prices. "My job is to freak out about the minor details that nobody will ever need to know, never see," he says. "That's what I do."

Part II

Labor and Its Discontents

New York Times

Exploited workers are paying the price for low-cost manicures and pedicures. Many are illegal immigrants working for little or no pay or even paying cash to "train" as unpaid interns. The work can be demeaning, and the highest-paid job in the salons, sculpting fake nails out of acrylic dust, can lead to serious health issues, including miscarriages. Sarah Maslin Nir vividly describes the trials faced by these women, whose workplaces received little attention from regulators before her exposé. Then Governor Andrew Cuomo announced a task force to investigate nail salons and put in place rules to protect workers and a campaign to educate them about their rights. New York mayor Bill de Blasio asked the city's Department of Consumer Affairs to investigate potentially harmful health effects and employment agencies that put workers in salons and to enforce the minimum wage.

Sarah Maslin Nir

5. The Price of Nice Nails

The women begin to arrive just before eight a.m., every day and without fail, until there are thickets of young Asian and Hispanic women on nearly every street corner along the main roads of Flushing, Queens.

As if on cue, cavalcades of battered Ford Econoline vans grumble to the curbs, and the women jump in. It is the start of another workday for legions of New York City's manicurists, who are hurtled to nail salons across three states. They will not return until late at night, after working ten- to twelve-hour shifts, hunched over fingers and toes.

On a morning last May, Jing Ren, a twenty-year-old who had recently arrived from China, stood among them for the first time, headed to a job at a salon in a Long Island strip mall. Her hair neat and glasses perpetually askew, she clutched her lunch and a packet of nail tools that manicurists must bring from job to job.

Tucked in her pocket was one hundred dollars in carefully folded bills for another expense: the fee the salon owner charges each new employee for her job. The deal was the same as it is for beginning manicurists in almost any salon in the New York area. She would work for no wages, subsisting on meager tips, until her boss decided she was skillful enough to merit a wage.

It would take nearly three months before her boss paid her. Thirty dollars a day.

Once an indulgence reserved for special occasions, manicures have become a grooming staple for women across the economic spectrum. There are now more than 17,000 nail salons in the United States, according to census data. The number of salons in New York City alone has more than tripled over a decade and a half to nearly 2,000 in 2012.

But largely overlooked is the rampant exploitation of those who toil in the industry. The *New York Times* interviewed more than 150 nail salon workers and owners, in four languages, and found that a vast majority of workers are paid below minimum wage; sometimes they are not even paid. Workers endure all manner of humiliation, including having their tips docked as punishment for minor transgressions, constant video monitoring by owners, even physical abuse. Employers are rarely punished for labor and other violations.

Asian-language newspapers are rife with classified ads listing manicurist jobs paying so little the daily wage can at first glance appear to be a typo. Ads in Chinese in both *Sing Tao Daily* and *World Journal* for NYC Nail Spa, a second-story salon on the Upper West Side of Manhattan, advertised a starting wage of ten dollars a day. The rate was confirmed by several workers.

Lawsuits filed in New York courts allege a long list of abuses: the salon in East Northport, N.Y., where workers said they were paid just $1.50 an hour during a sixty-six-hour workweek; the Harlem salon that manicurists said charged them for drinking the water yet on slow days paid them nothing at all; the minichain of Long Island salons whose workers said they were not only underpaid but also kicked as they sat on pedicure stools and verbally abused.

Last year, the New York State Labor Department, in conjunction with several other agencies, conducted its first nail salon sweep ever—about a month after the *Times* sent officials there an inquiry regarding their enforcement record with the industry. Investigators inspected 29 salons and found 116 wage violations.

Among the more than one hundred workers interviewed by the *Times*, only about a quarter said they were paid an amount that was the equivalent of New York State's minimum hourly wage. All but three workers, however, had wages withheld in other ways that would be considered illegal, such as never getting overtime.

The juxtapositions in nail salon workers' lives can be jarring. Many spend their days holding hands with women of unimaginable affluence, at salons on Madison Avenue and in Greenwich, Conn. Away from the manicure tables they crash in flophouses packed with bunk beds or in fetid apartments shared by as many as a dozen strangers.

Ms. Ren worked at Bee Nails, a chandelier-spangled salon in Hicksville, N.Y., where leather pedicure chairs are equipped with iPads on articulated arms so patrons can scroll the screens without smudging their manicures. They rarely spoke more than a few words to Ms. Ren, who, like most manicurists, wore a fake name chosen by a supervisor on a tag pinned to her chest. She was "Sherry." She worked in silence, sloughing off calluses from customers' feet or clipping dead skin from around their fingernail beds.

At night she returned to sleep jammed in a one-bedroom apartment in Flushing with her cousin, her cousin's father, and three strangers. Beds crowded the living room, each cordoned off by shower curtains hung from the ceiling. When lights flicked on in the kitchen, cockroaches skittered across the countertops.

Almost all of the workers interviewed by the *Times*, like Ms. Ren, had limited English; many are in the country illegally. The combination leaves them vulnerable.

Some workers suffer more acutely. Nail salons are governed by their own rituals and mores, a hidden world behind the glass exteriors and cute corner shops. In it, a rigid racial and ethnic caste system reigns in modern-day New York City, dictating not only pay but also how workers are treated.

Korean workers routinely earn twice as much as their peers, valued above others by the Korean owners who dominate the industry and who are often shockingly plain-spoken in their disparagement of workers of other backgrounds. Chinese workers occupy the next rung in the hierarchy; Hispanics and other non-Asians are at the bottom.

The typical cost of a manicure in the city helps explain the abysmal pay. A survey of more than 105 Manhattan salons by the *Times* found an average price of about $10.50. The country-wide average is almost double that, according to a 2014 survey by *Nails Magazine*, an industry publication.

With fees so low, someone must inevitably pay the price.

"You can be assured, if you go to a place with rock-bottom prices, that chances are the workers' wages are being stolen," said Nicole Hallett, a lecturer at Yale Law School who has worked on wage-theft cases in salons. "The costs are borne by the low-wage workers who are doing your nails."

In interviews, some owners readily acknowledged how little they paid their workers. Ms. Ren's boss, Lian Sheng Sun, who goes by Howard, at first denied doing anything wrong but then said it was just how business was done. "Salons have different ways of conducting their business," he said. "We run our business our own way to keep our small business surviving."

Many owners said they were helping new immigrants by giving them jobs.

"I want to change the first generation coming here and getting disgraced, and getting humiliated," said Roger Liu, twenty-eight, an immigrant from China, seated inside the salon he owned, Relaxing Town Nails and Spa in Huntington Station, N.Y. As he spoke last summer, an employee, a woman in her fifties, paced the salon, studying a scrap of paper scribbled with the steps of a pedicure, chanting them to herself quietly in Chinese.

It was her first week working in a salon, she said. Mr. Liu was not paying her.

Compelled to work endless hours just to get by, the manicurists live lives that unspool almost entirely within the walls of their salons. An underground economy has sprung up in Flushing and other city neighborhoods where salon workers live, to help them cope. On weekdays, women walk from door to door like Pied Pipers, taking nail salon workers' children to school for a fee. Many manicurists pay caregivers as much as half their wages to take their babies six days a week, twenty-four hours a day, after finding themselves unable to care for them at night and still wake up to paint nails.

Jing Ren usually spent days sleeping in her slim pallet a few feet from the bed of her twenty-four-year-old cousin, Xue Sun, also a manicurist. She had no time to make other friends.

She eventually started taking English classes, hoping to grasp onto a new life, but she feared the gravitational pull of this one.

"I would feel petrified," she said, "thinking that I'll be doing this for the rest of my life."

Low Prices, Low Pay

As far as small businesses go, it is relatively easy to open a nail salon.

Just a few thousand dollars is needed for things like pedicure chairs with whirlpool baths. Little English is required, and there are few licensing hoops to jump through. Many skip them altogether. Overhead is minimal: rent and some new bottles of polish each month—and the rock-bottom wages of workers.

Beyond the low barriers for entry, manicurists, owners, and others who have closely followed the nail industry are hard pressed to say definitively why salons have proliferated.

In the 1990s, nail-polish brands began to market more directly to consumers, helping to fuel demand, according to *Nails Magazine*. Polishes also became more sophisticated; they last longer and are easier to remove.

Census data show the number of salons in New York surged through the 2000s, far outstripping the rest of the country. Growth dimmed slightly during the recession, as lacquered nails remained an affordable treat for many, before climbing again.

But as nail salons have mushroomed, it has become harder to turn a profit, some owners said. Manicure prices have not budged much from 1990s levels, according to veteran workers. Neither have wages.

With their gleaming glass fronts, the salons seem to display their inner workings as transparently as a department store displays a holiday window. But much of how salons operate and how workers are treated is kept deliberately opaque to the outside world.

Among the hidden customs are how new manicurists get started. Most must hand over cash—usually $100 to $200, but sometimes much more—as a training fee. Weeks or months of work in a kind of unpaid apprenticeship follows.

Ms. Ren spent almost three months painting on pedicures and slathering feet with paraffin wax before one afternoon in the late summer when her boss drew her into a waxing room and told her she would finally be paid.

"I just burst into laughter unconsciously," Ms. Ren said. "I have been working for so long while making zero money; now finally my hard work paid off."

That night her cousins threw her a party. The next payday she learned her day wage would amount to under three dollars an hour.

Step into the prim confines of almost any salon and workers paid astonishingly low wages can be readily found. At May's Nails Salon on Fourteenth Street in the West Village of Manhattan, where a photo of the singer Gwen Stefani with a manicurist hung on the wall, new employees must pay $100, then work unpaid for several weeks, before they are started at $30 or $40 a day, according to a worker. A man who identified himself as the owner, but would give his name only as Greg, said the salon did not charge employees for their jobs but would not say how much they are paid.

At Sona Nails on First Avenue near Stuyvesant Town, a worker said she made thirty-five dollars a day. Sona Grung, the owner of Sona Nails, denied paying below minimum wage, yet defended the practice, particularly of underpaying new workers. "When a beginner comes in, they don't know anything, and they give you a job," she said. "If you work in a nail salon for thirty-five dollara, it's very good."

Nail salon workers are generally considered "tipped workers" under state and federal labor laws. Employers in New York are permitted to pay such workers slightly less than the state's $8.75 minimum hourly wage, based on a complex calculation of how much a worker is making in tips. But interviews with scores of workers revealed rates of pay so low that the so-called tip calculation is virtually meaningless. None reported receiving supplemental pay from their bosses, as is legally required when their day's tips fall short of the minimum wage. Overtime pay is almost unheard-of in the industry, even though workers routinely work up to twelve hours a day, six or even seven days a week.

Inside the hive of the salon, there are typically three ranks of workers. "Big Job" employees are veterans, experts at sculpting false nails out of acrylic dust. It is the most lucrative salon job, yet many younger manicurists avoid it because of the specter of serious health issues, including miscarriages and cancer, associated with inhaling fumes and clouds of plastic particles. "Medium Job" workers do regular manicures, while "Little Job" is the category of the beginners. They launder hot hand towels and sweep toenail clippings. They do work others do not want to do, such as pedicures.

More experienced workers usually earn fifty to seventy dollars per day, sometimes even eighty. Their pay, though, still typically amounts to significantly less than minimum wage, given their long hours.

In the poorer pockets of the city, at low-traffic salons in the Bronx and Queens, many workers are not paid a base wage at all, only a commission.

Nora Cacho was paid about 50 percent of the price of every manicure or lip wax she did at a Harlem shop that was part of a chain, Envy Nails. She frequently earned about $200 for each sixty-six-hour workweek—about $3 an hour. In sandal season, if she was lucky, she left the shop with slightly more—$300 each week, she said. On snowy days, Ms. Cacho, who is part of a class-action lawsuit against the chain, would return home with nothing. The chain's lawyer did not respond to requests for comment.

Ms. Cacho, who is from Ecuador, initially saw the industry as her financial salvation, as do many other immigrants. But what seems a way up usually gives way to a grinding existence.

Salon workers describe a culture of subservience that extends far beyond the pampering of customers. Tips or wages are often skimmed or never delivered, or deducted as punishment for things like spilled bottles of polish. At her Harlem salon, Ms. Cacho said she and her colleagues had to buy new clothes in whatever color the manager decided was fashionable that week. Cameras are regularly hidden in salons, piping live feeds directly to owners' smart phones and tablets.

Qing Lin, forty-seven, a manicurist who has worked on the Upper East Side for the last ten years, still gets emotional when recounting the time a splash of nail polish remover marred a customer's patent Prada sandals. When the woman demanded compensation, the $270 her boss pressed into the woman's hand came out of the manicurist's pay. Ms. Lin was asked not to return.

"I am worth less than a shoe," she said.

An Ethnic Caste System

As the throngs of manicurists gather in Flushing, Queens, every morning, the patter of "good mornings" is mostly in Chinese and

Spanish, with the occasional snatches of Tibetan or Nepali. Korean is hardly ever heard among these workers heading to salons outside New York City, many of them hours away.

But to the customer settling into the comfort of a pedicure chair in Manhattan, it can seem as if nearly the entire work force is Korean.

The contrast stems from the stark ethnic hierarchy imposed by nail salon owners. Seventy percent to eighty percent of salons in the city are Korean-owned, according to the Korean American Nail Salon Association.

Korean manicurists, particularly if they are youthful and attractive, typically have their pick of the most desirable jobs in the industry—shiny shops on Madison Avenue and in other affluent parts of the city. Non-Korean manicurists are often forced into less desirable jobs in the boroughs outside Manhattan or even farther out from the city, where customers are typically fewer and tips often paltry.

In general, Korean workers earn at least 15 percent to 25 percent more than their counterparts, but the disparity can sometimes be much greater, according to manicurists, beauty-school instructors, and owners.

Some bosses deliberately prey on the desperation of Hispanic manicurists, who are often drowning under large debts owed to "coyotes" who smuggled them across the border, workers and advocates say.

Many Korean owners are frank about their prejudices. "Spanish employees" are not as smart as Koreans or as sanitary, said Mal Sung Noh, sixty-eight, who is known as Mary, at the front desk of Rose Nails, a salon she owns on the Upper East Side.

Ms. Noh's salon sits behind the construction barricades of the Second Avenue subway line. Perhaps as a result, she employs a handful of Hispanic women. (Less lucrative shops on out-of-the-way streets or on the second stories of buildings tend to be more diverse.) Ms. Noh said she kept her Hispanic manicurists at the lowest rung of work. "They don't want to learn more," she said.

Ethnic discrimination imbues other aspects of salon life. Male pedicure customers are despised by many manicurists for their thick toenails and hair-covered knuckles. When a man comes into the store, almost invariably a non-Korean worker is first draft for his foot bath, salon workers said.

Ana Luisa Camas, thirty-two, an Ecuadorean immigrant, said that at a Korean-owned Connecticut salon where she worked, she and her Hispanic colleagues were made to sit in silence during their entire twelve-hour shifts, while the Korean manicurists were free to chat. "For two years I suffered from headaches," she said. "It was just the stress that was killing me."

Lhamo Dolma, thirty-nine, a manicurist from Tibet who goes by Jackey, recalled a former job at a Brooklyn salon where she had to eat lunch every day standing in a kitchenette with the shop's other non-Korean workers while her Korean counterparts ate at their desks.

"Their country people, they are completely free," she said in an interview in her house in Queens, seated on a low settee beneath her household's Buddhist shrine. She began to cry. "Why do they make us two different?" she said. "Everybody is the same."

A Scared Newcomer

There was a bright blue Siamese fighting fish in a Mason jar in a corner of the one-bedroom apartment where Ms. Ren lived with her cousin and four other adults. It rested on a table made from a broken cabinet door. Its name was July, after the month she was told she would finally earn a wage.

It was a rare moment of accomplishment for Ms. Ren, now twenty-one, in her early days in New York City. She had holed up indoors for weeks after arriving, too scared to go outside.

She wished she could be like her older cousin and roommate, Ms. Sun, who emerged from their apartment in Flushing each morning looking more like her customers than a manicurist, in bargain-store imitations of Hermès and Chanel. Ms. Sun woke up early each morning to steam her outfit—even her denim shorts—so that all traces of their grim quarters stayed shut up behind the apartment door.

When business at the salon began to slow in late 2013, Ms. Sun, who goes by Michelle, had an idea. She hopped a cheap bus south to Florida, a place she knew little about other than that it was always warm. She figured sandals—and pedicures—were year-round staples. She wandered from shop to shop until she found work.

Upon her return in spring 2014, Ms. Sun was upset to find Ms. Ren nearly a shut-in. Ms. Sun cajoled her younger charge to call salons listing openings online, taking the phone from her when she was too scared to speak to shop owners.

The day after, Ms. Ren stood on the corner of Franklin Avenue and Kissena Boulevard, her lunchbox in hand, waiting for a van to deliver her to her new salon—where, she did not know.

At Bee Nails, the salon in Hicksville, Ms. Ren fumbled even the most simple tasks at first, overwhelmed by nerves. She spent her days making piles of paper twists to swaddle pedicured toes, or cleaning up nail clippings. Her hands trembled when she tried to paint even her own nails in the break room. She refused to join the other Little Job workers for practice sessions, watching shyly.

A week in, her first manicure was on a man. His girlfriend sat next to him, whispering to him about the manicurist's shaking hands. Ms. Ren said later her hands only shook harder.

"I tried to calm down on my way back in the van—it's a long trip and quiet," she said. "I told myself that I have to prove that I'm capable of conquering all these difficulties and make it."

At home she stayed up late practicing manicures on her cousin and drafted careful ledgers of her expenses. Her sole income was a few dollars a day in tips, but she was meticulous, tabulating each banana and even her first ice cream from a chiming truck.

Beside a doodle of a cone, she wrote "$1.50." Next to it, in English: "It's good!"

By October, Ms. Ren had mostly tamed her anxiety. One Sunday morning, as a visitor watched, she sat balanced froglike on a small stool as she hoisted up the feet of a woman in a pink Juicy Couture track suit, deftly scratching off calluses with a roughened foam brick. The woman scrolled on her phone and picked at her cuticles. She addressed Ms. Ren once, when she warned the manicurist of a blister on her heel. Every so often, Ms. Ren sent a nail polish bottle or cuticle nipper flying, but she covered up her error with a titter and useful English phrases her boss encouraged her to practice. "So sorry," she whispered.

Some evenings, Ms. Sun's father, a line cook in Manhattan, would whip up elaborate meals of soft-shelled turtle and taro for the young women that reminded them of home. At night, he tucked them into bed with words of encouragement, before drawing closed the wall of curtain that separated his bed from theirs. Try to think of customers' feet as pig's feet, he would urge. Don't they love that Chinese delicacy when he makes it?

As the cold set in, a time of year when many bosses fire much of their salon staff, Ms. Ren grew anxious again. On slow days, she was sent to stand beside the highway in front of the salon in her green uniform bib, waving fliers. A customer review on the salon's Yelp page described it as "basically a sweatshop," and she felt it. Sometimes, she spent entire days dusting hundreds of individual plastic boxes of customers' personal nail tool kits.

"I felt what I had to do was so pointless," she later said.

Behind the Mercedes

A gold pendant embossed with Chinese characters and entwined with red thread hangs on the door of a two-story house in Center Moriches, on Long Island, about an hour's drive east from where Ms. Ren works in Hicksville. A wide creek that empties into Moriches Bay lies on the other side of the street. A Mercedes-Benz sport utility vehicle parks in the driveway.

It is the home of the owner of Nail Love, a salon in a nearby shopping center. The charm on the door invokes financial prosperity for the house's inhabitants. But the lives of the half-dozen manicurists who bunk in the basement are anything but prosperous.

They are employees of Nail Love. Their dimly lit warren is a barracks provided by the salon's owner, a common arrangement for workers in salons outside commuting distance from New York City. It saves owners money and sometimes even turns a profit. In some other such situations, workers must pay rent to their bosses.

Nail salon owners are often the success stories of their immigrant communities. Some owners rose from the ranks of manicurists themselves. In interviews, many owners expressed a vision of themselves as heroic, shouldering the burden of training workers and the risk of employing people who are not legally permitted to work in the United States. Fees extracted from new workers like Ms. Ren are proper compensation for the inconvenience of providing training, they said. Several owners said they felt betrayed when their workers quit or sued.

"They don't stop to think how difficult it is nowadays to keep the door of our business open to service people," Romelia M. Agudo, the former owner of a Park Slope salon, Romy's Nails, wrote in an affidavit asking a judge to dismiss a lawsuit by two of her employees who said they were underpaid and denied lunch breaks.

Many owners defended their business methods as the only way to stay afloat.

Ansik Nam, former president of the Korean American Nail Salon Association, said that in the early 2000s, scores of owners held an emergency meeting at a Korean restaurant in Flushing, hoping to prevent manicure and pedicure prices from sagging further. He said no agreement was reached.

The association's current president, Sangho Lee, declined a request to address issues of underpayment. So many owners do not pay minimum wage, he said, that he believed answering any questions would hurt the industry.

Tucked between the hand dryers of NYC Nail Spa on the Upper West Side, where the beginners' wage is ten dollars a day, the grim math of the nail salon industry is seemingly laid bare on a neatly typed sign, urging customers in broken English to tip well: "Less tips make us hard to hire good workers, or we have to pay higher wages to hire them, which might also cause a raise on the price."

In an interview, the owner's wife, who would give only her first name, Hwu, said the salon's sales exceeded $400,000 a year but there were significant expenses as well, like rent and payroll. Speaking at the salon in February, shortly after her husband dropped her off in their Cadillac SUV, she said some of her beginners were not paid ten dollars a day. She pointed to a male manicurist on his first day on the job: If he did not show promise, she said, he would not be paid at all.

The owners of Iris Nails, a chain with shops in Manhattan and Brooklyn, had seven stores that generated sales of $8 million per year, according to a 2012 article in *Korea Daily*, a Korean American newspaper. At the two Iris salons on Madison Avenue on the Upper East Side, longtime workers described starting out at wages of thirty and forty dollars a day. The owners did not respond to requests for comment.

The contrast between owners' and workers' lives can be stark.

Sophia Hong, who owned Madison Nails in Scarsdale, N.Y., prides herself on her art collection, including at least one work by Park Soo Keun, a Korean artist who had a painting sell for nearly $2 million at Christie's in 2012. The art hangs in her home in Bayside, Queens, one of several properties she owns, according to property records, including a Manhattan apartment in a luxury building overlooking Columbus Circle. In 2010, she was sued by an employee at her Scarsdale salon for failing to pay overtime. The case was settled. Ms. Hong declined to comment.

In rare instances when owners have been found guilty of wage theft, salons have often been quickly sold, sometimes to relatives. The original proprietors vanish, along with their assets, according to prosecutors. Even if they do not, collecting back wages is difficult. Owners can claim they do not have the means to pay, and it is often impossible to prove otherwise, given how unreliable salons' financial records are.

Despite winning a landmark court award of over $474,000 in 2012 for underpayment, six manicurists from a chain of Long Island salons under the name Babi have so far received less than a quarter of that, they said. The chain's owner, In Bae Kim, said he did not have the money, even though records show he sold his house for $1.13 million and a commercial property for $2 million just before the trial.

Mr. Kim was arrested last year by the state attorney general's office on charges of harassing a manicurist at the worker's new job. He pleaded guilty to disorderly conduct on January 3 and was sentenced to time served—eight days in jail.

Lack of Investigations

During the nearly three months Ms. Ren worked unpaid in the Long Island nail salon, like many manicurists, she had no idea that it was against the law or that the thirty-dollar day wage her boss finally paid her was also illegally low. As an immigrant, she felt happy to have any work at all, she said, and scared to complain. Furthermore, who would listen?

The Labor Department is the New York State agency responsible for monitoring wage violations. An examination by the *Times* of the department's enforcement database dating from 2008, obtained under the state's Freedom of Information Law, found the department typically opens two or three dozen nail salon cases a year across the entire state. According to census data, there were more than 3,600 nail salons in the state in 2012, the most recent year for which figures were available.

The department opened a vast majority of these cases in response to worker complaints, as opposed to initiating its own investigations, the data show.

A team of investigators regularly performs undercover sweeps of businesses suspected of breaking the law, but the agency had never conducted a sweep of nail salons until last year, said Christopher White, a spokesman for the Labor Department. He declined last month to say more about the salons in the operation or the violations found, because the investigation had not yet been closed. But a review of the thirty-seven cases opened in 2014 showed that almost one-third of them involved shops from a single chain, Envy Nails, the one facing a class-action lawsuit from its workers.

When the department does investigate a salon, more than 80 percent of the time the agency finds workers have been unpaid or underpaid and tries to recover the money, The *Times* analysis showed.

The department declined to make anyone available to discuss its investigative work on the record. It took nine months of repeated inquiries from the *Times* for the department to turn over part of its enforcement database.

Only a small number of the workers interviewed by the *Times* said they had ever seen an investigator, from any government agency, at their salon.

Among the Labor Department's 115 investigators statewide—56 are based in New York City—18 speak Spanish and 8 speak Chinese, essential tools for questioning immigrant workers to uncover whether they are being exploited. But just two speak Korean, according to the department. Department officials say all of their inspectors have access to interpreting services.

When investigators try to interview them, manicurists are frequently reluctant to cooperate, more so than in any other industry, according to a Labor Department official involved who spoke on the condition of anonymity because the official was not permitted to talk with reporters. "It's really the only industry we see that in," the person said, explaining that it most likely indicated just how widespread exploitation is in nail salons. "They are totally running scared in this industry."

Manicurists are also required to be licensed, but this is another area where enforcement is lax. There are nearly 30,000 licensed nail technicians in the state, according to the New York Department of State, but numerous manicurists work without licenses. Licenses are frequently fabricated, bought, and sold.

Manicurists say that even when government agencies do check on their employers, evasion is easy.

Lili, a manicurist from Ecuador who is picked up every morning in Flushing near Ms. Ren, laughs when she recalls the time state inspectors visited the Westchester County salon where she works. Spotting them, her boss barked for all the unlicensed workers—there were ten—to hustle out the back door.

"So we left, we got in the car, and we took a spin around the neighborhood," said Lili, who declined to give her surname because she is in this country illegally. "Twenty, thirty minutes later we returned. After they'd gone. We put our uniforms back on and we returned to work."

No Refunds

This past fall, Ms. Ren's parents arrived from China. Work had dried up for her mother, an insurance saleswoman, and father, a sometime chef, and they missed their only child. The visitors stuffed the one-bedroom with a total of eight bodies before Ms. Ren, her mother, and her father had to move out. The manicurist packed up her pet fish, and the family installed itself a few blocks down Union Street in a dank basement apartment, where for $830 a month the three share one bedroom.

At work Ms. Ren earned a raise, lifting her spirits. She now made forty dollars a day.

Inspired by her cousin, who had enrolled again in English classes, Ms. Ren signed up as well in October, three days a week. School, she hoped, would be a way out of a job she had come to loathe, but some days her hands ached too much to go to class—she could not hold a pencil. Other days she was just too tired.

Around the time her first semester of English classes wrapped up, Ms. Ren asked for another raise. It was then she learned there are actually two price lists at her salon. One is for customers. The other is jotted down in a hidden-away notebook and lists the prices employees must pay the owner to learn new skills: such as one hundred dollars for eyebrow waxing, one hundred dollars to learn how to apply gel and cure it with ultraviolet light. A raise would require a new skill—her boss suggested eyebrows and gel—and the cash fee.

She was in the nail salon van when her boss told her of the fee, as he drove her to a different Long Island salon he owns. He shuttles employees between the two shops, depending upon which is busiest. An iPad propped on the dashboard played video feeds from both salons. Ms. Ren responded to the new fee with uncharacteristic furor.

Her boss relented: He would give her a 50 percent discount. She refused.

"I already paid when I first came," she said. "Now I'm an employee and have been here for so long. Why do I still have to pay to pick up new skills?"

In an interview, Mr. Sun, Ms. Ren's boss, said the fees were "deposits" so employees did not leave with their new skills for another salon and were eventually refunded. Ms. Ren said she never got back the hundred dollars she had paid.

For weeks after the van ride, she dreamed of quitting. But there was another semester of English classes in the spring, and though her parents pledged to help support her, they could not do it alone.

The final affront was a red envelope embossed in gold, a traditional Lunar New Year gift her boss placed in her hands in February, the Chinese character for happiness and luck gleaming from the paper. She opened it to find just twenty dollars.

She quit on March 8. Her boss said nothing; one colleague hugged her goodbye. After ten months she had made about $10,000, she said.

Last month, she found a sixty-five-dollar-a-day job at another nail salon.

By then, her parents had also found work. Her father is a cook at a restaurant.

Her mother? She became a manicurist, for thirty dollars a day.

Associated Press

"If Americans and Europeans are eating this fish, they should remember us": so says Hlaing Min, an Indonesian caught up in an age-old practice that has reemerged in the global fishing industry: slavery. Rising prices have increased the demand for commercial fishing, one of the most dangerous jobs in the world. This has led to the rise of a new breed of agent that will go to any lengths, including kidnapping, to find workers. A team from the Associated Press crisscrossed the globe to gather damning evidence.

Robin McDowell,
Margie Mason, and
Martha Mendoza

6. Are Slaves Catching the Fish You Buy?

Benjina, Indonesia—The Burmese slaves sat on the floor and stared through the rusty bars of their locked cage, hidden on a tiny tropical island thousands of miles from home.

Just a few yards away, other workers loaded cargo ships with slave-caught seafood that clouds the supply networks of major supermarkets, restaurants, and even pet stores in the United States.

But the eight imprisoned men were considered flight risks—laborers who might dare run away. They lived on a few bites of rice and curry a day in a space barely big enough to lie down, stuck until the next trawler forces them back to sea.

"All I did was tell my captain I couldn't take it anymore, that I wanted to go home," said Kyaw Naing, his dark eyes pleading into an Associated Press video camera sneaked in by a sympathetic worker. "The next time we docked," he said nervously out of earshot of a nearby guard, "I was locked up."

Here, in the Indonesian island village of Benjina and the surrounding waters, hundreds of trapped men represent one of the most desperate links criss-crossing between companies and countries in the seafood industry. This intricate web of connections separates the fish we eat from the men who catch it and obscures a brutal truth: Your seafood may come from slaves.

The men the AP interviewed on Benjina were mostly from Myanmar, also known as Burma, one of the poorest countries in the world. They were brought to Indonesia through Thailand and forced to fish. Their catch was then shipped back to Thailand, where it entered the global stream of commerce.

Tainted fish can wind up in the supply chains of some of America's major grocery stores, such as Kroger, Albertsons, and Safeway; the nation's largest retailer, Wal-Mart; and the biggest food distributor, Sysco. It can find its way into the supply chains of some of the most popular brands of canned pet food, including Fancy Feast, Meow Mix, and Iams. It can turn up as calamari at fine dining restaurants, as imitation crab in a California sushi roll, or as packages of frozen snapper relabeled with store brands that land on our dinner tables.

In a year-long investigation, the AP talked to more than forty current and former slaves in Benjina. The AP documented the journey of a single large shipment of slave-caught seafood from the Indonesian village, tracking it by satellite to a gritty Thai harbor. Upon its arrival, AP journalists followed trucks that loaded and drove the seafood over four nights to dozens of factories, cold-storage plants, and the country's biggest fish market.

The tainted seafood mixes in with other fish at a number of sites in Thailand, including processing plants. U.S. Customs records show that several of those Thai factories ship to America. They also sell to Europe and Asia, but the AP traced shipments to the United States, where trade records are public.

By this time, it is nearly impossible to tell where a specific fish caught by a slave ends up. However, entire supply chains are muddied, and money is trickling down the line to companies that benefit from slave labor.

The major corporations contacted would not speak on the record but issued statements that strongly condemned labor abuses. All said they were taking steps to prevent forced labor, such as working with human rights groups to hold subcontractors accountable.

Several independent seafood distributors who did comment described the costly and exhaustive steps taken to ensure their supplies are clean. They said the discovery of slaves underscores how hard it is to monitor what goes on halfway around the world.

Santa Monica Seafood, a large independent importer that sells to restaurants, markets, and direct from its store, has been a leader in improving international fisheries and sends buyers around the world to inspect vendors.

"The supply chain is quite cloudy, especially when it comes from offshore," said Logan Kock, vice president for responsible sourcing, who acknowledged that the industry recognizes and is working to address the problem. "Is it possible a little of this stuff is leaking through? Yeah, it is possible. We are all aware of it."

The slaves interviewed by the AP had no idea where the fish they caught was headed. They knew only that it was so valuable, they were not allowed to eat it.

They said the captains on their fishing boats forced them to drink unclean water and work twenty- to twenty-two-hour shifts with no days off. Almost all said they were kicked, whipped with toxic stingray tails, or otherwise beaten if they complained or tried to rest. They were paid little or nothing as they hauled in heavy nets with squid, shrimp, snapper, grouper, and other fish.

Some shouted for help over the deck of their trawler in the port to reporters as bright fluorescent lights silhouetted their faces in the darkness.

"I want to go home. We all do," one man called out in Burmese, a cry repeated by others. The AP is not using the names of some men for their safety. "Our parents haven't heard from us for a long time. I'm sure they think we are dead."

Another glanced fearfully over his shoulder toward the captain's quarters, and then yelled: "It's torture. When we get beaten, we can't do anything back. . . . I think our lives are in the hands of the Lord of Death."

In the worst cases, numerous men reported maimings or even deaths on their boats.

"If Americans and Europeans are eating this fish, they should remember us," said Hlaing Min, thirty, a runaway slave from Benjina. "There must be a mountain of bones under the sea. . . . The bones of the people could be an island, it's that many."

·　　　·　　　·

For Burmese slaves, Benjina is the end of the world.

Roughly 3,500 people live in the town that straddles two small islands separated by a five-minute boat ride. Part of the Maluku chain, formerly known as the Spice Islands, the area is about 400 miles north of Australia and hosts small kangaroos and rare birds of paradise with dazzling bright feathers.

Benjina is impossible to reach by boat for several months of the year, when monsoon rains churn the Arafura Sea. It is further cut off by a lack of Internet access. Before a cell tower was finally installed last month, villagers would climb nearby hills each evening in the hope of finding a signal strong enough to send a text. An old landing strip has not been used in years.

The small harbor is occupied by Pusaka Benjina Resources, whose five-story office compound stands out and includes the cage with the slaves. The company is the only fishing operation on Benjina officially registered in Indonesia and is listed as the owner of more than ninety trawlers. However, the captains are Thai, and the Indonesian government is reviewing to see if the boats are really Thai-owned. Pusaka Benjina did not respond to phone calls and a letter and did not speak to a reporter who waited for two hours in the company's Jakarta office.

On the dock in Benjina, former slaves unload boats for food and pocket money. Many are men who were abandoned by their captains—sometimes five, ten, or even twenty years ago—and remain stranded.

In the deeply forested island interiors, new runaways forage for food and collect rainwater, living in constant fear of being found by hired slave catchers.

And just off a beach covered in sharp coral, a graveyard swallowed by the jungle entombs dozens of fishermen. They are buried under fake Thai names given to them when they were tricked or sold onto their ships, forever covering up evidence of their captors' abuse, their friends say.

"I always thought if there was an entrance there had to be an exit," said Tun Lin Maung, a slave abandoned on Benjina, as other men nodded or looked at the ground. "Now I know that's not true."

The Arafura Sea provides some of the world's richest and most diverse fishing grounds, teeming with mackerel, tuna, squid, and many other species.

Although it is Indonesian territory, it draws many illegal fishing fleets, including from Thailand. The trade that results affects the United States and other countries.

The United States counts Thailand as one of its top seafood suppliers, and buys about 20 percent of the country's $7 billion annual exports in the industry. Last year, the State Department blacklisted Thailand for failing to meet minimum standards in fighting human trafficking, placing the country in the ranks of North Korea, Syria, and Iran. However, there were no additional sanctions.

Thailand's seafood industry is largely run off the backs of migrant laborers, said Kendra Krieder, a State Department analyst who focuses on supply chains. The treatment of some of these workers falls under the U.S. government's definition of slavery, which includes forcing people to keep working even if they once signed up for the jobs or trafficking them into situations where they are exploited.

"In the most extreme cases, you're talking about someone kidnapped or tricked into working on a boat, physically beaten, chained," said Krieder. "These situations would be called modern slavery by any measure."

The Thai government says it is cleaning up the problem. On the bustling floor of North America's largest seafood show in Boston earlier this month, an official for the Department of Fisheries laid out a plan to address labor abuse, including new laws that mandate wages, sick leave, and shifts of no more than fourteen hours. However, Kamonpan Awaiwanont stopped short when presented details about the men in Benjina.

"This is still happening now?" he asked. He paused. "We are trying to solve it. This is ongoing."

The Thai government also promises a new national registry of illegal migrant workers, including more than 100,000 flooding the seafood industry. However, policing has now become even harder because decades of illegal fishing have depleted stocks close to home, pushing the boats farther and deeper into foreign waters.

The Indonesian government has called a temporary ban on most fishing, aiming to clear out foreign poachers who take billions of dollars of seafood from the country's waters. As a result, more than fifty boats are now docked in Benjina, leaving up to 1,000 more slaves stranded onshore and waiting to see what will happen next.

Indonesian officials are trying to enforce laws that ban cargo ships from picking up fish from boats at sea. This practice forces men to stay on the water for months or sometimes years at a time, essentially creating floating prisons.

Susi Pudjiastuti, the new fisheries minister, said she has heard of different fishing companies putting men in cells. She added that she believes the trawlers on Benjina may really have Thai owners, despite the Indonesian paperwork, reflecting a common practice of faking or duplicating licenses.

She said she is deeply disturbed about the abuse on Benjina and other islands.

"I'm very sad. I lose my eating appetite. I lose my sleep," she said. "They are building up an empire on slavery, on stealing, on fish[ing] out, on massive environmental destruction for a plate of seafood."

·   ·   ·

The story of slavery in the Thai seafood industry started decades ago with the same push-and-pull that shapes economic immigration worldwide—the hope of escaping grinding poverty to find a better life somewhere else.

In recent years, as the export business has expanded, it has become more difficult to convince young Burmese or Cambodian migrants and impoverished Thais—all of whom were found on Benjina—to accept the dangerous jobs. Agents have become more desperate and ruthless, recruiting children and the disabled, lying about wages, and even drugging and kidnapping migrants, according to a former broker who spoke on condition of anonymity to avoid retribution.

The broker said agents then sell the slaves, usually to Thai captains of fishing boats or the companies that own them. Each slave typically costs around $1,000, according to Patima Tungpuchayakul, manager of the Thai-based nonprofit Labor Rights Promotion Network Foundation. The men are later told they have to work off the "debt" with wages that don't come for months or years or at all.

"The employers are probably more worried about the fish than the workers' lives," she said. "They get a lot of money from this type of business."

Illegal Thai boats are falsely registered to fish in Indonesia through graft, sometimes with the help of government authorities. Praporn Ekouru, a Thai former member of parliament, admitted to the AP that he had bribed Indonesian officials to go into their waters, and complained that the Indonesian government's crackdown is hurting business.

"In the past, we sent Thai boats to fish in Indonesian waters by changing their flags," said Praporn, who is also chairman of the Songkhla Fisheries Association in southern Thailand. "We had to pay bribes of millions of baht per year, or about 200,000 baht [$6,100] per month. . . . The officials are not receiving money anymore because this order came from the government."

Illegal workers are given false documents because Thai boats cannot hire undocumented crew. One of the slaves in Benjina, Maung Soe, said he was given a fake seafarer book belonging to a Thai national, accepted in Indonesia as an informal travel permit. He rushed back to his boat to dig up a crinkled copy.

"That's not my name, not my signature," he said angrily, pointing at the worn piece of paper. "The only thing on here that is real is my photograph."

Soe said he had agreed to work on a fishing boat only if it stayed in Thai waters, because he had heard Indonesia was a place from which workers never came back.

"They tricked me," he said. "They lied to me. . . . They created fake papers and put me on the boat, and now here I am in Indonesia."

The slaves said the level of abuse on the fishing boats depends on individual captains and assistants. Aung Naing Win, who left a wife and two children behind in Myanmar two years ago, said some fishermen were so depressed that they simply threw themselves into the water. Win, forty, said his most painful task was working without proper clothing in the ship's giant freezer, where temperatures drop to 39 degrees below zero.

"It was so cold, our hands were burning," he said. "No one really cared if anyone died."

·　　·　　·

The shipment the AP tracked from the port of Benjina carried fish from smaller trawlers; AP journalists talked to slaves on more than a dozen of them.

A crane hoisted the seafood onto a refrigerated cargo ship called the *Silver Sea Line*, with an immense hold as big as fifty semi-trucks. At this point, by United Nations and U.S. standards, every fish in that hold is considered associated with slavery.

The ship belongs to the Silver Sea Reefer Co., which is registered in Thailand and has at least nine refrigerated cargo boats. The company said it is not involved with the fishermen.

"We only carry the shipment and we are hired in general by clients," said owner Panya Luangsomboon. "We're separated from the fishing boats."

The AP followed the *Silver Sea Line* by satellite over fifteen days to Samut Sakhon. When it arrived, workers on the dock packed the seafood over four nights onto more than 150 trucks, which then delivered their loads around the city.

One truck bore the name and bird logo of Kingfisher Holdings Ltd., which supplies frozen and canned seafood around the world. Another truck went to Mahachai Marine Foods Co., a cold-storage business that also supplies to Kingfisher and other exporters, according to Kawin Ngernanek, whose family runs it.

"Yes, yes, yes, yes," said Kawin, who also serves as spokesman for the Thai Overseas Fisheries Association. "Kingfisher buys several types of products."

When asked about abusive labor practices, Kingfisher did not answer repeated requests for comment. Mahachai manager Narongdet Prasertsri responded, "I have no idea about it at all."

Every month, Kingfisher and its subsidiary KF Foods Ltd. sends about 100 metric tons of seafood from Thailand to America, according to U.S. Customs Bills of Lading. These shipments have gone to Santa Monica Seafood, Stavis Seafoods—located on Boston's historic Fish Pier—and other distributors.

Richard Stavis, whose grandfather started the dealership in 1929, shook his head when told about the slaves whose catch may end up at businesses he buys from. He said his company visits processors and fisheries, requires notarized certification of legal practices, and uses third-party audits.

"The truth is, these are the kind of things that keep you up at night," he said. "That's the sort of thing I want to stop. . . . There are companies like ours that care and are working as hard as they can."

Wholesalers like Stavis sell packages of fish, branded and un-branded, that can end up on supermarket shelves with a private label or house brand. Stavis'S customers also include Sysco, the largest food distributor in the United States; there is no clear way to know which particular fish was sold to them.

Sysco declined an interview, but the company's code of conduct says it "will not knowingly work with any supplier that uses forced, bonded, indentured or slave labor."

Gavin Gibbons, a spokesman for National Fisheries Institute, which represents about 75 percent of the U.S. seafood industry, said the reports of abuse were "disturbing" and "disheartening." "But these type of things flourish in the shadows," he said.

A similar pattern repeats itself with other shipments and other companies, as the supply chain splinters off in many directions in Samut Sakhon. It is in this Thai port that slave-caught seafood starts to lose its history.

The AP followed another truck to Niwat Co., which sells to Thai Union Manufacturing Co., according to part-owner Prasert Luangsomboon. Weeks later, when confronted about forced labor in their supply chain, Niwat referred several requests for comment to Luangsomboon, who could not be reached for further comment.

Thai Union Manufacturing is a subsidiary of Thai Union Frozen Products PCL., the country's largest seafood corporation, with $3.5 billion in annual sales. This parent company, known simply as Thai Union, owns Chicken of the Sea and is buying Bumble Bee, although the AP did not observe any tuna fisheries. In September, it became the country's first business to be certified by Dow Jones for sustainable practices after meeting environmental and social reviews.

Thai Union said it condemns human rights violations, but multiple stakeholders must be part of the solution. "We all have to admit that it is difficult to ensure the Thai seafood industry's supply chain is 100 percent clean," CEO Thiraphong Chansiri said in an e-mailed statement.

Thai Union ships thousands of cans of cat food to the United States, including household brands like Fancy Feast, Meow Mix, and Iams. These end up on shelves of major grocery chains, such as Kroger, Safeway, and Albertsons, as well as pet stores; again, however, it's impossible to tell if a particular can of cat food might have slave-caught fish.

Thai Union says its direct clients include Wal-Mart, which declined an interview but said in an e-mail statement: "We care about the men and women in our supply chain, and we are concerned about the ethical recruitment of workers."

Wal-Mart described its work with several nonprofits to end forced labor in Thailand, including Project Issara, and referred the AP to Lisa Rende Taylor, its director. She noted that slave-caught seafood can slip into supply chains undetected at several points, such as when it is traded between boats or mingles with clean fish at processing plants. She also confirmed that seafood sold at the Talay Thai market—to where the AP followed several trucks—can enter international supply chains.

"Transactions throughout Thai seafood supply chains are often not well-documented, making it difficult to estimate exactly how much seafood available on supermarket shelves around the world is tainted by human trafficking and forced labor," she said.

Poj Aramwattananont, president of an industry group that represents Thai Union, Kingfisher and others, said Thais are not "jungle people" and know that human trafficking is wrong. However, he acknowledged that Thai companies cannot always track down the origins of their fish.

"We don't know where the fish come from when we buy from Indonesia," said Poj of the Thai Frozen Foods Association. "We have no record. We don't know if that fish is good or bad."

•   •   •

The seafood the slaves on Benjina catch may travel around the world, but their own lives often end right here, in this island village.

A crude cemetery holds more than graves strangled by tall grasses and jungle vines, where small wooden markers are neatly labeled, some with the falsified names of slaves and boats. Only their friends remember where they were laid to rest.

In the past, former slave Hla Phyo said, supervisors on ships simply tossed bodies into the sea to be devoured by sharks. But after authorities and companies started demanding that every man be accounted for on the roster upon return, captains began stowing corpses alongside the fish in ship freezers until they arrived back in Benjina, the slaves said.

Lifting his knees as he stepped over the thick brush, Phyo searched for two grave markers overrun by weeds—friends he helped bury.

It's been five years since he himself escaped the sea and struggled to survive on the island. Every night, his mind drifts back to his mother in Myanmar. He knows she must be getting old now, and he desperately wants to return to her. Standing among so many anonymous tombs stacked on top of each other, hopelessness overwhelms him.

"I'm starting to feel like I will be in Indonesia forever," he said, wiping a tear away. "I remember thinking when I was digging, the only thing that awaits us here is death."

Dissent

Francesca Mari dissects the class implications of the personal-assistant economy in this fascinating analysis of the pipeline that funnels liberal-arts graduates into the elite worlds of Hollywood, publishing, and finance. The Ivy-educated personal assistant, both "privileged and exploited," is expected to perform an important person's grunt work with élan. "If you weren't brought up with these manners, you can't help but acquire them, at least to some degree, at an elite college. Manners are the mark of social and class affiliations, and assistantships, won by means of manners, ensure that exclusive professions remain the province of a certain class."

Francesca Mari

7. The Assistant Economy

I n 1975 Susan Sontag, the American intellectual famous for *On Photography* and *Against Interpretation*, was diagnosed with stage 4 breast cancer and survived after a radical mastectomy, extensive radiation treatments, and thirty months of debilitating chemotherapy. In the aftermath, she needed someone to help her catch up on her correspondence. Her editors at the *New York Review of Books* recommended a former *Review* assistant named Sigrid Nunez, who lived near Sontag on the Upper West Side.

Strictly speaking, Nunez was Sontag's assistant for a very short while. But the psychological fallout was significant. The first time Nunez arrived for work, Sontag grilled her for gossip about the *Review*. The second time, Nunez met Sontag's mother. The third time, Nunez was set up with Sontag's son, the nonfiction writer David Rieff. Soon they began dating, and Sontag invited Nunez to move in because she couldn't bear the thought of her son moving out.

Nunez was no longer an assistant, but Sontag still expected deference. Nunez, then an aspiring novelist (now an established one), would wake up early to try to snatch the solitude she needed to write, only for Sontag to knock on her door and cajole her into eating breakfast. Sontag wanted to edit Nunez's fiction, and she was hurt when Nunez didn't accept her suggestions. Nunez found the whole relationship difficult, perplexing, and at times almost obliterating.

She also learned a great deal about books and culture from Sontag and through her met some interesting people. In the case of the poet Joseph Brodsky, Sontag's one-time boyfriend, she ate Chinese food with them. "Do I even need to say what an enormous privilege it was to hear them both?" Nunez writes in her memoir of Sontag, *Sempre Susan*. "Looking back, I only wish that I could feel more joy—or, at least, that I could find a way of remembering that is not so painful." But why was it painful? While Nunez grew into her own as a writer, Sontag could only ever see her as a naïve student. Much later, when Sontag called Nunez to congratulate her on winning the prestigious Rome Prize, Sontag added, "You know, they offered that prize to me once." Thirty years later, writing her memoir, Nunez was still trying to explain the depth of the wound.

When I was an undergrad at Harvard, the English Department produced fancy brochures about the opportunities available to its majors: teacher, editor, Rhodes scholar. Personal assistant was not listed. I hadn't even heard of such positions until senior year, when older friends, artistically inclined friends, started snagging them. It's the position I think I've heard most about now.

Nearly every exclusive field runs on assistants. The actor James Franco, like Buddha before him, had an assistant keep track of his meals and school assignments. The critic and writer Daphne Merkin has employed a steady stream of Ivy-educated elves. They're tasked with everything from editing to returning dead houseplants. Best-selling novelist John Irving (*The Cider House Rules, A Prayer for Owen Meany*) has an assistant who types up his roughly twenty-five pages of handwritten manuscript a day. He recruits exclusively from liberal arts schools in cold climates like Middlebury and Vassar to ensure his hires can survive the winter at his home in Dorset, Vermont. During the 2008 presidential season, recent Harvard grad Eric Lesser impressed senior advisor to the president David Axelrod with his color-coded system for tracking Obama's campaign luggage. Lesser was taken on as Axelrod's "special assistant," assuming responsibility for everything from supervising his boss's diet to organizing the first-ever presidential seder.

Welcome to the main artery into creative or elite work—highly pressurized, poorly recompensed, sometimes exhilarating, sometimes menial secretarial assistance. From the confluence of two grand movements in American history—the continued flight of women out of the home and into the workplace, and the growing population of arts- and politically oriented college graduates struggling to survive in urban epicenters that are increasingly ceded to bankers and consultants—the personal assistant is born.

According to the Bureau of Labor Statistics, there were almost 4 million secretaries and administrative assistants in the United States in 2012. "Office and administrative positions" is one of the largest occupational groups in the United States and continues to grow. And yet the title "secretary" is all but nonexistent in the arts. Doctors and lawyers have secretaries or administrative assistants. Artists, intellectuals, politicians, and "creatives" have *personal* assistants—aptly named because the job responsibilities are so intimately bound up in the personality of the employer. And because of this, because of the ambitious nature of the people these assistants serve as well as the ambitious nature of the work assistants someday hope to do themselves, personal assistants are simultaneously more devoted to the job than an administrative assistant and less.

I. Recruiting

One of the most exceptional—and mysterious—personal assistantship programs is run by a hedge-fund billionaire in New York. For years, his human resources staff used to tuck the same discreet, neatly boxed advertisement in alongside the dense criticism of the *New Republic* and the *New York Review of Books*, as well as in Ivy League alumni magazines:

RESEARCH ASSOCIATE/PERSONAL ASSISTANT New York City—Highly intelligent, resourceful individuals with exceptional communication skills sought to undertake research projects and administrative tasks for one of Wall Street's most successful entrepreneurs. We welcome applications from writers, musicians, artists, or others who may be pursuing other professional goals in the balance of their time. $90–110k/yr to start (depending on qualifications). Resume to: gen8R@sps find.com

The firm recruits and interviews year-round, whether there are openings or not. In addition to ads, the billionaire's people e-mail Phi Beta Kappa and summa students from top colleges about openings at the firm, though they are also likely scouting for assistants. "Although much of our work involves the use of advanced mathematical and computational techniques," the e-mail reads, "we are equally interested in speaking with brilliant liberal arts graduates, regardless of major, who are open to the possibility of a career they may never have previously considered." It might be the only time in their lives that art students or English majors are courted by a potential employer. "The firm," the email continues, "can give serious consideration only to individuals having extraordinary intellectual capabilities, communication skills, and general 'real world' competence." Of the many who apply, a handful are called to New York, where their "real world competence" is quantified in no fewer than five management-consulting-style interviews. Interviewees sign nondisclosure forms and, if hired as personal assistants, are essentially barred from saying where they work. When pressed, they might say they are writing books or "making music."

The truth about this job is stranger than fiction, but, given the nondisclosure forms, only fiction can hint at what it's like to work in positions like these. Here is Edna, the protagonist of *The Mistakes Madeline Made*, a play by Elizabeth Meriwether (creator of *New Girl*), who once worked as an assistant herself:

> I am one of fifteen assistants to a family. . . . This family may be the Platonic Essence of Rich. Their rich is a higher order of being . . . Dad runs his home the way he runs his hedge fund— using a model to protect his family against the possibility of loss or waste or even just the unexpected. Oh. Oh. I hate them all.

Edna especially hates Beth, the overachieving (and older) leader of the "Household System." Beth is introduced to the audience glorying in the team's latest achievement: "I have finally received email confirmation that George likes the pair of sneakers we bought—listen to this—I believe he told Judith: 'Yay. Mommy. Yay. I love my sneakies.'"

Socially demeaning labor may be par for the postgraduate course, but it's uncanny how people like the hedge fund billionaire and others knew to target the creative types. It's as if they've spotted an inefficiency in the market of underemployed, educated people and turned it to their advantage. Agencies like the Celebrity Personal Assistant Network have also been cropping up to match assistants with employers. Countless other powerful people, however, find impressive assistants through their networks alone.

II. Snagging an Assistantship

The assistants I know didn't get their jobs through agencies or learn their craft from handbooks. One Harvard sophomore approached *New Yorker* writer Adam Gopnik after a reading and offered her assistance over the summer. She postponed her first semester of junior year to extend her stay. A classmate of hers took his fall 2008 semester off to assist former White House deputy chief of staff Karl Rove, whom he became acquainted with when, as president of the Harvard Republicans, he had invited Rove to speak on campus. As he recalled, at the time, the speech was one of the only ones that Rove had given at a college campus that went off without a hitch. Rove wrote him a thank-you card and then that summer sent a signed letter to his home in the oil-rich city of Midland, Texas, asking if he knew of anyone interested in an internship. He certainly did.

In other words, the assistants I know capitalized on what is perhaps the greatest benefit provided to them by their elite universities: access. The ones who snagged assistantships—and ultimately advanced from them—were not necessarily smarter or more creative, but they were more socially competent. They excelled at chat—a skill that comes naturally to those accustomed to attending their parents' cocktail parties and less naturally to many a middle-class nerd who has previously had no reason to doubt the meritocracy.

Harvard's Office of Career Services told me they do not have advice for a student looking to become a personal assistant. "If you have a passion for something," an OCS spokesperson told me, "you find a way to get in front of the people you want to work for." The skills required are really more like manners: a feel for how to mix deference, intelligence, and, most importantly, shared cultural references into conversation with a successful person. If you weren't brought up with these manners, you can't help but acquire them, at least to some degree, at an elite college. Manners are the mark of social and class affiliations, and assistantships, won by means of manners, ensure that exclusive professions remain the province of a certain class.

I asked the counselor if Harvard kids were actually any good at serving others. "A lot of students are used to running things on campus," she said. "And Harvard students are strong both orally and in communication and can multitask."

Did she know any students assisting someone famous? She knew a sophomore who had assisted Dustin Hoffman over the summer, but he hadn't found the job through OCS. "A family friend put him in touch with somebody, though I know he did a lot of theater around here."

"Do you know anyone else?" I asked.

"Don't you?" she said. "Oh, there's one other person. He works in the White House now. I think he carried Obama's bags. He made sure they got from one hotel to another. . . . He was written up in the *Times*."

III. Tasks

As a postproduction assistant working with the film director Robert Altman, CJ Gardella, a recent graduate from the School of Visual Arts, recounted how assistants from time to time helped fabricate fan mail, like:

Dear Mr. Altman,
    I loved Mash. I loved Nashville. You've got to make MASHVILLE!

                Love,
                Your biggest fan

As it happened, Gardella and the others genuinely liked and revered Altman; the notes were, in their own way, earnest. They were then tucked into the newspapers cushioning the materials being mailed to Altman—the "questionable materials," as Gardella referred to them, meaning weed. By Gardella's account, one package arrived ripped and empty, but most of the others made it to Altman in London or Los Angeles or, during the summer of 2005, in Minnesota, where he was shooting his final film, *A Prairie Home Companion.*

Gardella's father, a contractor, was renovating a home for a friend of one of Altman's producers when he learned that Altman needed an assistant. (He already knew, of course, that his son was looking for work.) Gardella interviewed and started as an unpaid intern in 2005 and after several months entered the payroll as a postproduction assistant. He logged footage, ordered lunch, dispensed "questionable" mailings, and made DVD "dups" (duplicates of footage). He toted Altman's lifetime achievement Oscar across town in a grocery bag. "The eagle has landed," he remembered Altman saying when he saw it in the office.

Gardella's position bore all the marks of an elite assistantship. It was prestigious: when people heard about his job, they were impressed. The work was both high-pressure and menial, not always the most pleasant combination, but he was also invited to screenings and exposed to industry giants. Gardella saw all the e-mails and phone calls that got a movie made, and, luckiest of all, he loved his boss. "With Altman I was [literally] wearing his shoes," Gardella told me. "They were black Pumas and everyone who saw me wear them said they were old man shoes. But in the office, they were the coolest."

Longitudinal studies of the data in the Internet Movie Database (IMDb) have found that the status of one's employer and project typically matters much more than the skill level and responsibilities of one's position. Over time, researchers suggest that assistantships tend to move towards mentorship, especially among those of the same gender. The ideal gig offers persistent contact with an employer, even if the job is more about fetching coffee and less about substantive creative work.

In 2010, *New York* magazine ran an infographic—"The Amazing Human Launching Pads"—about employers whose underlings go on to great things. It included people like chef Jean-Georges Vongerichten, TV writer-producer David Chase, and Robert Silvers, the editor and cofounder of the *New York Review of Books*. A staffer at the *NYRB* told me that every assistant in the office sent the charticle to his parents as proof that they weren't wasting the $160,000 that had been spent on their college education.

But make no mistake: today's assistantship is not an apprenticeship, which would be tightly regulated to ensure its utility. Apprentices training to be anything from an able seaman to an elevator constructor "earn as they learn"—on average $16.01 an hour from the first day. Apprentices have on-the-job mentors, and they get additional training from technical schools and community colleges. The average apprentice makes $33,301 per year—as much, if not more than, the average assistant. Upon completion of his or her training, an apprentice earns $54,829, or nearly double the salary of an assistant. (The hedge fund billionaire, because he himself is so far removed from what the people he hires want to be doing, must pay much more.)

An assistantship, then, may be more like an internship. The very word "intern," as Ross Perlin writes in *Intern Nation*, connotes both "privilege and exploitation." Privilege because of the intern's proximity to prestige and because of his (presumed) ability to forgo a salary, exploitation because of the menial and un(der)paid work. Like an intern, an assistant typically learns by observation and performs nebulous duties particular to the personality of the boss. In both cases, what's earned, if anything, is less valuable than the perceived professional benefits—the condoned voyeurism, the network of current and former assistants, the interesting e-mail addresses, friendly introductions, free galleys, and so on.

And the sheer ubiquity of assistantships and access to the most intimate details of one's boss has fed a pop-culture boomlet—the assistantship novel as contemporary upstairs/downstairs narrative. More than a hundred novels about glamorous and beleaguered personal assistants have been published, almost all since 2000. *The Devil Wears Prada* is the best known, but there are countless others: *Boss Lady, Safe at Second, As Long as She Needs Me, Life with My Sister Madonna, Chore Whore, A Total Waste of Makeup, The Lying Tongue, Final Witness,* and—rather wistfully—*Out-foxxed.*

As in *The Devil Wears Prada,* fear of the boss and the ever-present threat of dismissal line the personal assistant's work with both dread and excitement. Scott Rudin, the superproducer behind so many Oscar-nominated movies every year (in 2008, Rudin's *There Will Be Blood* and *No Country for Old Men* were nominated for eight Oscars each), is notorious for his temper (revealed on the front pages most recently by the Sony leak, in which he called Angelina Jolie a "minimally talented spoiled brat"). He has four or five assistants at any one time, and his former underlings now fill some of Hollywood's most prominent positions. But while practically every studio head has once served Rudin, the majority of his assistants don't survive the fourth month. The *Wall Street Journal* once quoted an estimate by some of Rudin's assistants that he had gone through 250 of them in five years. Rudin admitted to 119, excluding the kids who hadn't survived what he referred to as the two-week "trial period." Sometimes he fires them all at once. They tramp to the café across the street to await a call from the office manager, who often rehires them.

And to think: Rudin was once himself an assistant to the Broadway director and impresario Kermit Bloomgarden. "When I'd come home, my mother would ask, 'How was your day?'" Rudin told the *LA Times.* "And I'd say, 'I made lunch for Burt Lancaster.'"

IV. Advancement

Senior year of college, a friend of mine who was majoring in film struck up a lengthy e-mail correspondence with the assistant to director Darren Aronofsky (*Pi, Black Swan, The Wrestler*). He eventually learned that the assistant would soon be leaving and snagged the job. After my friend's first day, he went out to dinner to celebrate. At eight p.m., he remembers receiving a call and was about to silence it when he saw it was his new boss. "Do you have a paper and pencil?" Aronofsky allegedly asked. My friend took a second too long to respond. "The first rule of the job," he remembered Aronofsky saying, "is that you have a paper and pencil. Call me back."

What made the position appealing, my friend told me, was the implication that "if you do this job, you can do what I do." Not in terms of the creativity, but in terms of the time commitment, the need for organization, the need to deal with people, the practical things. "It's not like, 'If you do this job for me, I'll let you make movies.'" What distinguishes one smart kid from another, in a world full of them, are organizational skills and an up-for-anything diligence.

One problem is that the assistant's diligence cannot lead to a promotion. Technically, promotions don't exist. You can't become the person you assist, and so the strategic assistant curries favor, an especially fickle and undignified form of wage labor. In his memoir, *The Man in the Gray Flannel Skirt*, Jon-Jon Goulian, a former assistant to the *NYRB*'s Bob Silvers, wrote about the decision to quit a job that had once seemed so perfect:

> There was the matter of my ego. When Bob was thirty-four years old, he was commander in chief, at the helm of the ship, steering the *New York Review* to greatness. When I was thirty-four I was sharpening his pencils, and feeding him dried blueberries.

It didn't take more than a couple of years for Jon-Jon to accidentally call Bob "Baba," a bastardized version of what Jon-Jon called his father—Dada. It was a frightening slip because isn't the point of getting a job to begin to grow up?

V. Stagnation

When Gardella's gig with Robert Altman ended, he became director Noah Baumbach's (*The Squid and the Whale*, *Kicking and Screaming*) assistant. According to Gardella, although the two sat in adjacent rooms, Baumbach communicated almost exclusively by e-mail, requesting groceries, cars, and flight confirmations. Gardella says he learned by osmosis and by being around during initial cuts of the film. When Baumbach first screened *Margot at the Wedding*, Gardella distributed blank sheets of paper and pencils to the audience, who were instructed to write whatever occurred to them freely and anonymously. As Gardella waited to collect the responses, he took a sheet and wrote what he thought the director would most want to hear, simply "so good." He recalled that the next day, Baumbach brought out a stack of responses with that one on top. "See that?" he said. Gardella nodded.

When *Margot* wrapped, Gardella was out of work. He became an assistant to Gene Stavis, an influential film historian and one of Gardella's former teachers at the School of Visual Arts. "It's like an ever-descending spiral for you," Stavis joked. Gardella put all of his savings into the shooting of his first feature, *Shunka*. "I gave [the film] to Noah and he didn't get back to me," Gardella told me. "But, you know, he's busy."

Indeed, this may be just the job for Noah Baumbach's new assistant.

VI. Resignation

Nothing becomes an assistant so much as leaving his or her job. "The worst thing to be called," Aronofsky's assistant told me, long after he'd moved on, "is a really good assistant."

Diligence and deference have an expiration date, or at least they should. Assistantship fiction, usually written by former assistants, enacts countless fantasies of escape. In *Chore Whore*, by Heather H. Howard ("a personal assistant to some of the biggest names in Hollywood for more than two decades," according to her bio), a Hollywood PA named Corki, no longer young and no longer quite so enamored of backstage grit, gets out. Or, rather, she's replaced—the cowboy boyfriend of her boss of twenty years swaps in two twenty-year-olds from one of his foursomes. But regardless of whether Corki quit or was let go, the dignity that leaving affords her is just the same. In Meriwether's play, Edna eventually rebels against the tyranny of the Household System by stealing the hypoallergenic handiwipes, specially ordered from abroad for the son and, in doing so, precipitates the system's hysteric meltdown. Most famously, in the book *The Devil Wears Prada*, after a year of servility to the icy and abusive Anna Wintour–like fashion magazine editor named Miranda Priestly, twenty-three-year-old Andrea is too terrified to ask to leave Paris Fashion Week when her best friend is hospitalized after a drunk driving accident. Ashamed of prioritizing her job, she quits at Priestly's next tirade and, in short order, starts publishing her writing. In other words, these books always end with liberation from bondage. Assistant fiction is incapable, it seems, of imagining any other narrative arc.

For my own part, I graduated from college having spent three years working on a literary magazine, where it was considered uncouth to talk about a professional future. In high school, I'd never felt there was anything embarrassing about buying a study guide for an AP exam, but I never thought of buying one of the professional success books that fill the shelves at Barnes & Noble and the warehouses at Amazon. My assumption that I didn't need conventional career guidance betrayed a privilege I was as yet unaware of. Though I wasn't able to articulate it as such at the time, I believed that the creative class was immune to professional plotting and monetary concerns—that if I just worked hard enough on my essays and articles, I'd make enough money later in life, doing interesting work. I was the first in my family to attend a four-year college, and, needless to say, I was very naïve.

In some ways, I lucked out. An essay I wrote caught the eye of a professor who recommended me to the *New Republic* just when they were looking for a literary assistant, and a friend guided me through the application process. After a year and a half in Washington, I moved to New York, where I freelanced and took on fact-checking gigs, surviving on oatmeal, cereal, and Negra Modelo. My 2009 tax returns show an income of $14,000. The only food I bought out was two falafels and a meal with another former assistant, who asked me out on a date and then argued that I wasn't that poor if I could afford milk (eating cereal, he said, was expensive). When it was time to pay, he had no cash—and this West Village restaurant didn't take cards. Then I found another literary assistantship. It was to be my last.

Years after Sigrid Nunez broke up with Sontag's son and moved out, Sontag decided that she wanted an actual personal assistant. She called up Nunez for a recommendation, and when Nunez suggested a young girl they knew, Sontag raged, "I don't want some kid! I'm not looking for a typist! I need someone who knows me and knows my work and the things I care about. Oh, just forget it. Clearly, you have no idea what it means to be in my situation."

Sontag was chronically lonely, never more so than when she was left to her own thoughts. Not every boss's hunger for daily affirmation and support is quite so palpable. But often, an assistant is hired as much for the fawning as for the typing—whether it's conveyed through knowledge or attentiveness or actual praise. Ideally, the assistant is a forgiving fan, the perfect receptacle for inchoate ideas.

But inevitably, the boss's inchoate ideas and preferences press upon the assistant, sometimes forever. "Boring, like servile, was one of her favorite words," Nunez writes.

Another was *exemplary*. Also, *serious*. "You can tell how serious people are by looking at their books." She meant not only what books they had on their shelves but how the books were arranged.... Because of her, I arranged my own books by subject and in chronological rather than alphabetical order. I wanted to be serious.

But perhaps the real expense of this work is how much the boss—and the idea of the boss—occupies his assistants after hours. Witnessing the behavior of a man or woman with no time for privacy only makes his or her inner life more fascinating. Is he aware that his mind has flip-flopped? Or that he just assumed his assistant's idea? Whom is he angry at when he chucks a no. 2 pencil across the room? Look at that love letter! This mythologizing is relentless and trifling, but it fills a real need: the need to justify your job by making your boss as big and as marvelous as possible. And that, after all, is what the boss always wanted.

Businessweek

Claire Suddath takes to the cover of Bloomberg's *Businessweek* to show what a backwater the United States is when it comes to maternity (and paternity) leave. The only other country in the world that doesn't guarantee paid maternity leave is impoverished Papua New Guinea. This lack has huge consequences not only for quality of life but also for the U.S. economy. Suddath looks to Scandinavia to show what a more modern system—one that doesn't nudge women out of the workforce—looks like.

Claire Suddath

8. Can the U.S. Ever Fix Its Messed-Up Maternity Leave System?

One week into her new job, Letitia Camire learned she was pregnant. It was 2011, and she'd just been hired as the office manager for United Tool and Machine, a small, family-owned tool and die company outside Boston. Her salary was $30,000 a year. Camire clicked with her coworkers immediately. Her boss, the owner and president, started asking her about long-term career goals. "They seemed so family-oriented," says Camire, now thirty-two. So when her morning sickness became noticeable ("I just sat at my desk looking like death warmed over"), she felt she owed her new work family an explanation. She was only a few weeks along when she walked into the president's office one morning, shut the door, and told him she was pregnant.

"His face immediately changed," she says. "The first words out of his mouth were, 'You know you're still on your ninety-day probation period.' So I pretty much knew what that meant." A few weeks later, she was let go. The company told her it was a reorganization move, but she didn't buy it. She knew that according to the 1978 Pregnancy Discrimination Act, firing or demoting an employee because she's pregnant is illegal, but she also knew discrimination can be hard to prove. The U.S. Supreme Court recently considered the case of Peggy Young, a United Parcel Service employee who was forced into unpaid leave when she told her company she was pregnant and couldn't carry packages heavier than twenty pounds. Young has lost in lower courts because UPS's accommodation of disabilities not caused by workplace injuries is gender-neutral. The court will issue its decision later this year. "I didn't have the financial resources to fight," Camire says. United Tool and Machine says Camire was let go because her job was eliminated, and that the president was unaware she was pregnant at the time.

Camire soon found herself in the awkward position of interviewing for jobs while pregnant. She wasn't showing yet, but she told recruiters anyway. "I just didn't want to waste anyone's time," she says. Luckily, the Israel-based electronics company Orbotech had no qualms about hiring her. Camire was a new employee, though, so she didn't qualify for the short-term disability insurance that it, like many companies, uses as a workaround to give maternity leave. Instead, she ran through her sick days and vacation time and relied on her husband's salary to allow her to take nine weeks off, unpaid. "We put a lot of things on credit cards," she says. They stopped going out to dinner. They streamlined their grocery budget, drove their cars as little as possible, and gave up—for a while, anyway—the idea of saving for retirement. "Financially, I probably should've been back even sooner than that," Camire says. But she couldn't find a local day-care center that would take such a young baby.

Her story isn't unusual. Unless you work for a company that voluntarily offers it, or in one of three states, paid maternity leave doesn't exist in the United States. A law called the Family and Medical Leave Act (FMLA) grants up to twelve weeks of unpaid leave every year, but it applies only to full-time workers at companies with fifty or more employees. About half of all working Americans are covered by FMLA. The other half—freelancers, contract workers, entrepreneurs, people who work at small businesses—are on their own. Paid leave is even rarer: Only 12 percent of American workers have access to it in the United States, according to the Bureau of Labor Statistics.

This comes as a shock to a lot of young women. "Wait, what?" Kathryn, thirty-three, says about the moment she realized the New York media startup she'd recently joined didn't offer maternity leave. "I thought we had laws about this." (Kathryn asked to have her last name withheld because of a nondisclosure agreement with her former company.)

Most new mothers are in their twenties or thirties, which means they grew up in a world of female Supreme Court justices, politicians, and astronauts. They have more college degrees than men, they entered the workforce in near-equal numbers, and they chose their careers assuming that having children wouldn't mean losing money. Almost two-thirds of women with children under six work, about twice the rate of the previous generation. "I went to college and found something I loved. I got a job. I married and had babies and just assumed maternity leave was something that existed," says Annalisa Spencer, thirty-one, an electrical engineer in Salt Lake City who has three children and got no leave for the third. "Nobody told me it would be like this."

In 2013, Senator Kirsten Gillibrand (D-N.Y.) introduced legislation that would make employers offer new parents three months of paid leave at 66 percent of their salary, but the bill, the Family Act, has been stalled in Congress for more than a year. Even if it passes, it won't fix a system that paints a huge segment of the workforce into a corner. In a country where the median household income is $53,000, 66 percent of a salary might not be enough to support a family. But the Family Act would drastically change the lives of many American workers. One of the reasons women make less than men—sixteen cents per dollar less, according to the Pew Research Center—is that they're clustered in lower-paying fields or in positions where they work fewer hours.

Yet young women right out of college experience almost no gap at all. The discrepancy grows as they get older and advance—or fail to advance—in their careers. And the first bump in the road seems to happen right as they start to have children.

. . .

According to the United Nations' International Labour Organization, there are only two countries in the world that don't have some form of legally protected, partially paid time off for working women who've just had a baby: Papua New Guinea and the United States.

The United States is also way behind the seventy-eight countries that also offer leave to fathers. Forcing mothers back to work early can have consequences for children. When they're on maternity leave, their children are more likely to be breast-fed and taken to the doctor for checkups. Studies have found that a year after having a baby, women who took at least a month of leave reported higher salary increases.

With no federal action, some states have stepped in. Five states pay new mothers through their disability insurance programs. In 2004, California passed the country's first paid parental leave law, open to both mothers and fathers. There, new parents get up to six weeks off at 55 percent of their current paycheck, up to about $1,000 a week. Since then, New Jersey and Rhode Island have followed.

The policies vary widely across industries and pay grades. A BLS survey of "business, management, and finance" workers—basically, those in white-collar jobs—found that 26 percent of them get paid leave. At many Silicon Valley companies, which compete for talent, new parents have it made. Facebook offers a little more than four months to everyone. Google offers five for mothers and three for fathers or new adoptive parents. The company developed its policy a few years ago when it noticed that many new mothers were quitting their jobs. After it added two more months and offering full pay, the number of new mothers who left the company dropped by half.

Some older companies also have generous policies. Goldman Sachs offers four paid months, and General Electric offers two months to moms and two weeks to dads or other parents. Waitresses and sales clerks are often out of luck; only 6 percent of service workers get anything at all. That means the ability to adjust to parenthood, learn to breast-feed, and manage a newborn becomes a luxury only certain people can afford. "We have these policies set up from the *Mad Men* era when dads worked and moms stayed at home. But that doesn't reflect the American workforce anymore," says Gillibrand, who as partner at the Manhattan law firm Boies, Schiller & Flexner wrote the firm's maternity leave policy in 2002.

Recently, some companies have started to offer leave to fathers. This decreases the likelihood that an employer will shy away from hiring young women, and it destigmatizes the idea that new dads need time off, too. In the ten years since California adopted its policy, the number of requests submitted by men has gone up each year and stands at 26 percent. In general, the amount of time they take off is much shorter, typically no more than a week or two. And as children age, the cost of day care and nannies starts to squeeze families' income, sometimes prompting one of the parents to go part-time or decide to stay home. Even today, that person is usually the mother.

In most places, the only parent offered time off is the mother; she qualifies for short-term disability insurance after she physically gives birth. That's what Spencer, the electrical engineer in Utah, used when she got six weeks at half pay after she had her first child. (She skipped payments on her 401(k) to take another six unpaid.) By the time her third child came along, she had dropped down to part-time so she wouldn't have to pay so much for rising day-care costs, which meant she didn't get any maternity leave at all. "I'm hourly now, so it's not like I'm getting paid for time I'm not working," she says. She spent her last maternity leave working from home.

Even women in high-income positions have trouble figuring out how the patchwork of policies applies to them. "I have three months of paid leave, forty-six days of unused vacation time that I saved up, and then the six weeks that California offers, but I don't know if it runs concurrently with my vacation time. It was very confusing. For a while I didn't even know what day my leave officially ended," Jeanette Barzelay, a civil litigation attorney in San Francisco, told me. Because Barzelay lives in California, she's covered under the state's paid-leave law.

Despite the confusing system, Barzelay did take a lot of time off—six months, partially paid. But most people, even in California, aren't that lucky. Colleen, a fast-talking forty-four-year-old television director in Los Angeles, didn't use California's paid leave when she had her second child in 2008 because it doesn't include job protection. For years, she has worked sixty-five- to seventy-hour weeks with studios such as Walt Disney and Nickelodeon. (Colleen asked to have her last name withheld because she doesn't want to jeopardize her relationship with the studios.) She's highly paid, but as with most production workers in Hollywood, her contracts for TV shows run from week to week. Because she's a contract employee, FMLA doesn't cover her, and California's law, which does, doesn't require studios to let her keep her job. "There's this kind of unwritten, unspoken thought that you could be replaced at any moment," she says. So when a TV studio asked her to return to work three weeks after having a C-section, she had to show up. "I told them I needed to recover from major surgery before I go back to running around on set all day. They were like, 'Umm, we really need you back,'" she says. "I wasn't in a position to argue with them."

Gillibrand's bill would apply to every company, no matter what size, and would keep people like Camire from having to rely on credit cards or people like Colleen from working right after a C-section. It includes fathers, adoptive parents, and same-sex parents and would be paid through a new payroll tax of two-tenths of 1 percent. It's endorsed by groups such as the National Partnership for Women and Families and the Small Business Majority. The U.S. Chamber of Commerce and the National Restaurant Association, which have historically opposed paid leave, haven't come out against it. Furthermore, polls suggest that paid family leave is overwhelmingly supported by men and women across the political spectrum.

So why is the Family Act at a standstill? Gillibrand says Congress doesn't think it's important enough. "The issue isn't being raised because too many of the members of Congress were never affected by it," she says, pointing out that 80 percent of Congress is older and male. "They're not primary caregivers. Most members of Congress are affluent and are able to afford help or able to support their [wives]. It's not a problem for most of them." Hillary Clinton has also admitted that while she supports paid leave, it's a political battle the United States isn't ready to fight. "I don't think, politically, we could get it [passed] now," she said in a CNN town-hall meeting last June.

Washington won't be able to ignore this forever. "You're finally starting to see momentum on this issue," says Debra Ness, president of the National Partnership for Women and Families. Over the past decade, Ness has noticed that young parents are becoming increasingly angry at the lack of employer support when they start to have children. "This will be part of the conversation during the next election," she says. "The sleeping giant is waking up."

Before it was passed, California's law was vehemently opposed by manufacturing and small-business associations, which argued that it would be too hard for companies with just a few employees to handle someone's six-week absence. The California Chamber of Commerce called it a "job killer." To get it passed, lawmakers agreed to fund the law by taxing people's paychecks, not businesses. As a result, a 2011 survey found that 91 percent of California business owners said the law either helped or had no effect on their profitability. The National Bureau of Economic Research found that California women in low-wage jobs were more than three times as likely to take some sort of maternity leave under the law and returned to their old jobs in higher numbers. Over time their wages were higher, too. "Businesses in California don't seem to be reporting a strong negative effect. I haven't seen evidence of a significant downside," says Christopher Ruhm, a professor of public policy and economics at the University of Virginia.

Gillibrand's bill is a sweeping piece of legislation that would, as Carrie Lukas, the managing director of the conservative Independent Women's Forum, puts it, "rewrite employment contracts for every working American." Lukas is against the act because she's "worried about the way it'll change women's employment prospects. It's written in gender-neutral language, but every employer in their right mind knows who's going to take advantage of these benefits." As hard as it might be for paid-leave advocates to accept, she has a point. That's exactly what happened in Sweden.

·   ·   ·

In any discussion of parental leave, Sweden is the promised land. Parents are given sixteen months of paid leave, two of which are reserved just for fathers, and they can divide the rest however they like until their child is eight years old. While on leave, the government pays 80 percent of the parent's income, even if she's self-employed.

"We've got it so good here," says Christine Demsteader, a single mother living in Stockholm. She runs her own communications company but still took sixteen months off when her only child was born a few years ago. "The thing is, we have only one system for doing things: Women take a year off, then they go back to work and the kid goes into day care," she says. "You don't have another option."

"And it's understood that a woman who becomes a mother cannot have the same career as a man," adds her friend Lisa Rydberg, who'd run over to Demsteader's house when she heard that an American journalist was calling.

For all Sweden's efforts at gender equality, men still make about 35 percent more than women, according to a 2012 Swedish government report. And although the top five spots on the World Economic Forum's Global Gender Gap index are all held by Nordic countries, their percentage of female chief executive officers is no higher than the 5 percent achieved by Fortune 500 companies in the United States. "I just know I'd get a promotion three years later than a colleague who is a man," says Rydberg. "That's how it is."

Intentionally or not, Sweden seems to have routed women onto the "mommy track," a slower, less demanding career path for women with children. In the United States it often comes under the guise of the purposefully vague term "caregiver status," which companies use when offering reduced hours and a lower salary to parents who need flexibility. In academia, universities will often pause the so-called tenure clock for female professors who take time off to have children. Some of these policies can be helpful. But they also have the side effect of segregating those who use them into positions where they're just not expected to advance.

Most women try to get around this by gaming the system. A biology professor at the University of Pittsburgh planned her pregnancy so that she'd give birth during the summer, when she already had time off. (Unpaid, of course.) Colleen the TV director tried to have her kids between TV seasons; she succeeded two out of three times. Of course, this method assumes a woman gets pregnant only when she wants to, she has a healthy pregnancy and delivery, and her baby doesn't need special care. "I had this one window when I had to have the baby," Kate Lytton, a ballet teacher in Akron, told me. Lytton had her daughter in July and took six weeks off unpaid but could do that only because classes weren't in session. "When she was a week late, I worried she'd cut into my leave time."

In fields without a seasonal break, women put off having children until they're in a senior position, then cross their fingers and hope it's not too late. "The standard practice for women in law is to make partner first and then start a family," says Chelsea Petersen, a partner at the law firm Perkins Coie in Seattle. Nine years ago she was thirty-four and a midlevel associate at the firm, which is exactly the wrong time—professionally—to have kids. "That's when you're really working hard, trying to prove yourself. But with my age, I couldn't wait another seven years," she says. A year after having her first and only child, Petersen found herself crying in a fetal position on the floor of her office, suffering from exhaustion. "Days would go by where I wouldn't have eaten a real meal or taken care of myself for five minutes," she says. Over the years, Perkins Coie has extended its leave policy to cover fathers and created a support group for working parents. Still, Petersen can count at least ten women in her department who've left, many because the demands on their time were too much. As far as she knows, she's the only one who had a baby, made partner, and stayed full-time.

Not everyone can work as hard as Petersen. Or even wants to. "Listen, I know Sheryl Sandberg wants me to lean in," Colleen told me. In her book *Lean In* and her 2010 TED Talk, the Facebook COO urged women to accept promotions or go for new jobs even when they knew they might be pregnant soon. "Well, OK, Sheryl, I think that's a really great notion," Colleen says. "But it's different for us. It just flat out is. There is nothing we can do about it, because biologically it's like, well, you're having babies now."

Luckily, there is some middle ground between the American patchwork and Swedish sabbatical—and the best example of it is Canada. "Unlike the Scandinavian countries, Canada's tax rate isn't radically different from the U.S.," says Ruhm at the University of Virginia, which means any program it has could conceivably be implemented in the United States. "I've become an incrementalist—try something small, see if it's working, and then tweak it. That's what Canada does." Canada passed its first national maternity leave law in 1971 and has been adjusting it ever since. In 2000 it lengthened its available leave from six months to a year. About four months of that is reserved for mothers; the rest is available to all parents. They receive 55 percent of their salary (up to an income limit), paid through the country's unemployment insurance program, and are guaranteed their jobs when they go back to work.

Gillibrand's Family Act looks a lot like Canada's model. And because it has never been debated or amended—the Senate Finance Committee has been quietly ignoring it for more than a year—it hasn't yet been muddied up with loopholes or concessions. It won't turn working motherhood into anything resembling "easy." But it may be the closest thing to a workable solution.

·   ·   ·

Nine weeks after Camire had her baby, a daughter she named Catherine, she went back to work at Orbotech. "I was like, thank God I get to talk to someone other than a lump!" she laughs. She stayed at the company for two years, where she oversaw sales and shipping. In 2013 she became pregnant with her second child. This time, Camire qualified for the company's short-term disability pay, which allowed her six weeks off at two-thirds of her salary. (FMLA provided another six, unpaid.) Then she started thinking about the future. Day-care costs for her children would run about $25,000 a year in Boston. When she factored in gas, meals, and other costs, the amount of money she'd be able to provide for her family was laughably small. So three months before she was supposed to go on maternity leave, Camire told her manager she wouldn't be coming back.

"The company was completely shocked," she says. Sure, she could've taken the leave and then refused to come back afterward, but Camire didn't want to do that. "I would've burned bridges personally and professionally. That sat heavily on me."

For the next few years, she'll stay at home. Her son, Charlie, is seven months old. Catherine is almost three. Camire's days are filled with diapers and bottles and nap times that never seem to align. In some ways, raising a child while working was easier, she says. "At day care, I had someone to help me figure out the developmental milestones. They'd send a note saying, y'know, Catherine takes an eight-ounce bottle now instead of six. With Charlie, I have to figure that out on my own." She misses Orbotech sometimes and plans to go back to work in a few years once the kids are in school. She just hopes no one minds the long employment gap on her résumé.

Washington Post

Catherine Rampell jars readers with the story of Charles Gladden, a man who works in the United States Senate and lives near the White House. But Gladden is no power broker. He works in the Senate cafeteria, makes eleven dollars an hour, and sleeps in a Metro station. In showing how the inequities of twenty-first-century America run through even its most hallowed democratic institutions, Rampell illuminates the disconnect between the ruling class and its servants.

Catherine Rampell

9. The Homeless Man Who Works in the Senate

I n the basement of the Dirksen Senate Office Building, sixty-three-year-old Charles Gladden works alongside some of the nation's most powerful people. For eight years, he has greeted senators, staffers, and lobbyists in the hallways and the cafeteria, at exclusive banquets and special functions. He reflects fondly on some of the warmer colleagues who he says got the boot too soon.

But unbeknown to any of these bigwigs, or even to his employer, Gladden is homeless. He works in the Senate cafeteria, and he has not had a fixed address for the past five years.

The reasons are complicated. He said he has made decisions he regrets—not least leaving George Washington University, where he'd been studying fine arts on a scholarship. (Truancy and trouble with the law landed him in a juvenile institution as a teenager; he got the scholarship after winning second place in an art show.) After dropping out, he spent years in low-paying jobs: painting houses, laying bricks, delivering food.

Today he gives much of his meager paycheck to his three daughters and their grandchildren, who have also struggled to find steady housing and employment. He says that he needs the money less than they do, that he knows how to brave "the elements" and make good use of food pantries and free health clinics. He has, after all, been homeless intermittently over two decades. He has always managed.

"I want to provide for them," he says of his family, "not burden them."

Gladden also, of course, does not make very much money.

For a week's work at the Senate cafeteria—sweeping floors, mopping bathrooms, cleaning dishes, composting leftovers, transporting laundry—he says his take-home pay is about $360. And while he takes enormous pride in serving the country's public servants, he is not sure these public servants are returning the favor.

"Our lawmakers, they don't even realize what's going on right beneath their feet," he says. "They don't have a clue."

So Gladden—as in, "you've got to be glad, and I need a den," to borrow his preferred mnemonic—decided to give them a clue by participating in a one-day strike on Wednesday. Alongside hundreds of other federal contract workers, he protested the fact that our government, the single biggest (indirect) creator of low-wage jobs in the country, doesn't require the companies it does business with to pay what he considers a living wage.

His case is, he knows, atypical. But he says his story illustrates the limited choices and daily instability facing low-wage workers, including those lucky enough to work full time and those lucky enough to work in what, to outsiders, looks like a cushy government job.

Gladden, like many low-income people, suffers from chronic illness. He was diagnosed with diabetes over a decade ago. As his vision dimmed and he developed problems in his feet and hands, he decided to find less physically taxing work. So he sought out a food-service job on Capitol Hill.

But after Congress privatized its dining services, Gladden says, his new employer, Restaurant Associates, shrank the employee head count and worsened hours. Some days, when he got roped into special events, he says he clocked in at ten a.m. and out at three a.m. (Restaurant Associates declined to comment on personnel matters for this column.)

The extra pay is helpful, but Gladden's diabetes has made it difficult to stay on his feet for so many hours a day. He shuffles a bit when he walks, having had three toes amputated in the past year and a half. The missed work because of hospital stays has been devastating, and in the months since he was last discharged, he's had trouble coming up with the co-pay for his insulin. Sometimes he panhandles, on the weekends and when he effectively gets laid off for weeks because the Senate is in recess.

The biggest challenge, though, is finding a safe place to store his insulin.

"I tried to live in a shelter, but guys kept stealing my medication because they think they can get high off of it," he said.

Hence his nights at the McPherson Square Metro Station, about 2,000 feet from the White House. He knows his nearby neighbor has signed an executive order requiring new government contract bids to promise to pay at least $10.10 an hour, less than Gladden earns. Gladden thinks President Obama, and the senators he sees every day, can do more. That perhaps they will do more, once they learn what his life is like.

"But first," he says, "they need to know."

New York Times

Gretchen Morgenson pulls together three research papers that make a compelling case that "too big to fail" does more than require taxpayer bailouts. One study found that overall productivity gains were dragged down in economies with rapidly growing financial industries because banks tend to invest in industries with lots of assets, such as real estate and construction, which are not as productive as such industries as research and development start-ups. So what should policy makers do? Maybe, Morgenson suggests, they should assess the financial industry's purpose and try to determine whether it adds value in our society.

10. Smothered by a Boom in Banking

Attendees at last week's JPMorgan Chase annual investor day once again asked the question that no big bank executive wants to hear. Wouldn't shareholders be better off if the company were smaller or broken up?

No, no, and no, JPMorgan replied. "Scale has always defined the winner in banking," said Marianne Lake, the company's chief financial officer.

It is to be expected that all big-bank executives believe in big finance. They benefit from being giant, after all.

For the rest of us, though, it's worth noting that the effects of a dominant financial industry are far less beneficial.

Certainly, as we learned in 2008, when megabanks get into trouble, they line up for bailouts. This imperils taxpayers.

But even during good times the impact of big finance can be negative for the world at large. According to a compelling new paper published two weeks ago by the Bank for International Settlements, high-growth financial sectors actually hurt the broader economy by dragging down overall growth and curbing productivity.

The paper's coauthors are Stephen G. Cecchetti, economics professor at Brandeis International Business School, and Enisse Kharroubi, senior economist at the BIS. Their findings are a great addition to the debate about how much is too much when it comes to the role finance should play in our economy.

The paper is titled "Why Does Financial Sector Growth Crowd Out Real Economic Growth?" and it builds on past research that found that overall productivity gains were dragged down in economies with rapidly growing financial industries.

This idea seems almost counterintuitive. Wouldn't a booming finance industry mean that money is humming through all parts of the economy, financing growth in all kinds of industries? In the new paper, the authors looked for an answer. They studied thirty-three manufacturing industries in fifteen advanced economies around the world.

They found that financial booms were especially harmful to certain industries. Bankers, they say, act in predictable ways. They tend to lend money to projects with assets that can be pledged as collateral, such as those in real estate or construction. This is understandable—bankers want to be able to seize assets if a borrower gets into trouble on a loan, and they prefer those assets to be tangible.

But these industries are also among the least productive, and that leaves fewer dollars for more promising research-and-development start-ups that may have only intangibles, such as knowledge and ideas, to offer a banker as collateral. Even though such start-ups have far more potential than projects backed by tangible collateral, they don't attract the financing they need.

This is true during slow-growth economic times as well, but during boom times, so much money crowds into less productive sectors that the overall economy suffers.

"By draining resources from the real economy," the authors wrote, "financial-sector growth becomes a drag on real growth."

The impact is sizable.

"We find unambiguous evidence for very large effects of financial booms on industries that either have significant external financing needs or are R.&D.-intensive," the authors concluded in their paper. Even in economies where finance is growing quickly, industries that require a lot of research and development trail the performance of other industries in economies where finance is experiencing slower growth, they found. In fact, that productivity growth appeared to be two percentage points lower per year. Two percentage points a year is an enormous difference.

Another pernicious element is at work, the authors said. When finance is ascendant in an economy, it attracts an inordinate number of highly skilled workers who might otherwise take their productivity and brains to nonfinancial industries.

I spoke with Professor Cecchetti last week about the paper. "When I was in college long ago, all my friends wanted to figure out how to cure cancer," he said. "But by the 1990s, everyone wanted to become hedge fund managers. Do we want to have more hedge fund managers or more people trying to figure out how to solve our energy and environmental problems or otherwise improving our lives? That's the way I think about the problem."

There may be hope on that score. Some 31 percent of the Yale class of 2000 were employed in finance a year after graduation; among last year's class, 17 percent went to work in the industry, according to a university survey.

Still, finance was the most popular pursuit among Yale graduates last year; the next industry down the list was education, with 11.9 percent.

Thomas Philippon, a finance professor at New York University's Stern School of Business, is another academic who has studied the role of finance in the economy.

In a November 2012 article in *The Quarterly Journal of Economics*, Mr. Philippon and Ariell Reshef, an economist at the University of Virginia, reported on wages in the United States financial industry from 1909 to 2006. Among their findings: Finance accounted for 15 to 25 percent of the overall increase in wage inequality between 1980 and 2006.

Also questioning the dominance of finance in our society is Luigi Zingales, professor of entrepreneurship and finance at the University of Chicago Booth School of Business. In his 2012 book,

A Capitalism for the People, he wrote that the financial sector, "thanks to its resources and cleverness, has increasingly been able to rig the rules to its own advantage."

If big finance can have such injurious implications, what should policy makers do? "In some countries we see governments that are very protectionist of financial companies," Professor Cecchetti said. "The two issues you want to worry about are what happens when there is too much debt and financing in your economy, and if you are subsidizing it, you might want to think about that pretty hard."

One way we subsidize debt in this country is by providing tax deductions for mortgage interest. That policy encourages borrowers to take on bigger home loans than they otherwise might.

Even now, as the mortgage crisis recedes into the distance, it remains critical that we assess the financial industry's purpose and try to determine whether it adds value in our society.

Ideally, finance should propel an economy by helping create jobs and wealth for a broad portion of the population. But clearly, there's a point when finance sucks too much oxygen out of the room, leaving the rest of us gasping for air.

Bigger, in finance, it seems, is not better.

Part III

Technology:
Behind the Screen

Wired

The security specialist Matt Malone calls himself a "for-profit archaeologist." He cruises alleys and shopping-mall dump zones in his pickup looking for discarded items to sell for a profit, but he's also looking for insight. And he gets a lot of raw material from a consumer culture that produces an estimated 7.1 pounds of trash per person per day. He came to the dumpster-diving calling by accident, when an employer asked him to conduct a "zero-knowledge attack" on an Austin-based company. Not only did he find a lot of the company's business in its dumpster, he found valuable stuff—and a second calling.

Randall Sullivan

11. The Pro Dumpster Diver Who's Making Thousands Off America's Biggest Retailers

att Malone doesn't mind being called a professional dumpster diver. He tells me this a little after two a.m. on the morning of July 7 as we cruise the trash receptacles behind the stores of a shopping center just off the Capital of Texas Highway in Austin. Given the image that conjures, though, it's worth pointing out that Malone has a pretty good day job, earning a six-figure salary as a security specialist for Slait Consulting. He is also founder of Assero Security, a startup that he says has recently been offered seed money by not one but two separate investors. Nevertheless, the thirty-seven-year-old Malone does spend a good many of his off-hours digging through the trash. And the fact is, he earns a sizable amount of money from this activity—more per hour than he makes at his Slait job.

Malone stops his Chevy Avalanche next to the dumpster in back of an Office Depot. Within seconds, he's out of the truck and sticking his magnetized flashlight to the inside of the dumpster's wall. He heaves himself up onto the metal rim to lean inside and begins digging through a top layer of cardboard and packing materials. Half a minute later I hear what I will learn is Malone's version of eureka: "Hell yes! Hell yes!" He comes out with a box containing a complete Uniden Wireless Video Surveillance System—two cameras and a wireless monitor—which normally retails for $419. A quick inspection reveals that it's all in perfect condition, although someone has clearly opened and repacked it. "A return," he says, then plunges back into the dumpster.

Ten minutes later, when he's again behind the wheel of the Avalanche, Malone continues to tell me about the material benefits of dumpster diving. If he were to dedicate himself to the activity as a full-time job, he says, finding various discarded treasures, refurbishing and selling them off, he's confident he could pull in at least $250,000 a year—there is that much stuff simply tossed into dumpsters in the Austin area. He lists a few recent "recoveries": vacuums, power tools, furniture, carpeting, industrial machines, assorted electronics. Much of it needs a little love, he says, but a lot of it, like this Uniden system, is in perfect condition.

But, he quickly adds, his foraging isn't just about dollars. It's also about the knowledge he acquires and the people he shares it with. He prefers to be known as a "for-profit archaeologist." After all, archaeologists have always studied garbage. The esteemed William Rathje, who established the Garbage Project at the University of Arizona, observed shortly before his 2012 death that refuse, more than anything else human beings produce, "gives us insight into the long-term values of a civilization."

As for Malone, the main insight he's obtained from digging through our civilization's trash is that most people don't place a lot of value in value anymore.

·　　·　　·

Malone started dumpster diving nine years ago, when he was working at a lower-level corporate security job. His employer had assigned him to conduct what's called a "zero-knowledge attack" on an Austin-based company. "That means you hire me and don't give me any information about your operation," Malone explains. "I'm just a random guy who wants to break into your system." The most effective way to do this was to dig through his client's trash; many hacks and identity thefts come from information left in dumpsters. Sure enough, after just a couple of weeks of looking through the dumpsters outside the client's offices, he had amassed a box full of documents, loaded with the confidential information of thousands of customers. ("It made quite an impression" on his client, he recalls.)

But he also discovered something else. One night while doing his research, he decided to poke around in neighboring trash bins, including the dumpster at OfficeMax. Inside he discovered "a whole bunch of printers, discontinued lines that were still in the boxes." He took the printers home and put them in his garage. But he couldn't stop wondering what else was out there in the dumpsters of Austin. Before long, he went back out to see what else he could find.

A short and wiry man whose manic enthusiasm and radiant smile lend him a quirky charm, Malone says that at first he looked for items he could use himself, especially in his main passion, building and riding "mini chopper" motorcycles. On a hunch he checked the dumpster behind the Emerson Electric warehouse in an industrial park near his home, where he discovered several discarded motors that would provide enough power to move a mini chopper along at forty to fifty miles per hour. Then, out of curiosity, he turned his attention to the dumpsters at Home Depot, Harbor Freight, Big Lots, Sears, Best Buy, and a few others. He was astounded at what he found: building materials, power tools, HEPA filters, and a dizzying array of electronics.

At first, Malone mainly used his discoveries for various hobby projects. Along with his mini-choppers, he built an electric skateboard, a set of plasma speakers, several 3-D projectors, and a computer that ran while submerged in mineral oil. "People would come over and ask, 'Man, where'd you get that?'" he recalls. "I'd say, 'Well, I made it.' I didn't say right away that I made it mostly from stuff I got out of dumpsters." Inevitably his friends would ask to buy his various toys, and—usually already bored with them and having moved on to a new project—he would agree to sell. Even so, his garage soon overflowed, and Malone decided he should make some space by staging a weekend yard sale.

That sale provided several revelations. The biggest was what sold with the drive-by public. "I had all my cool stuff out front, a couple of very nice computers, mini-choppers, some high-end printers—the big-ticket stuff—thinking, 'This is what's going to make me the money.'" It wasn't. Instead, people flocked to "the small stuff": the photo paper and toner he'd pulled out of the dumpsters at OfficeMax and Office Depot, the hand tools he'd found in the trash at Harbor Freight, the CDs from GameStop dumpsters, the assorted seasonal tchotchkes that had been tossed by the employees at Pier 1 and Cost Plus. "I eventually figured out that I had to sell the big stuff on Amazon or Craigslist," Malone says. But all those small sales added up: By Sunday afternoon he had collected a little more than $3,000 in cash. "And that was when I realized, 'This has the potential to be something.'"

At the time, Malone explains, he was working for a company called Vintage IT and making only about half of his current salary, so he appreciated the opportunity to augment his income. He began to organize his approach, making daily checks of the various malls and business parks closest to his home to ascertain what days and times dumpsters were most likely filled with desirable items. Within a few weeks he knew exactly when the trash was collected at every store and business on his route so he could time his visits for when the dumpsters were fullest. He also learned to look for stores that were changing locations or—better yet—going out of business. Store remodels were also good targets. "I was learning as I went along and designing a kind of collection system before I even realized that was what I was doing."

As we drive by a shopping center just off the Mopac Expressway, Malone remembers the weeks when the Circuit City that once anchored this mall was closing. "I went back day after day after day," he says. "I got brand-new stereos, GPS devices, some really nice cameras, flatscreen TVs. I got a boom box there that was bigger than I am. And what was great was that you could sell it at retail, because it was all still in the boxes."

Suddenly, Malone spots a huge "yarder" dumpster directly behind Bealls department store—an indication the store may be remodeling. Within moments he has pulled his truck alongside the yarder and used the truck bed to climb in. Wading through the cardboard and bubble wrap, Malone quickly finds three slightly used dress-form mannequins that he is sure can be sold to an owner of one of the pop-up clothing stores that have become popular in Austin. That's just the beginning, though. During the next fifteen minutes, he's so deep in the bowels of the dumpster that at moments all I can see are his shoulders and the back of his head; he exclaims "Hell yes!" at least a half dozen times. When Malone is finished there are two large stacks of laminated MDF boards and plate-glass panels from discarded store displays in the back of the truck. He can use the boards at a workshop that he maintains in a small business park a couple of minutes from his North Austin home. "These precut boards are really expensive," Malone says. "That's money I won't be spending." Malone has operated a number of trash-related enterprises out of his shop, often with names like Chinese Scooter Repair.

Malone can get downright philosophical about the empire he's managed to build out of garbage. "We can only do what we do here because we live in a society where most people have been conditioned to look past what's right in front of them."

•   •   •

So how did we get that way? The search for an answer leads at least as far back as 1945. The United States had come out of World War II as the only major power that was both richer and more powerful than it had been going in. Prosperity was becoming a kind of secular religion, and its visionary torchbearer was J. Gordon Lippincott. Today, Lippincott is remembered mainly as the father of corporate branding, the engineer-cum-marketer who created the Campbell's Soup label and the Coca-Cola logo. He was also, however, the high priest of planned obsolescence. "Our willingness to part with something before it is completely worn out is a phenomenon noticeable in no other society in history," he wrote. The phenomenon "is soundly based on our economy of abundance. It must be further nurtured even though it is contrary to one of the oldest inbred laws of humanity—the law of thrift."

By the 1950s the United States had emerged as the planet's first full-fledged consumer society. And the pace of obsolescence only increased with the rise of the digital age. As Gordon E. Moore so famously predicted, the integrated circuits that drove the next generation of innovation were doubling in power every eighteen months. This rapid rate of improvement meant that consumer technology quickly became outdated—unable to perform the same functions as the latest gadgets and machines. The trend, buttressed by corporate stockholders who wanted ever-increasing sales numbers and by advertising and media that constantly pushed the latest breakthrough or advancement, soon created a culture in which people don't simply want the latest devices—they also see little or no value in the old ones.

"People got trained to throw stuff away," Malone says.

So they did. By 2004, according to an extensive Columbia University and BioCycle study, the United States had become a country that every day produced an estimated 7.1 pounds of trash for each man, woman, and child. Edward Humes, whose 2012 book, *Garbology*, is perhaps the most comprehensive consideration of the subject, recalls his visit to Southern California's giant Puente Hills Landfill before its closure. "You stand atop this 500-foot plateau of trash so big that you could put Dodger Stadium on top of it—with parking—and it literally boggles the mind. This is a landfill that serves just LA County, and the plateau has 130 million tons of trash in it," he says. "Some of it's worthless, but a lot of it isn't. We're throwing away tremendous value."

Malone sees himself as a kind of bridge between not only the philosophies of abundance and sustainability but also the haves and have-nots. Lots of people—even in the United States—can't afford the newest device. "But you can make a huge difference in their lives if you can sell them a computer that works well for $200," he says.

It helps his cause that Malone is not only mechanically gifted but loves to learn new things. For instance, he acquired much of what he knows about scooter repair from the mechanics at a company called Austin Motor Sport, which hired him to set up its computer system. While there, Malone met a customer who kept bringing in old, nonfunctioning electric scooters and selling them for about fifty dollars each. It turned out that the customer drove a garbage truck; people on his route were throwing these scooters away. Malone soon discovered that they weren't broken; it was just that their twelve-volt batteries had died. Replacement batteries tended to cost almost as much as an entire scooter, so most people junked them. But Malone knew how to power the scooters for next to nothing. He had previously recovered a hundred emergency exit lights discarded at a construction site where an office building was being renovated. Each of those lights housed a twelve-volt battery, one that could be repurposed to power an electric scooter. "At this point," Malone says, "I figure I've sold more than 100 recycled electric scooters, and I've made an average of about $150 on each one." His profit margin on Roombas—which also often just need replacement batteries—is even higher.

·   ·   ·

Malone pauses while deciding whether to take a huge plastic bag filled with hundreds of brand-new Srixon range balls, which he's just pulled out of a Golfsmith dumpster. He's got a fondness for this particular location, he explains, owing to the huge assortment of racket covers he found here when the store decided to eliminate its line of tennis products. He can't remember who told him tennis racket covers sold for pretty close to their retail price on Amazon, but they were right, Malone says: "I made a shitload of money on them." Ultimately he decides to keep the Srixons, shoving the bag into the bed of his Avalanche.

Malone is not alone in his pursuits. Indeed, he has discovered an entire community of trash collectors in the Austin area. These scavenger entrepreneurs are overwhelmingly white and working-class, hustlers who tend to carry a ton of personal baggage and yet are "still more willing to share what they know than just about any people I've ever met," Malone says.

Take his friend Coulter Luce. It was Luce who taught Malone to see beyond commercial dumpsters and look around the apartment complexes surrounding the University of Texas campus, especially at the end of the academic year. "The first time I went over there I found so many computers in the trash that I couldn't believe it," Malone recalls. "Plus all this other stuff that had just been dumped by rich kids in a hurry to get home." Luce, who had gotten into dumpster diving after losing his job and descending into financial distress, went so far as to befriend several building managers, who would tell him when a student was being evicted for nonpayment of rent. Frequently, Luce says, kids just leave all their stuff behind. "And that stuff went straight into the dumpsters, where I'd be waiting." He claims to have made $65,000 that first year, even though he was using methamphetamine. "I was tweaking and it messed me up," Luce admits.

Malone called Luce in 2006 after stumbling upon a huge find in the parking lot of Discount Electronics, a local Austin chain. The store was clearing out its warehouse and had hauled everything to the parking lot of its main store on Anderson Lane. Malone focused on the forty prototypes of Dell's newest high-end desktop computer, which Discount Electronics had contracted to test. He was still loading them when Luce showed up and walked right past the computers to the photo paper and toner. "Coulter taught me to stop going after the big prize and get the consumables," Malone says. People aren't going to need new printers that often, but they constantly need paper and toner.

As for the forty Dell computers, Malone still considers them a missed opportunity. "They were all damaged," he says. "The way Discount Electronics had tested these prototypes was to put them on a superpowerful heat sink for a solid month, to see how much they could take." If he had waited a few months until the model had gone on the market, Malone estimates, he could have fixed them up with replacement parts and made about $1,000 in profit on each machine. Instead he rushed to sell the broken computers, which meant he mostly ended up giving them away. Luce, meanwhile, made a killing on the consumables he had collected.

Luce also pioneered a unique method for targeting storage units. When people move their stuff out of storage, he figured, they make a lot of decisions about what to cull. Most leave things behind, either in or near the facility's dumpsters. People who have gone through a divorce or are coming to collect the possessions of a deceased loved one inevitably toss an amazing array of valuable items. Luce explained to Malone that he could rent the smallest storage unit in a facility, usually a locker-sized space that cost $20 per month, and have 24/7 access to a place where treasures were discarded on a daily basis. "I got an entire shop's worth of power tools, all brand-new, right after I rented my first storage unit," recalls Malone, who now has units in four different facilities. "What's great is that you have places to stash your loot and protected dumpsters that only you can get into."

Another of Malone's trash-hunting friends was a man named Mike Miller, whom Malone calls "my personal guru of dumpster diving." Miller, who died of heart disease a few years ago, taught Malone to collect all the pieces of disassembled or broken items, because they could almost certainly find use in different projects down the line. It's a lesson that Malone adheres to as we drive through Austin. At Discount Electronics, he collects an assortment of circuit boards, wafers, and tiny screw-down connectors that can be fitted into dozens of electronic devices. Later, in the dumpster at yet another Office Depot, Malone finds a brand-new office chair with a claim slip indicating that some parts are missing. When he returns to his office and looks up the serial number on the Internet, he will discover that the chair—which retails for $339—is only missing a pair of washers. "I'll probably sell it on Amazon for half of what Office Depot charges," he says, "but that's still $170" for what he estimates to be a total of twenty minutes of work.

Once, while sorting through the dumpster at this same Office Depot store, Malone came across a boxy machine that he didn't recognize. The thing was brand-new, though, so he followed Miller's mantra: "When in doubt, take it!" When Malone looked up the serial number online, he discovered it was a Martin Yale business card slitter with a retail price of $1,850. He sold it for $1,200 through Craigslist.

·   ·   ·

For Malone, Luce, and the community of scavengers they are a part of, one big threat looms: the increasingly widespread use of commercial-size trash compactors.

Big-box stores like Walmart have praised compactors for reducing the volume of trash they send to landfills, but to Malone and other dumpster divers the machines are utterly evil, creating far more waste than they eliminate. Josh Vincik, another Austin-area trash hunter, says that when he started dumpster diving, he'd routinely find ten to twenty models of kids' bicycles in the Walmart dumpster—bikes he could usually sell for roughly half of what Walmart charged, often to kids who otherwise might not have been able to afford them. "Those bikes—along with a lot of other stuff that's basically brand-new—are still being thrown out," Vincik says, "but now they're locked inside that compactor, where they're slowly being crushed."

It's the same at Best Buy, Bed Bath & Beyond, and any number of companies that have gone to trash compactors, says Malone, who has opened a number of compactors to look inside. He's found destroyed "lawn mowers, bicycles, Weed Eaters, barbecue pits, home theater systems, portable air-conditioning units, fishing poles, boom boxes, and a ton—I mean a ton—of electronics. You open one of these things up and it's literally an ocean of products inside."

When *Wired* asked Walmart about Malone's and Vincik's claims, the company responded with a statement that didn't address the questions directly but rather touted the company's public commitment to "reaching zero waste to landfill by 2025" and said that "total annual waste generated from our operations in the US has decreased by 3.3 percent, compared to our 2010 baseline." Bed Bath & Beyond responded with a similar statement, while Best Buy declined to respond to questions about the compactors.

Author Humes, who has in the past extolled Walmart's reduction of landfill-bound waste, reacted with dismay to Malone's and Vincik's reports. "The fact that a company that has made such a public—and I think sincere—commitment to reducing waste is still sending so many things people could use to landfills is really disturbing," he said. "I think it probably says more about our society and the economy in general than it does about Walmart in particular."

While researching his book, Humes obtained what was one of the last interviews with William Rathje, the late University of Arizona garbage researcher. During that conversation, the archaeologist said that U.S. overconsumption reminded him of the ancient civilizations he had studied, in which the moment that extravagance began to outstrip resources always seemed to signal the descent into contraction and decline. In *Garbology*, Humes urged a break with that historical pattern and an all-out commitment to cutting waste. But in his conversation with Rathje, the university researcher noted one big problem with this idea: "No great civilization of the past has ever pulled this off," Humes says Rathje told him. "None."

.   .   .

Malone warned me that starting out on the Sunday of the July 4 holiday weekend would likely mean a relatively scant selection of discarded merchandise. Nevertheless, he still expected to back up his claim that he can make a quarter-million dollars a year from trash. In fact, he's thought long and hard about dumpster diving full-time, only he doesn't want to give up his work as a computer security specialist. After all, he's just back from a trip that took him across a wide arc of the eastern seaboard. In New York, he says, he helped a posh fashion house defend itself from a hacker attack, "which was great, because I really liked those people." In Virginia, he says, he was assigned by a government agency he won't name to expose any vulnerabilities to terrorist attack that might exist in its food supply chain. "I'm not going to walk away from those kinds of experiences. But at the same time I don't want to give up the treasure-hunt thrill I get from dumpster diving."

At the end of our second night together (which runs well into the early morning hours), Malone assembles his take and begins preparing a spreadsheet that includes both retail costs and probable sale prices. He does it scrupulously, assigning no value to the items he intends to use in his shop or his various businesses (the lumber, the MDF boards, the plate glass, the office supplies, the USB chargers, and the "various software" he's collected). The big scores are six Dell R200 servers, a single Dell 2950 server, a Cisco Catalyst 5500 Series switch, and a Cisco Catalyst 2960

Series switch. He looks up each item to ascertain the retail price, guessing conservatively that he can sell the gear for half of that amount.

The total retail value of these items comes to $10,182, meaning that Malone estimates he will earn $5,091 in sales. This adds up to more than $2,500 for each night out, which, despite a good deal of downtime answering my questions, is a pretty good haul. At that rate, if he were to work 240 days a year—a five-day workweek with four weeks of vacation—he would earn over $600,000 annually.

That startling figure leads to a thought: Maybe one way to ward off the dystopia of contraction and decline that William Rathje, Edward Humes, and so many others have foreseen in this wasteful country's future is to recognize, as Matt Malone has, that while America's streets have never been paved with gold, these days they are certainly littered with it.

Wired

It's a horror of a job, hours watching gore and filth and inhumanity to shield U.S. social-media users from it. Like most tough jobs, it is outsourced to poorer nations, including the Philippines. One expert estimates that there are "well over 100,000" content moderators scrubbing social-media sites, mobile apps, and cloud storage services. Adrian Chen traveled to Bacoor, outside Manila, where workers hunt for pornography, gore, sexual solicitation, racism, and other offenses in order to make social-media sites seem friendlier. The search takes a heavy psychic toll on the workers doing this dirty job.

Adrian Chen

12. The Laborers Who Keep Dick Pics and Beheadings Out of Your Facebook Feed

The campuses of the tech industry are famous for their lavish cafeterias, cushy shuttles, and on-site laundry services. But on a muggy February afternoon, some of these companies' most important work is being done 7,000 miles away, on the second floor of a former elementary school at the end of a row of auto mechanics' stalls in Bacoor, a gritty Filipino town thirteen miles southwest of Manila. When I climb the building's narrow stairwell, I need to press against the wall to slide by workers heading down for a smoke break. Up one flight, a drowsy security guard staffs what passes for a front desk: a wooden table in a dark hallway overflowing with file folders.

Past the guard, in a large room packed with workers manning PCs on long tables, I meet Michael Baybayan, an enthusiastic twenty-one-year-old with a jaunty pouf of reddish-brown hair. If the space does not resemble a typical startup's office, the image on Baybayan's screen does not resemble typical startup work: It appears to show a super-close-up photo of a two-pronged dildo wedged in a vagina. I say *appears* because I can barely begin to make sense of the image, a baseball-card-sized abstraction of flesh and translucent pink plastic, before he disappears it with a casual flick of his mouse.

Baybayan is part of a massive labor force that handles "content moderation"—the removal of offensive material—for U.S. social-networking sites. As social media connects more people more intimately than ever before, companies have been confronted with the Grandma Problem: Now that grandparents routinely use services like Facebook to connect with their kids and grandkids, they are potentially exposed to the Internet's panoply of jerks, racists, creeps, criminals, and bullies. They won't continue to log on if they find their family photos sandwiched between a gruesome Russian highway accident and a hardcore porn video. Social media's growth into a multi-billion-dollar industry and its lasting mainstream appeal have depended in large part on companies' ability to police the borders of their user-generated content—to ensure that Grandma never has to see images like the one Baybayan just nuked.

So companies like Facebook and Twitter rely on an army of workers employed to soak up the worst of humanity in order to protect the rest of us. And there are legions of them—a vast, invisible pool of human labor. Hemanshu Nigam, the former chief security officer of MySpace who now runs online-safety consultancy SSP Blue, estimates that the number of content moderators scrubbing the world's social media sites, mobile apps, and cloud storage services runs to "well over 100,000"—that is, about twice the total head count of Google and nearly fourteen times that of Facebook.

This work is increasingly done in the Philippines. A former U.S. colony, the Philippines has maintained close cultural ties to the United States, which content moderation companies say helps Filipinos determine what Americans find offensive. And moderators in the Philippines can be hired for a fraction of American wages. Ryan Cardeno, a former contractor for Microsoft in the Philippines, told me that he made $500 per month by the end of his three-and-a-half-year tenure with outsourcing firm Sykes.

Last year, Cardeno was offered $312 per month by another firm to moderate content for Facebook, paltry even by industry standards.

Here in the former elementary school, Baybayan and his co-workers are screening content for Whisper, an LA-based mobile startup—recently valued at $200 million by its VCs—that lets users post photos and share secrets anonymously. They work for a U.S.-based outsourcing firm called TaskUs. It's something of a surprise that Whisper would let a reporter in to see this process. When I asked Microsoft, Google, and Facebook for information about how they moderate their services, they offered vague statements about protecting users but declined to discuss specifics. Many tech companies make their moderators sign strict nondisclosure agreements, barring them from talking even to other employees of the same outsourcing firm about their work.

"I think if there's not an explicit campaign to hide it, there's certainly a tacit one," says Sarah Roberts, a media studies scholar at the University of Western Ontario and one of the few academics who study commercial content moderation. Companies would prefer not to acknowledge the hands-on effort required to curate our social-media experiences, Roberts says. "It goes to our misunderstandings about the Internet and our view of technology as being somehow magically not human."

I was given a look at the Whisper moderation process because Michael Heyward, Whisper's CEO, sees moderation as an integral feature and a key selling point of his app. Whisper practices "active moderation," an especially labor-intensive process in which every single post is screened in real time; many other companies moderate content only if it's been flagged as objectionable by users, which is known as reactive moderating. "The type of space we're trying to create with anonymity is one where we're asking users to put themselves out there and feel vulnerable," he tells me. "Once the toothpaste is out of the tube, it's tough to put it back in."

Watching Baybayan's work makes terrifyingly clear the amount of labor that goes into keeping Whisper's toothpaste in the tube. (After my visit, Baybayan left his job and the Bacoor office of TaskUs was raided by the Philippine version of the FBI for allegedly using pirated software on its computers. The company has since moved its content-moderation operations to a new facility in Manila.) He begins with a grid of posts, each of which is a rectangular photo, many with bold text overlays—the same rough format as old-school Internet memes. In its freewheeling anonymity, Whisper functions for its users as a sort of externalized id, an outlet for confessions, rants, and secret desires that might be too sensitive (or too boring) for Facebook or Twitter. Moderators here view a raw feed of Whisper posts in real time. Shorn from context, the posts read like the collected tics of a Tourette's sufferer. *Any bisexual women in NYC wanna chat?* Or: *I hate Irish accents!* Or: *I fucked my stepdad then blackmailed him into buying me a car.*

A list of categories, scrawled on a whiteboard, reminds the workers of what they're hunting for: pornography, gore, minors, sexual solicitation, sexual body parts/images, racism. When Baybayan sees a potential violation, he drills in on it to confirm, then sends it away—erasing it from the user's account and the service altogether—and moves back to the grid. Within twenty-five minutes, Baybayan has eliminated an impressive variety of dick pics, thong shots, exotic objects inserted into bodies, hateful taunts, and requests for oral sex.

More difficult is a post that features a stock image of a man's chiseled torso, overlaid with the text "I want to have a gay experience, M18 here." Is this the confession of a hidden desire (allowed) or a hookup request (forbidden)? Baybayan—who, like most employees of TaskUs, has a college degree—spoke thoughtfully about how to judge this distinction.

"What is the intention?" Baybayan says. "You have to determine the difference between thought and solicitation." He has only a few seconds to decide. New posts are appearing constantly at the top of the screen, pushing the others down. He judges the post to be sexual solicitation and deletes it; somewhere, a horny teen's hopes are dashed. Baybayan scrolls back to the top of the screen and begins scanning again.

.   .   .

Eight years after the fact, Jake Swearingen can still recall the video that made him quit. He was twenty-four years old and between jobs in the Bay Area when he got a gig as a moderator for a then-new startup called VideoEgg. Three days in, a video of an apparent beheading came across his queue.

"Oh fuck! I've got a beheading!" he blurted out. A slightly older colleague in a black hoodie casually turned around in his chair. "Oh," he said, "which one?" At that moment Swearingen decided he did not want to become a connoisseur of beheading videos. "I didn't want to look back and say I became so blasé to watching people have these really horrible things happen to them that I'm ironic or jokey about it," says Swearingen, now the social-media editor at Atlantic Media. (Swearingen was also an intern at *Wired* in 2007.)

While a large amount of content moderation takes place overseas, much is still done in the United States, often by young college graduates like Swearingen was. Many companies employ a two-tiered moderation system, where the most basic moderation is outsourced abroad while more complex screening, which requires greater cultural familiarity, is done domestically. U.S.-based moderators are much better compensated than their overseas counterparts: A brand-new American moderator for a large tech company in the United States can make more in an hour than a veteran Filipino moderator makes in a day. But then a career in the outsourcing industry is something many young Filipinos aspire to, whereas American moderators often fall into the job as a last resort, and burnout is common.

"Everybody hits the wall, generally between three and five months," says a former YouTube content moderator I'll call Rob. "You just think, 'Holy shit, what am I spending my day doing? This is awful.'"

Rob became a content moderator in 2010. He'd graduated from college and followed his girlfriend to the Bay Area, where he found his history degree had approximately the same effect on employers as a face tattoo. Months went by, and Rob grew increasingly desperate. Then came the cold call from CDI, a contracting firm. The recruiter wanted him to interview for a position with Google, moderating videos on YouTube. *Google!* Sure, he would just be a contractor, but he was told there was a chance of turning the job into a real career there. The pay, at roughly $20 an hour, was far superior to a fast-food salary. He interviewed and was given a one-year contract. "I was pretty stoked," Rob said. "It paid well, and I figured YouTube would look good on a résumé."

For the first few months, Rob didn't mind his job moderating videos at YouTube's headquarters in San Bruno. His coworkers were mostly new graduates like himself, many of them liberal arts majors just happy to have found employment that didn't require a hairnet. His supervisor was great, and there were even a few perks, like free lunch at the cafeteria. During his eight-hour shifts, Rob sat at a desk in YouTube's open office with two monitors. On one he flicked through batches of ten videos at a time. On the other monitor, he could do whatever he wanted. He watched the entire *Battlestar Galactica* series with one eye while nuking torture videos and hate speech with the other. He also got a fascinating glimpse into the inner workings of YouTube. For instance, in late 2010, Google's legal team gave moderators the urgent task of deleting the violent sermons of the American radical Islamist preacher Anwar al-Awlaki after a British woman said she was inspired by them to stab a politician.

But as months dragged on, the rough stuff began to take a toll. The worst was the gore: brutal street fights, animal torture, suicide bombings, decapitations, and horrific traffic accidents. The

Arab Spring was in full swing, and activists were using YouTube to show the world the government crackdowns that resulted. Moderators were instructed to leave such "newsworthy" videos up with a warning, even if they violated the content guidelines. But the close-ups of protesters' corpses and street battles were tough for Rob and his coworkers to handle. So were the videos that documented misery just for the sick thrill of it.

"If someone was uploading animal abuse, a lot of the time it was the person who did it. He was *proud* of that," Rob says. "And seeing it from the eyes of someone who was proud to *do* the fucked-up thing, rather than news reporting on the fucked-up thing—it just hurts you so much harder, for some reason. It just gives you a much darker view of humanity."

Rob began to dwell on the videos outside of work. He became withdrawn and testy. YouTube employs counselors whom moderators can theoretically talk to, but Rob had no idea how to access them. He didn't know anyone who had. Instead, he self-medicated. He began drinking more and gained weight.

It became clear to Rob that he would likely never become a real Google employee. A few months into his contract, he applied for a job with Google but says he was turned down for an interview because his GPA didn't meet the requirement. (Google denies that GPA alone would be a deciding factor in its hiring.) Even if it had, Rob says, he's heard of only a few contractors who ended up with staff positions at Google.

A couple of months before the end of his contract, he found another job and quit. When Rob's last shift ended at seven p.m., he left feeling elated. He jumped into his car, drove to his parents' house in Orange County, and slept for three days straight.

.   .   .

Given that content moderators might very well constitute as much as half the total workforce for social media sites, it's worth pondering just what the long-term psychological toll of this work can be. Jane Stevenson was head of the occupational health and welfare department for Britain's National Crime Squad—the UK equivalent of the FBI—in the early 2000s, when the first wave of international anti-child-pornography operations was launched. She saw investigators become overwhelmed by the images. Even after she left her post, agencies and private organizations continued to ask for her help dealing with the fallout, so she started an occupational-health consultancy, Workplace Wellbeing, focused on high-pressure industries. She has since advised social-media companies in the UK and found that the challenges facing their content moderators echo those of child-pornography and antiterrorism investigators in law enforcement.

"From the moment you see the first image, you will change for good," Stevenson says. But where law enforcement has developed specialized programs and hires experienced mental-health professionals, Stevenson says that many technology companies have yet to grasp the seriousness of the problem.

"There's the thought that it's just the same as bereavement or bullying at work, and the same people can deal with it," Stevenson says. "All of us will go through a bereavement, almost all of us will be distressed by somebody saying something we don't like. All of these things are normal things. But is having sex with a two-year-old normal? Is cutting somebody's head off—quite slowly, mind you; I don't mean to traumatize you but beheadings don't happen quickly—is that normal behavior? Is that something you expect?"

In Manila, I meet Denise (not her real name), a psychologist who consults for two content-moderation firms in the Philippines. "It's like PTSD," she tells me as we sit in her office above one of the city's perpetually snarled freeways. "There is a memory trace in their mind." Denise and her team set up extensive monitoring systems for their clients. Employees are given a battery of psychological tests to determine their mental baseline then interviewed and counseled regularly to minimize the effect of disturbing images. But even with the best counseling, staring into the heart of human darkness exacts a toll. Workers quit because they feel desensitized by the hours of pornography they watch each day and no longer want to be intimate with their spouses. Others report a supercharged sex drive. "How would you feel watching pornography for eight hours a day, every day?" Denise says. "How long can you take that?"

·　　·　　·

Nearby, in a shopping mall, I meet a young woman whom I'll call Maria. She's on her lunch break from an outsourcing firm, where she works on a team that moderates photos and videos for the cloud storage service of a major U.S. technology company. Maria is a quality-assurance representative, which means her duties include double-checking the work of the dozens of agents on her team to make sure they catch everything. This requires her to view many videos that have been flagged by moderators.

"I get really affected by bestiality with children," she says. "I have to stop. I have to stop for a moment and loosen up, maybe go to Starbucks and have a coffee." She laughs at the absurd juxtaposition of a horrific sex crime and an overpriced latte.

Constant exposure to videos like this has turned some of Maria's coworkers intensely paranoid. Every day they see proof of the infinite variety of human depravity. They begin to suspect the worst of people they meet in real life, wondering what secrets their hard drives might hold. Two of Maria's female coworkers have become so suspicious that they no longer leave their children with babysitters. They sometimes miss work because they can't find someone they trust to take care of their kids.

Maria is especially haunted by one video that came across her queue soon after she started the job. "There's this lady," she says, dropping her voice. "Probably in the age of fifteen to eighteen, I don't know. She looks like a minor. There's this bald guy putting his head to the lady's vagina. The lady is blindfolded, handcuffed, screaming and crying."

The video was more than a half hour long. After watching just over a minute, Maria began to tremble with sadness and rage. Who would do something so cruel to another person? She examined the man on the screen. He was bald and appeared to be of Middle Eastern descent but was otherwise completely unremarkable. The face of evil was someone you might pass by in the mall without a second glance.

After two and a half years on the cloud storage moderation team, Maria plans to quit later this year and go to medical school. But she expects that video of the blindfolded girl to stick with her long after she's gone. "I don't know if I can forget it," she says. "I watched that a long time ago, but it's like I just watched it yesterday."

New Republic

Franklin Foer calls for the breakup of Amazon in this controversial cover story about a company that has come to dominate both shopping on the Web and, somewhat quietly, much of the infrastructure of the Web as well. Foer makes a persuasive case that the brutal tactics of Jeff Bezos and his company have violated antitrust law and that Amazon's pricing power gives it too much control over too many vital industries, not the least of which is publishing.

13. Amazon Must Be Stopped

B efore we speak ill of Amazon, let us kneel down before it. Twenty years ago, the company began with the stated goal of creating a bookstore as comprehensive as the great Library of Alexandria and then quickly managed to make even that grandiloquent ambition look puny. Amazon could soon conjure the full text of almost any volume onto a phone in less time than a yawn. Its warehouses are filled with an unabridged catalogue of items that comes damn close to serving every human need, both basic and esoteric—a mere click away, speedily delivered, and as cheap as capitalism permits.

Rather than pocketing the profits from this creation, Amazon has plowed revenue into bettering itself—into the construction of well-placed fulfillment centers that further hasten the arrival of its packages, into technologies that attempt to read our acquisitive minds and aptly suggest our next purchase. Shopping on Amazon has so ingrained itself in modern American life that it has become something close to our unthinking habit, and the company has achieved a level of dominance that merits the application of a very old label: monopoly.

That term doesn't get tossed around much these days, but it should. Amazon is *the* shining representative of a new golden age of monopoly that also includes Google and Walmart. Unlike U.S. Steel, the new behemoths don't use their barely challenged power to hike up prices. They are, in fact, self-styled servants of the consumer and have ushered in an era of low prices for everything from flat-screen TVs to paper napkins to smart phones.

In other words, we're all enjoying the benefits of these corporations far too much to think hard about distant dangers. Besides, the ideology of Silicon Valley suggests that we have nothing much to fear: If these firms no longer engineer breathtaking technologies, they will be creatively destroyed. That's why Peter Thiel, the creator of PayPal, has argued that the term "monopoly" should be stripped of its negative connotation. A monopoly, he argues, is really nothing more than a synonym for a highly successful company. Insulation from the brutish spirit of competition even makes them superior organizations—more beneficent employers, better able to both daydream and think clearly. In Tile's phrasing: "Creative monopolies aren't just good for the rest of society; they're powerful engines for making it better."

Thiel makes an important point: The Internet-age monopolies *are* a different species; they flummox our conventional ways of thinking about corporate concentration and have proved especially elusive to those who ponder questions of antitrust, the discipline of law that aims to curb threats to the competitive marketplace. Part of the issue is the laws themselves, which were conceived to manage an industrial economy—and have, over time, evolved to focus on a specific set of narrow questions that have little to do with the core problem at hand.

Whether Amazon, which does $75 billion in annual revenue, has technically violated antitrust laws is an important matter, of course. But descending into the weeds of predatory-pricing statutes also obscures the very real threat. In its pursuit of bigness, Amazon has left a trail of destruction—competitors undercut, suppliers squeezed—some of it necessary and some of it highly worrisome. And in its confrontation with the publisher Hachette, it has entered a phase of heightened aggression unseen even when it tried to crush Zappos by offering a $5 rebate on all its shoes or when it gave employees phony business cards to avoid paying sales taxes in various states.

In effect, we've been thrust back a hundred years to a time when the law was not up to the task of protecting the threats to democracy posed by monopoly, a time when the new nature of the corporation demanded a significant revision of government.

.   .   .

The progressive era's most venomous screeds against monopoly came from the pen of one of its stodgiest characters, Louis Brandeis. In the early 1900s, before he became a Supreme Court justice, he took on a series of clients whose cases exposed him to the Gilded Age's worst excesses. It radicalized his thinking. "If the Lord had intended things to be big, he would have made man bigger—in brains and character," he wrote his daughter. He believed that the new corporations had only managed to thrive by dint of their dirty tactics: secret contracts, price fixing, and the purchase of potential competitors. On a level playing field, he lectured a Senate Committee in 1911, "these monsters would fall to the ground."

Brandeis often wrote on behalf of exploited American consumers, but they were hardly his primary objects of concern. In the great Jeffersonian tradition, his heart truly bled for the small producers and sellers squashed by the monopolists. To protect these businessmen, Brandeis launched a crusade for "fair trade," which revolved around a doctrine called Resale Price Maintenance. The idea was that manufacturers should legally control the retail value of their wares, rather than hand the power of pricing over to large chains and department stores, whose size gave them the unstoppable advantage of offering deep discounts. If this campaign forced consumers to pay slightly higher prices, Brandeis didn't mind one bit. In an essay he wrote for *Harper's Weekly* in 1913, he excoriated the consumer who cared only about short-term prices: "Thoughtless or weak, he yields to the temptation of trifling immediate gain, and, selling his birthright for a mess of pottage, becomes himself an instrument of monopoly." And in the generation that followed Brandeis, Midwestern liberals, Southern populists, and assorted other politicians continued to inveigh against the debasement of small businessmen.

By the postwar period, however, the producer was edged out of liberal thinking and replaced by a figure better suited to the affluence of the times. In the 1960s, Ralph Nader portrayed the consumer as the true victim of corporate greed. (Michael Sandel elegantly narrates this transformation of liberal thought in his book, *Democracy's Discontent*.) To the Naderites, antitrust laws remained as necessary as ever, but only for the sake of driving down the very prices that Brandeis had once hoped to maintain. Mark Green, a leading disciple of Nader's, wrote that the "primary focus of antitrust enforcement" should be "efficient production and distribution—not the local farmer, local druggist, or local grocer."

Conservatives, it turned out, were only too happy to hear such talk. After years of defending monopoly as perfectly justifiable, they began publishing books and articles conceding that consumer welfare was a legitimate purpose of antitrust, perhaps the only one. Robert Bork denounced all of Brandeis's attempts to protect small producers as a "jumble of half-digested notions and mythologies." A cottage industry of like-minded critiques emanated from the University of Chicago's Law School and then traveled straight to Republicans in Washington. In the hands of Ronald Reagan's Justice Department, not to mention the judges he appointed to the federal bench, efficiency and low prices provided the justification for dismantling much of the old antitrust infrastructure. No subsequent administration, either Democratic or Republican, has meaningfully tried to revive it.

And Amazon is the price we're paying for that bipartisan turn in thinking. As he built the company, Jeff Bezos carefully studied the example of Walmart, America's largest retailer. He borrowed his personal style from the parsimonious Sam Walton and also poached from his C-suite. Walmart's executives aren't extravagantly compensated; neither are Amazon's. For a time, they didn't even receive reimbursements for office parking. Meanwhile, both companies have studiously avoided unionization and treat their workers miserably. In one famous incident, Amazon hired paramedics to revive heat-sick employees at a Pennsylvania warehouse rather than buy an air-conditioning unit.

Still, the biggest lesson that Bezos drew from the Waltons was in how to handle suppliers. Both Amazon and Walmart promise its customers the same feat—undercutting their competition on price. But frugality and innovation can only go so far in keeping prices headed southward, especially in the face of the stock market's impatience. Growing profit margins depend, therefore, on continually getting a better deal from suppliers. At Walmart, this tactic is enshrined in policy. The company has insisted that suppliers of basic consumer goods annually reduce their prices by about 5 percent, according to Charles Fishman's book *The Walmart Effect*.

It's hard to overstate how badly these price demands injure the possibility for robust competition. But when Amazon engages in the same behavior, it acquires a darker tint. Where Walmart is essentially a large-scale, cut-rate version of the old department store and grocer, Amazon doesn't confine its ambitions to any existing template. Without the constraints of brick and mortar, it considers nothing too remote from its core business, so it has grown to sell server space to the CIA, produce original televisions shows about bumbling congressmen, and engineer its own line of mobile phones.

And as it amasses economic power, it also acquires greater influence in the cultural and intellectual life of the nation. Consider Amazon's relationship to the publishing industry. A recent survey conducted by the Codex Group, released in March, found that Amazon commands a 67 percent share of the e-books market (not at all surprising given that it invented a wildly popular device for consuming digital tomes). And when it comes to the sale of all new books—hard, soft, and electronic—Amazon accounts for 41 percent.

Even though the five major publishing houses have political connections and economic power of their own, they just can't compete. When Amazon first set the price for e-books at $9.99, it did so unilaterally and didn't inform publishers in advance of its live-streamed announcement. The company continually finds new schemes for exacting tribute from the houses. Amazon requires a contribution to a "marketing development fund"—which hits publishers for an additional 5 to 7 percent of their gross sales. All the wondrous tools on the Amazon site are open to publishers, but only if they write appropriately sized checks: Preorder buttons, appearance in search results, and personalized recommendations are hardly enlightened services provided by your friendly bookseller. Sure, Barnes and Noble and other chains have long charged fees for shelf placement, but Amazon has invented a steroidal version of that old practice. There seems to be no limit to Amazon's demands—and its current negotiations with Hachette prove the point. The *New York Times* has reported that Amazon apparently wants to increase its cut of each e-book it sells, from 30 percent to 50.[1]

To justify this approach with publishers, Amazon portrays them as deserving of rough treatment. One ex-Amazon employee told *The New Yorker*'s George Packer that the company views publishers as "antediluvian losers with rotary phones and inventory systems designed in 1968 and a warehouse full of crap." In the mid-2000s, the company famously launched an initiative

---

1. Amazon has subsequently attempted to claw back ground in public opinion by casually injecting an altogether different proposal: "We believe 35% should go to the author, 35% to the publisher and 30% to Amazon."

called the Gazelle Project to extract better terms from small publishers. Its moniker was derived from a Bezos suggestion that his team pursue its prey as a cheetah tracks a "sickly gazelle." (Lawyers a bit more sensitive to antitrust laws renamed it the "Small Publisher Negotiation Program.") Or as one executive charged with dealing with the book industry confessed to the reporter Brad Stone, "I did everything I could to screw with their performance."

In their desperation, publishers have tried various gambits to alter this dynamic. They have attempted to fight size with size—a misbegotten notion that led them to collude with Apple in blatant violation of price-fixing laws. And in the same spirit, they have accelerated the old tendency to seek safety in mergers. Just last year, Random House joined Penguin to form a mega-house, which controls 25 percent of the book business, in the dim hope that this new brawn would insulate them from Amazon's harshest demands. But even a giant corporation ultimately has to bend to the will of their big buyer. That's been the iron law of Walmart, which imposes its terms on the largest corporations in the world. As the New America Foundation's Barry Lynn has described, "Walmart . . . has told Coca-Cola what artificial sweetener to use in a diet soda, it has told Disney what scenes to cut from a DVD, it has told Levi's what grade of cotton to use in its jeans, and it has told lawn-mower makers what grade of steel to buy."

So, no matter how large they grow, publishers will continue to strip away costs to satisfy Amazon. And more attention will fall on a strange inefficiency at the heart of the business: the advances that publishing houses pay their writers. This upfront money is the economic pillar on which quality books rest, the great bulwark against dilettantism. Advances make it financially viable for a writer to commit years of work to a project.

But no bank or investor in its right mind would extend that kind of credit to an author, save perhaps Stephen King. Which means that it won't take much for this anomalous ecosystem to collapse. Amazon might decide that it can only generate enough revenue by further transforming the e-book market—and it might try to drive sales by deflating Salman Rushdie and Jennifer Egan novels to the price of a Diet Coke. Or it can continue to prod the publishing houses to change their models, until they submit. Either way, the culture will suffer the inevitable consequences of monopoly—less variety of products and lower quality of the remaining ones. This is depressing enough to ponder when it comes to the fate of lawn-mower blades.

$$\bullet \qquad \bullet \qquad \bullet$$

In confronting what to do about Amazon, first we have to realize our own complicity. We've all been seduced by the deep discounts, the monthly automatic diaper delivery, the free Prime movies, the gift wrapping, the free two-day shipping, the ability to buy shoes or books or pinto beans or a toilet all from the same place. But it has gone beyond seduction, really. We *expect* these kinds of conveniences now, as if they were birthrights. They've become baked into our ideas about how consumers should be treated.

These expectations help fuel our collective denial about Amazon. We seem to believe that the Web is far too fluid to fall capture to monopoly. If a site starts to develop the lameness of an AltaVista or Myspace, consumers will unhesitatingly abandon it. But while that meritocratic theory might be true enough for a search engine or social media site, Amazon is different. It has a record of shredding young businesses, like Zappos and Diapers.com, just as they begin to pose a competitive challenge. It uses its riches to undercut opponents on price—Amazon was prepared to lose $100 million in three months in its quest to harm Diapers.com—then once it has exhausted the resources of its foes, it buys them and walks away even stronger.

This big-footing necessitates a government response. It is often said that the state is too lead-footed to keep pace with tech companies; that by the time it decides to take action against a firm, the digital economy will have galloped off into the distance. But there's a long history that suggests the opposite.

It starts with AT&T's Bell Labs in the late 1940s. Even though scientists there developed a slew of great inventions—automatic dialing, new switchboards—executives atop the monopoly essentially shoved the new gizmos into a filing cabinet, where they languished. (Unchallenged monopolists have little incentive to disrupt industries they already control.) Under pressure from the government, AT&T began licensing its technology to other firms, including a device called the electronic transistor—which, in the hands of Texas Instruments, became the basis for the computer.

Or take IBM, a company that constantly flirted with breaking the law. The Justice Department hounded Big Blue in the 1950s and 1960s. And though IBM complained about the intrusions, it would always settle with the government and promise to reform its ways. In truth, it should have thanked the trustbusters. With the government at its elbow, IBM turned away from the business of tabulating machines to enter computing, a field it would revolutionize. Then there's IBM's successor, Microsoft. The company was known for using its dominance to squash small rivals who made superior products. But the government's prosecution caused it to back away from that tactic, which, in turn, allowed nascent companies like Google and Skype to grow. "Antitrust gets some credit for restoring uncontested American technological preeminence," says Tim Wu, author of *The Master Switch*. "It made sure the web would stay open."

These stories sound impressive now, but it took decades of experimentation, mostly unsuccessful, before a serviceable approach for curbing monopolies finally emerged. In the earliest days of the Progressive Era, the country was quick to discover the danger of huge corporations and acted with alacrity to legislate it into oblivion, passing the Sherman Antitrust Act in 1890. But wishing the problem away is very different from solving it. Progressives never could agree on how to think about monopolies— would they permit them to exist, carefully regulated by the state, or smash them into bits? The creation of the Federal Trade Commission in 1914 was meant to be the culmination of that long struggle, yet it came to embody all the conceptual fuzziness of the debate. Even Brandeis considered it a "stupid administration."

It took a Great Depression to provide the clarity that progressives never did manage. When all of Roosevelt's efforts to revive the economy sputtered, he waged all-out war on monopoly. In 1940 alone, his Justice Department brought 92 new cases and filed 3,412 complaints; it went after big-time players like Alcoa, General Motors, and the American Medical Association. Monopoly no longer stirred emotions, as it had in Brandeis's time, but Roosevelt's triumphs set precedents that ensured future victories. He implanted antitrust more securely in government, a technocratic tool for managing the health of the economy.

Perhaps the debate over Amazon won't take as many fits and starts. There are already a few ideas percolating—one would strip Amazon of the power to set prices; another would deprive it of the ability to use its site to punish recalcitrant suppliers. Those ideas feel like tentative jabs at the problem, rather than coherent solutions to it. Still, if we don't engage the new reality of monopoly with the spirit of argumentation and experimentation that carried Brandeis, we'll drift toward an unsustainable future, where one company holds intolerable economic and cultural sway. Unfortunately, a robust regulatory state is one item that can't be delivered overnight.

The Atlantic

While some in Silicon Valley are mining the mundane for riches, plenty of companies are aiming for something a bit more ambitious than laundry delivery. Google's skunkworks operation, for instance, is working on projects such as self-driving cars and artificial brains. The firm is working on a delivery service, too, but it's no Washio. Google plans to use drones to deliver packages to people across the world within minutes of their orders. The idea may be crackpot or it may be the future, but Alexis Madrigal's story offers fascinating insights into how Google thinks and solves problems.

14. Inside Google's Secret Drone-Delivery Program

A zipping comes across the sky.

A man named Neil Parfitt is standing in a field on a cattle ranch outside Warwick, Australia. A white vehicle appears above the trees, a tiny plane a bit bigger than a seagull. It glides towards Parfitt, pitches upward to a vertical position, and hovers near him, a couple hundred feet in the air. From its belly, a package comes tumbling downward, connected by a thin line to the vehicle itself. Right before the delivery hits the ground, it slows, hitting the earth with a *tap*. The delivery slows, almost imperceptibly, just before it hits the ground, hardly kicking up any dust. A small rectangular module on the end of the line detaches the payload and ascends back up the vehicle, locking into place beneath the nose. As the wing returns to flying posture and zips back to its launch point half a mile away, Parfitt walks over to the package, opens it up, and extracts some treats for his dogs.

The Australian test flight and thirty others like it conducted in mid-August are the culmination of the first phase of Project Wing, a secret drone program that's been running for two years at Google X, the company's whoa-inducing, long-range research lab.

Though a couple of rumors have escaped the Googleplex—because *of course* Google must have a drone-delivery program—Project Wing's official existence and substance were revealed today. I've spent the past week talking to Googlers who worked on the project, reviewing video of the flights, and interviewing other people convinced delivery by drone will work.

Taken with the company's other robotics investments, Google's corporate posture has become even more ambitious. Google doesn't just want to organize all the world's *information*. Google wants to organize all *the world*.

During this initial phase of development, Google landed on an unusual design called a tail sitter, a hybrid of a plane and a helicopter that takes off vertically then rotates to a horizontal position for flying around. For delivery, it hovers and winches packages down to the ground. At the end of the tether, there's a little bundle of electronics they call the "egg," which detects that the package has hit the ground, detaches from the delivery, and is pulled back up into the body of the vehicle.

That Parfitt would be the man on the receiving end of the tests was mostly happenstance. Google's partner in the country, Phil Swinsburg of Unmanned Systems Australia, convinced him to take part in the demonstration deliveries launched from a nearby farm. (Australia's "remotely piloted aircraft" policies are more permissive than those in the United States.)

Standing with Parfitt as he received dog treats from a flying robot was Nick Roy, the MIT roboticist who took a two-year sabbatical to lead Project Wing. In all the testing, Roy had never seen one of his drones deliver a package. He was always at the takeoff point, watching debugging information scroll up the screen and anxiously waiting to see what would happen. "Sergey [Brin] has been bugging me, asking, 'What is it like? Is it actually a nice experience to get this?' and I'm like, 'Dude, I don't know. I'm looking at the screen,'" Roy told me.

So, this time, as he prepared to end his tour of duty at Google X and return to MIT, he watches as the Wing swoops and delivers. Recalling that moment, he struggles not to sound too rapturous or lose his cool technical objectivity. "Once the package is down and the egg is back up, the vehicle gains altitude and does this beautiful arc, and it's off again," he said. "That was delightful."

The parting between Roy and Google X seems amicable. When Astro Teller, director of the lab, described it to me in an interview in Mountain View, he literally patted Roy on the knee. "Nick was super ultra-clear with us from day one, despite lots of pressure from me,"—Teller pats Roy on the knee—"that he was going to leave after two years." But the timeline was good, Teller maintained, because it gave the project shape and a direction.

In the two years, Roy's goal was simple: figure out if the idea of drone delivery made sense to work on. Should Google pursue creating a real, reliable service? Was it possible? Could a self-flying vehicle be built and programmed so that it could take off and land anywhere, go really fast, and accurately drop a package from the air?

The answer, Roy and Teller say, is yes. They have not built a reliable system Google users can order from yet, but they believe the challenges are surmountable. Now, Google will begin growing the program in an ultimate push to create a service that will deliver things people want quickly via small, fast "self-flying vehicles," as they like to call them.

Teller has found a replacement for Roy in Dave Vos, a twenty-year veteran of automating flying machines, who sold his drone software company, Athena Technologies, to Rockwell in 2008. Where Roy got to play what-if and why-not, Vos must transform the Wing into a service that real people might use.

"What excited us from the beginning was that if the right thing could find anybody just in the moment that they need it, the world might be radically better place," Teller said.

There are already dozens of Googlers working on the project, concocting everything from new forms of the vehicle to the nature of its delivery mechanism to the user experience of the app for ordering drones. There will be more recruits soon. Google will enter the public debate about the use of civilian unmanned aerial vehicles. Regulators will start hearing from the company. Many packages will be dropped from the sky on a tiny winch from a robot hovering in the air.

This may sound crazy. This may *be* crazy. But Google is getting serious about sending packages flying through the air on tiny drones. And this is how that happened.

.   .   .

Of course Google wants the world to believe in delivery by drone as part of the natural progression of technological society to deliver things faster and faster. This is how the world works, according to Google cofounder, Sergey Brin.

Imagine Brin in 2011. Perhaps he's wearing a Google Glass prototype and a long-sleeved technical T-shirt, maybe even Vibram FiveFinger footwear. He is rich beyond all comprehension, a billionaire many times over. In his thirty-ninth year on earth, he has decided to grow a beard, wisdom-enhancing salt-and-pepper sprinkled around his chin.

While Larry Page runs the mainline cash cow Internet advertising business, Brin (or Sergey, as everyone at Google X invokes him) is building a second, much wilder company inside the envelope of the old one. Over the next few years, he will unveil self-driving cars, Google Glass; help acquire eight robotics companies and a high-altitude, solar-powered drone maker; and do whatever else Google is doing in secret.

And one day in 2011—before any of us had seen these new ideas—he is talking with Astro Teller, whose goatee is more salt than pepper, and they make an observation about the world.

"The original observation felt most like this," Teller said. "When the Pony Express came along, it really reshaped society to be able to move things around fairly reliably at that speed, which was measured in many days. The U.S. Postal Service—growing partly out of the Pony Express and having it be even more reliable and starting to shorten the time—really did change society again.

"FedEx overnight delivery has absolutely changed the world again. We're starting to see same-day service actually change the world," he continued. "Why would we think that the next 10x— being able to get something in just a minute or two—wouldn't change the world?"

If there is one thing Google likes, it is changing the world. The company's framework for *societal* transformation has been conditioned by the relentless decrease in cost and increase in performance of computers. They believe order-of-magnitude changes can happen quickly because they've seen and participated in both the rise of the commercial Web and the astonishing growth of mobile computing.

To these technical changes, they attach the concept of progress, especially if Google, with its deeply held sense that it won't or can't be evil, is involved. As the company has matured, people like Teller seem willing to admit that perhaps all things aren't getting better all the time. But they argue the new "goods" outweigh the new "bads," especially if an honest accounting is made of the current alternatives.

"Google X has this experience all of the time in all of these different projects," Teller said. People count all the problems created by our current way of life as zero because that's what we're used to as the societal default, he contended. Conversely, people immediately see the negatives of any new thing. "We are not deaf to those issues and we're really eager to talk to society about how to mitigate those," Teller said. "But part of our conversation with society is about us listening, but also trying to remind the people that we talk to that the place we're starting from is not zero. In this case, for delivery, cars, airplanes create a very large carbon footprint and have a lot of safety issues."

So, of course, Google wants to help increase the speed of delivery and reduce the carbon footprint and safety of delivery. Ergo, the development of self-flying vehicles. "In principle that [speed improvement] could happen independent of self-flying vehicles," Teller concluded. "But it was obvious from the very beginning that it was going to have to be self-flying vehicles."

Google X began to come up with ideas and test them theoretically and experimentally. They considered many different wild options, sketching out new and wacky transportation systems. ("What if you took a glider up on a balloon with a super long string and the glider goes up, releases, and zooms down . . . You can—on paper—satisfy yourself that's not the right solution.") But eventually, Teller realized they needed an expert. They did a search and ended up pulling Roy across the county.

Roy was perhaps a less-than-obvious choice. For one, he'd never worked on drones flying outside. The challenges of the wind were new to him. Roy neither had a traditional aeronautics background nor had he dealt in logistics. Look back on his résumé from the early 2000s, as he prepared to finish his Ph.D. at Carnegie Mellon: There are almost no signs that he'd be the guy Google X would one day tap for a drone project. His most prominent work had been on tour guide and nursing robots.

But that leaves out one very important detail: Roy's thesis advisor was Sebastian Thrun, the founder of Google X and one of the most influential people in robotics. In the years before his tour at Google, Roy did important work with the support of the Office of Naval Research on indoor drone navigation in "GPS-denied" environments, where the vehicles can't rely on satellites to position themselves.

When Roy arrived in California, Project Wing's initial focus was on delivering defibrillators to help people who have had heart attacks. The key factor in the success of using a defibrillator is how quickly it is deployed, so saving a few minutes of transit time could make for a lifesaving application. But as time went on, the Google team realized that tying into the 911 system and other practical exigencies eliminated the speed advantage they thought they could deliver.

So, now, Teller's—and, by extension, I will assume Brin's—big-picture vision has shifted to the ways ubiquitous, two-minute delivery can transform people's relationship to stuff.

The idea goes like this: Because people can't assume near-instantaneous delivery of whatever they need, they stockpile things. They might have a bunch of batteries, slowly decharging in a drawer, or a drill that they use for ten minutes a year. Each of these things is a personal possession that sits around, embodying all this energy and industrial effort unproductively.

If this sounds familiar, it should: It is the argument—even down to the drill example—that organizations like Worldchanging made in the mid-2000s for the creation of "product-service systems." Those ideas, in turn, became key planks in the original conception of the "sharing economy," imagined as one in which the world could make much less stuff because efficient, digital logistics would let each asset be used by more people.

"It would help move us from an ownership society to an access society. We would have more of a community feel to the things in our lives," Teller preached. "And what if we could do that and lower the noise pollution and lower the carbon footprint, while we improve the safety of having these things come to you?"

And unicorns might win the Kentucky Derby, too! But one would need to find a unicorn first before it could enter the race.

Google had to build a vehicle and teach it to fly itself.

· · ·

Off one of the many hallways inside Google X's simple red brick building in Mountain View, there is a door labeled "The Hatchery." Roy swipes his badge and we step inside the guts of the secret Project Wing.

This is a workshop. Scattered about, I can see fishing line on a table, three colors of tape, a tall half-stuffed trash can, drawers of fasteners, spare antennae, several glue guns, and some drills. Off to my right, through glass doors, there are four identical plane bodies lined up, wingless. At the back, a man is hand-building some electronics, copper gleaming in the overhead lights.

Carapaces of different species of unmanned aerial vehicles are piled on shelving units and anywhere else they might fit. The horseshoe-crab shaped bodies of several editions of the current drone sit down at my feet. Their electronic innards are visible through clear plastic. Above me, a Cessna model hangs from the ceiling. On shelving units, there are the familiar buglike quad-copters, a strange craft with helicopter rotors built into its single wing, and a remote-control monster truck.

The main attraction, however, is the gleaming white prototype sitting atop the wheeled table in the center of the room labeled *Chickadee*. It sits on its tail in the angle of repose of the Space Shuttle, nose pointed to the sky. This is the tail-sitter, just like the one that dropped the dog treats in Australia.

The design is simple. There is a tail that serves as a stand, a central plastic body, and two wings made out of foam board covered in a thin skin for protection from the elements. There are four rotors attached to the vehicle, two on the underside closer to the body, and two on the outside towards the edges of the wings.

The build quality is fascinating. From afar, it looks shiny and complete, and it's loaded with custom-built electronics, but up close, it's clear that the body itself is handmade and hacked together. Fingerprint smudges smear it. Some pieces have been professionally fabricated, it seems, but other bits look made in the on-site shop. It is a work in progress.

The class of vehicles that it belongs to is not common. Most flying things are fixed wing—like a plane—or some type of helicopter, which uses one or more rotors to stay in the air. To fly, fixed-wing craft primarily move air horizontally while helicopters move air vertically. The tradeoffs are pretty obvious: The fixed wing craft are more aerodynamic and efficient. They can go farther, faster with less fuel. Meanwhile, the choppers can maneuver well in many different conditions, don't need a runway to take off or land, and can hover in place.

In the military drone world of Predators and Global Hawks, fixed wing, long-range craft predominate. In the hobbyist drone world, quadcopters like the DJI Phantom 2 and Parrot AR.Drone are most popular among enthusiasts, although a strong model-airplane community exists.

In aeronautics, hybrid craft that combine elements of fixed-wing planes and helicopters do exist, and certainly aerospace companies experimented with them. But they are more complex because they have to execute two entirely different tasks: moving air on different axes. In some cases, such as the new F-35B, Lockheed Martin built rotating jets into the plane body that can be pointed at the ground to achieve liftoff, then rotated in the air, to push the jets through the sky.

The tail-sitter configuration, in which the *whole craft* rotates from a vertical to a horizontal position, has also been a source of fascination through aeronautical history. The Nazis, for example, were considering such a craft. And there was an American defense program that resulted in the creation of two prototype aircraft by Lockheed and Convair. The photographs of these huge planes sitting vertically on runways—shiny and steel, unmistakably midcentury—feel retrofuturistic. None of the research efforts caught on, though, with a major problem being that there wasn't a good way for the pilot to deal with the change in orientation.

Obviously, that's not a problem with a drone, though. The "pilot" is housed in a desktop-class computer that sits towards the tail of the plane. The power system, batteries, cabling, and a big capacitor sit just above it. That's hooked to the motors, which also send back motor-performance data to the flight computer. Sensor data also come in from the inertial measurement unit (IMU) mounted to the left of the computer. The IMU uses accelerometers and gyroscopes to determine the X-Y-Z positioning of the craft, an essential part of flying. In the nose, we find the GPS unit, and in the tail, there's a camera pointed down. There's no on-board laser range-finding system in the current incarnation, but there are two communications radios, one high-bandwidth for sending telemetry data and one low-bandwidth for longer-range communications.

Google has not settled on this design for all its future program development, but it has formed the platform for much of their testing. While the hardware is a significant part of the problem, they seem largely agnostic about which flying machine might ultimately serve their needs best. The real challenges, Teller and Roy insist, come in the design of the rest of the system like, for example, the delivery mechanism.

Imagine all the possible ways one might get something from high in the air down to the ground. How about a tiny parachute à la *The Hunger Games*? Roy's team tried it. There was too much wind interference and they struggled with accuracy. How about literally firing them down, a ballistic approach? "We contemplated this," Roy said. "And then Sergey walked out from under a balcony and we almost hit him in a drop test." After that, they moved on.

Another obvious idea is to simply land the craft, drop the package, and then take off again. To test the premise, they brought in some of Google's user-experience researchers, who queried people about how they might react to such a delivery.

What they found was that individuals could not be stopped from trying to reach for their packages, even if they were told that the rotors on the vehicle were dangerous, which they are.

Finally, they settled on an idea that Roy had initially resisted: winching down a line with the package on it and then winding it back up into the craft.

Mechanical engineer Joanna Cohen, trained at Cal Tech and MIT, designed the contraption. It consists of a few key parts. The first is the winch itself, which spools out the high-grade fishing line. The second is the "egg," the little gadget that goes down with the package, detects that it has reached the ground, releases the delivery, and signals that it should be cranked back up to the hovering UAV. If something goes wrong, there is an emergency release mechanism at the top of the line—"basically a razor blade," Cohen told me—that allows the UAV to cut and fly.

When a package comes hurtling down, it moves at about 10 meters per second (about 22 miles per hour). When it gets close to the ground, the winch slows the fall to 2 meters per second for a relatively soft landing.

In the abstract, or under ideal conditions, this seems simple enough. But the project's hardware lead, James Burgess, said that out in the world, it's not so easy to make the deliveries work.

"If you can imagine a user case where we're going to someone's house, and the egg hits something—maybe it hit the power lines, maybe it hit the trees, maybe it hit the roof, maybe it hit the railing on the porch before it got to the porch. There are a lot of unknowns and environmental challenges," Burgess said.

"So the egg is smart enough to know that it hit something, but the vehicle also knows how high it is and the winch also knows how much line it is letting out. The egg says, 'I hit something,' and the vehicle says, 'But wait, you're not far enough down yet, so keep going because probably you bounced off something and don't arm yourself for [package] release.' So, all of our sensors and components work together in this network to make good decisions."

Or, for now, some kind of decision. When I asked how they planned to deal with power lines, which seem especially challenging to sense and avoid, the whole team demurred. "Remember: early days," Roy intoned. "We're not even close to that."

•　　　•　　　•

Like all autonomous robots, delivery drones have three fundamental tasks. They have to understand their position in the physical world. They have to reason where they should go next.

And they have to actually execute the control maneuvers to get there.

It turns out that the basics of getting from one place to another, under ideal conditions, are not that difficult. Some hobbyist drones can fly through a set of waypoints on their own. Others can follow a signal down on the ground. But these capabilities are more in the realm of autopilot than *autonomy*: They simply hold a bearing, altitude, and speed. It's kind of like cruise control in the sky. It's a pretty huge leap from cruise control to self-driving cars, and the same is true of the jump from autopilot to self-flying vehicles.

But what *is* hard is dealing with the thousands of unexpected scenarios and "edge cases" that would inevitably crop up if these systems were deployed at scale. It's the sum of how the vehicles handle all those difficult situations that add up to a reliable technology.

The analogy to Google's self-driving-car efforts is clear here: It's not that hard to build software that can drive a car on the freeway or even around Mountain View and deal with 99 percent of the things that happen.

But what about that 1 percent?

Finding and learning how to deal with all the possible edge cases and coming up with safety procedures for what to do when the robot doesn't know what to do is actually what forms the core of these big, long-term development programs.

In self-driving cars, Google keeps a massive database of all the times when a human operator had to take control of a car. They can simulate what would have happened if the human had not tagged in and try out different software approaches to teaching the system how to react, if, in fact, it would have made an error. Any time they change the system's logic, Google tests the alterations against that whole database to make sure they haven't broken something with the new fix.

Project Wing will probably adopt the same approach with both the database and the human operators. But instead of a single driver operating a single car, as has been the case in the autono-mous-vehicle program, Teller likes to imagine that there will be a relatively small number of operators controlling a number of drones, helping them make the right decisions in difficult situations.

"If a self-flying vehicle is trying to lower something and it goes down three feet and gets stuck, should it go home? Should it land? There's not a right answer to that," Teller told me. "That would be a good moment for it to raise its hand and say back to some-one looking at the delivery control software, 'What should I do?'"

This is a Google-y approach to the problem of ultra-reliabil-ity. Many of Google's famously computation-driven projects— like the creation of Google Maps—employed literally thousands of people to supervise and correct the automatic systems. It is one of Google's open secrets that they deploy human intelligence as a catalyst. Instead of programming in that last little bit of reliabil-ity, the final 1 or 0.1 or 0.01 percent, they can deploy a bit of cheap human brainpower. And over time, the humans work themselves out of jobs by teaching the machines how to act. "When the hu-man says, 'Here's the right thing to do,' that becomes something we can bake into the system and that will happen slightly less often in the future," Teller said.

One area where humans might be less helpful is the develop-ment of detect-and-avoid software that could help the drones deal with birds, other UAVs, helicopters, and the like. Some—*some*— of these issues could be solved by regulation that creates certain corridors or layers of air space for drones, as well as requiring transponders or other signaling mechanisms on all human-made flying things. But that's not a complete solution because as Teller put it, the birds aren't going to wear instruments.

Roy says the project is still in the very early days of develop-ing a mature, reliable detect-and-avoid system. But they are very far from having the right answers.

Think about what the problem really looks like: A camera or radar or laser is pointed at the sky in the direction that the vehicle is flying. The background could be either the sky or earthly terrain with all the variation that could imply. So the environment itself is pretty noisy. And the only signal that the drone was on a collision path with a distant object would be a few pixels in the image from, say, a camera. Working from those limited data, the software has to interpret those pixels as a type of flying thing and predict what it might do. And it has to do all that consistently under radically different lighting and visibility conditions.

Predicting others' flight paths requires that one's algorithm make some tradeoffs. At one end of the spectrum, one could program the software to say that other flying things could do *anything at any time*. But that makes it incredibly difficult to fly in normal airspace and is overly conservative. On the other end of the spectrum, one could assign fixed and rigid paths to all other flying things, assuming they move more or less in straight lines along a trajectory. But that, too, could lead to problems if a plane turns or a bird dives or a quadcopter reverses direction.

In the self-driving car space, Google has also had to build these sorts of models for cars and pedestrians and bicyclists, but roads—and the logic of the roads—heavily constrain what maneuvers are likely. Furthermore, it's easy to gather lots and lots of data about how drivers operate: All Google has to do is drive and drive and drive, loading ever more data into their models for how other vehicles move on the roads of California.

The sky is voluminous, and these vehicles are small. It's a lot less crowded than the country's road networks, and flying things can move in all directions. Roy's team found it difficult to even trigger their sense-and-avoid systems when they tried to do so intentionally by flying remote-controlled planes at them. So the self-flying vehicles need these systems for ultimate reliability and autonomy, but they are exceptionally difficult to build—and to test.

There are other problems, too. The task of simply orienting the UAV in space can be difficult depending on GPS availability and accuracy. The cargo loading process requires lots of manual intervention. The economics of delivery might end up making no sense. The batteries need to get better. The vehicles need to get quieter. The reliability of the parts in the drones needs to go up.

Google also has to convince the public that they *want* drones instead of UPS trucks. This isn't just about safety but also the very real concerns that drone delivery might generate new kinds of airborne pollution, electronic locusts jittering across the sky. Or that it might destroy delivery-truck-driver jobs, which are some of the last good blue-collar gigs around.

And even more fundamentally: What the hell is anyone really going to use drone delivery of anything in two minutes service for? It's a nice vision to consider the sharing economy delivered via robotic air, but what specific applications for these robots will actually make sense?

Recall that the initial application for drone delivery was sending defibrillators winging across cities. Well, many cities have solved this problem in a different way. They keep the machines geographically scattered across a city. That may be inelegant. That may be slightly wasteful. But it's simple, it's easy, and it does not require the invention and intervention of a flying robot.

·　　·　　·

Google, however, is not alone in thinking that delivery by drone is a plausible part of the future. Sure, there is Amazon, which announced a drone-delivery-development program last December. But there is also Andreas Raptopoulos and his company Matternet.

Forged out of some sessions at Singularity University, the off-the-wall futurology school in Silicon Valley, Matternet has been working to build a business around delivering medicines and other high-value goods in places without roads. They've tested in Haiti, the Dominican Republic, and Bhutan.

Since the Amazon announcement, interest in what they're doing has exploded, and Raptopoulos expects a similar increase in attention with Google's validation of their work. "We refer to our adoption curve as before and after Amazon. Things have really shifted in people's minds. People have started thinking at the corporate and organization level. There is an opportunity to solve a big problem," Raptopoulos told me. "And I think Google's announcement with accelerate that even further."

But Raptopoulous's vision for the future of drone delivery is very different from Google's. He imagines not an anywhere-to-anywhere free for all but that drones will carry goods to landing depots run by local people who build their own small businesses around the UAV service. He doesn't see this type of service cutting into the logistics business in rich countries, at least not for a long while.

There are other cargo-drone believers, even outside Silicon Valley. In Europe, there is an entire organization—the Platform Unmanned Cargo Aircraft (PUCA)—devoted to bringing people together around the idea. Their vision of the future would see large cargo planes carrying between two and twenty tons of cargo flying relatively slowly and cheaply from places underserved by the existing infrastructure. One controller on the ground could handle ten to thirty cargo planes flying at less than 300 miles per hour to save fuel. They could travel at all times of night and day, creating a more flexible in-filling logistics service to the current cargo system. In this scenario, cargo drones are like flying buses, not the speedy vanguard of two-minute delivery.

Founded by the Dutch business school professor Hans Heerkens, PUCA hosted a conference earlier this year that saw presentations from Airbus Defense and Space, the Dutch Air Force, and—most intriguingly—the journalist and novelist Jonathan Ledgard, who is heading up a project with the Swiss Federal Institute of Technology around cargo drones for Africa.

Ledgard, who wrote one of the best novels published this decade in *Submergence*, shared a draft of their vision with me—and it is fascinating in its mix of high and low technology, pessimism and optimism. He calls the robots in his plan "donkeys."

"The qualities of a donkey are similar to what is required for a cargo drone: sure-footed, dependable, intelligent, able to deal with dust and heat, cheap, uncomplaining," Ledgard wrote. "The choice of the name 'donkey' for cargo drones is deliberate. A donkey is not a Pegasus, associated with speed. It does not bomb, does not monitor. It flies stuff between here and there, that is all."

He imagines that specific cargo routes will develop in Africa at around Eiffel Tower height in what he calls "the lower sky." Unlike Google, he does not imagine that they will fly all around; it will not be Uber for stuff one can buy at CVS. "The routes will be geofenced: donkeys will only be able to fly in an air corridor about 200 metres wide and 150 metres high," Ledgard wrote. "Busier routes will resemble a high-speed ski gondola, without cables or supporting structures."

At the stops on the route, "every small town will have its own clean energy donkey station" that will "mix 3D printing and other advanced technology with low tech, presaging a Tatooine future where neural circuitry and simple materials will be matter-of-factly combined."

Ledgard believes "there isn't going to be enough cash for Africa to build out its roads." Yet, in previous generations, good roads were an enabling condition for industrialization and realizing jumps in the standard of living. How might African nations and citizens experience greater prosperity? The only way, Ledgard has concluded, is through the air.

A decade traveling the continent for *The Economist*, reporting on everything from jihadis to the spread of cheap Nokia cell phones, has convinced him that a technological paradox will permeate poor countries in the twenty-first century.

"A community will have access to a flying robot even though it will not have access to clean water, or security, or be able to keep its girls in school."

This may sound absurd, but that doesn't mean it won't be the future we live.

.   .   .

Google has a specific vision for the future of self-flying vehicles, but its mere public entry into the field will catalyze all the efforts enumerated here from Matternet's similar project to Ledgard's radically different donkey vision. Google simply showing interest in flying drones legitimizes all these efforts by people who are trying to marshal much greater resources than they currently have to make their initiatives work.

Beyond the reputation boost, the unmanned-cargo-plane booster, Heerkens, hopes that Google will develop its program in a way that allows other companies to tap into its infrastructure. "The significance of what Google does, to me, is less in the vehicles they use here and now," Heerkens said, "but the possibility in being a big organization of implementing the support infrastructure that's needed." For example, the detect-and-avoid systems will need to be certified, he believes, and Google could help governments figure out how to do so.

Matternet's Raptopoulos wondered, too, whether they might not launch a service but provide the cloud infrastructure for others to operate their own vehicles. "Google understands data infrastructure and mapping at the different levels better than almost anybody else. They may be thinking about an infrastructure play more than a service play," said Raptopoulos, who had spoken with Teller about the project. "But this is all speculation."

One area where Google will almost certainly have a major impact is in shaping the regulations that ultimately govern unmanned aircraft. "To a far greater degree than Amazon, Google has a history of working with policy makers and stakeholders on technology reform," the University of Washington's Ryan Calo, an expert on drone regulation, said. "Think net neutrality, fair use, privacy, and, recently, transportation. Adding Google's voice could have a significant effect on regulatory policy toward drones."

In Google's case, that may mean they do what they've done with self-driving vehicles, where they hired Ron Medford, a former official at the National Highway Traffic Safety Administration, to lobby regulators on their behalf. Medford, backed by Google, has had a clear influence on legislative processes in California, Nevada, and other states where self-driving-car laws have passed. In this case, Google could hire someone from the Federal Aviation Administration and perhaps make similar in-roads.

Teller confirmed that Google wants a seat at the regulatory table. "It's gonna take conversations with the public and with regulators. But so far in the conversations we've had over the last two years, and more intensely over the last couple months with regulators, I'm cautiously optimistic that everyone wants the same thing," he said. "Everyone wants the world to be a great place that's safe and has the benefits of the technology with as little or no downsides as possible."

Never were more Google-y words spoken.

Part IV

Business Accountability

InsideClimate News

Marcus Stern and Sebastian Jones join forces with InsideClimate News and the Weather Channel to tell the harrowing story of the transportation of highly volatile crude oil from North Dakota's Bakken shale across an aging railroad infrastructure in tank cars originally built to carry corn syrup and other less-dangerous liquids. One blew up in Lac-Mégantic in Canada, killing forty-seven people. It's a disaster waiting to happen in other locations that the trains cross almost without supervision, including Tuscaloosa, Ala., and the Chicago suburbs. Meanwhile, the oil industry successfully pushes back attempts at more regulation.

Marcus Stern and
Sebastian Jones

15. Boom: North America's Expensive Oil-by-Rail Problem

Regulators in the United States knew they had to act fast. A train hauling 2 million gallons of crude oil from North Dakota had exploded in the Canadian town of Lac-Mégantic, killing forty-seven people. Now they had to assure Americans a similar disaster wouldn't happen south of the border, where the U.S. oil boom is sending highly volatile crude oil every day over aging, often defective rails in vulnerable railcars.

On the surface, the response from Washington following the July, 6, 2013, explosion seemed promising. Over the next several months, the U.S. Department of Transportation issued two emergency orders, two safety alerts, and a safety advisory. It began drafting sweeping new oil-train regulations to safeguard the sudden surge of oil being shipped on U.S. rails. The railroad industry heeded the call, too, agreeing to slow down trains, increase safety inspections, and reroute oil trains away from populous areas.

But almost a year and a half later—and after three railcar explosions in the United States—those headline-grabbing measures have turned out to be less than they appeared. Idling oil trains are still left unattended in highly populated areas. The effort to draft new safety regulations has been bogged down in disputes between the railroads and the oil industry over who will bear the brunt of the costs. The oil industry is balking at some of the tanker upgrades, and the railroads are lobbying against further speed restrictions.

And rerouting trains away from big cities and small towns? That, too, has been of limited value because refineries, ports, and other offloading facilities tend to be in big cities.

InsideClimate News, the Weather Channel, and the Investigative Fund have monitored the regulatory response to oil-train explosions this year, focusing on whether the agency that oversees the railroads—the Federal Railroad Administration (FRA)— is able to ensure that the nation's aging railroad infrastructure can safely handle its latest task: serving as a massive, rickety network of pipelines on wheels.

We found that regulators don't have the resources to catch up with—let alone get ahead of—the risks posed by exploding oil trains. That has left the FRA politically outgunned by the railroad industry, leaving it largely to police itself.

Among the issues we identified:

- Too few government inspectors: The railroad agency has only 76 track inspectors, assisted by a few dozen state inspectors, to oversee the operations of some 780 railroad companies that manage 140,000 miles of track, plus railroad bridges. By its own estimate the agency can inspect less than 1 percent of the railroad activities under its oversight each year.

- Little oversight of railroad bridges: The FRA has set no engineering standards for railroad bridges, relying almost entirely on individual railroads to inspect, maintain, and repair their own bridges and trestles, some of them built more than a century ago. The agency doesn't keep an inventory or even a count of the bridges, estimated to number between 70,000 and 100,000.

- Secrecy: State and local governments can't independently assess the condition of local rail infrastructure because their inspectors don't have access to the railroads' design and maintenance records or to the tracks, trestles, and bridges themselves. The railroads consider such information proprietary; the tracks and bridges are their private property and disclosure of those materials is voluntary.

- Meager penalties: Fines are low, on the theory that the cost and consequences of an accident are sufficient incentive for railroads to properly maintain their tracks and bridges. In 2013, the FRA issued $13.9 million in fines to an industry whose top-seven revenue gainers alone took in nearly $84 billion

"How did it get missed?" Deborah Hersman, former chair of the National Transportation Safety Board, asked at an April NTSB hearing about the hazards of shipping crude oil by rail. "Unfortunately, I've seen too much of a tombstone mentality. Did it take derailments and body count for us to understand?"

But Then the Oil Trains Started Exploding

The economic rebirth of America's railroads is deeply entwined with the gusher of oil that began flowing from North Dakota's Bakken shale in the mid-2000s. With few pipelines to carry this liquid gold to refineries, producers turned to the railroads. Why wait to build politically contentious pipelines when they could transport huge volumes of crude by train?

Railcar shipments of oil soared from 9,500 in 2008 to more than 400,000 in 2013—most of it crude from North Dakota. Railroad revenue from transporting crude during that period rose from $25.8 million to $2.15 billion.

This bit of industrial alchemy helped keep oil prices from rising during the ongoing turbulence in the Middle East and created billions of dollars in investments in rail loading and unloading facilities, bringing more jobs to parts of America beyond North Dakota.

But then the oil trains from North Dakota started exploding. First in Lac-Mégantic, Canada. Then in Aliceville, Ala.; Casselton, N.D.; New Brunswick, Canada; and Lynchburg, Va.

The explosions triggered protests, lawsuits, and stormy community meetings: In Albany, N.Y., where Bakken crude is offloaded from railcars and sent down the Hudson River on barges; in Chicago suburbs that are crisscrossed with tracks; in Portland, Ore., a transit point for oil headed to Vancouver, Wash., and in the San Francisco Bay Area, where refineries receive the oil shipped in ocean tankers from Vancouver—and directly by rail from North Dakota.

"When you look at what could happen—and all of us are vulnerable—you'd think there would be more urgency," said Karen Darch, president of the Village of Barrington, one of several mayors in cities around Chicago alarmed by the rise of oil train traffic through their towns. "But it looks like the regulators are still keeping their fingers crossed that the next bad accident doesn't happen."

NTSB board member Christopher Hart said regulators need to respond to the new reality of oil by rail.

"Sometimes business models change quickly, and we need to figure out a way to keep the regulator up to speed with those changes—so that we don't have a disconnect between what's happening in the real world and where the regulations are," Hart said in an interview. Hart is now the NTSB's acting chairman.

Government officials and industry trade groups are still sparring over why North Dakota's crude is so much more volatile than other domestic oil, but many outside experts say the answer is clear: The Bakken's light crude is more like gasoline and rich in volatile natural-gas liquids, including methane, ethane, propane, and butane.

There's an ongoing controversy about how and how much of the natural-gas liquids should be removed. Currently, North Dakota doesn't have the equipment and pipelines to process and transport the gases for resale. Instead, some of the gas-laden oil is being shipped to coastal refineries, which are equipped to handle them. There, they can be sold separately, generating additional profits—but creating new dangers along the way.

During the rail journey, the natural-gas liquids separate from the oil and become gaseous, forming an explosive propane-butane blanket on top of the oil. If a railcar ruptures—and if some of the gas comes into contact with the outside air and a spark occurs—the railcar will explode and act as a blow torch on the car next to it. The result is a series of explosions like those captured on cell phones after the Lac-Mégantic, Aliceville, Casselton, and Lynchburg accidents—mushroom-shaped fireballs rising hundreds of feet into the sky.

The danger is compounded when trains are very long. The push to get North Dakota's oil to refineries as quickly as possible is so strong that trains sometimes stretch for a mile and a half, commonly pulling about one hundred railcars. Each car can carry roughly 30,000 gallons of oil, which means a single train can haul as much as 3 million gallons of oil—enough to fill a football field almost as high as the goal posts.

In the past, a train might have included five or ten cars of crude oil, said the NTSB's Christopher Hart. Today, "the entire train is nothing but this crude oil."

Dangers of Tanker Cars Known Since 1991

The type of railcar typically used to carry North Dakota's oil—the DOT-111—was never intended to haul volatile crude oil.

Designed in the 1960s, the cars originally carried corn syrup and other less explosive cargo.

Since 1991, the NTSB has warned repeatedly that the cars are prone to rupture during a derailment. Still, the ethanol industry used the DOT-111 as a workhorse in the mid-2000s, when the United States became the world's largest ethanol producer. It remained the ethanol industry's railcar even after thirteen DOT-111s ruptured at a railroad crossing in Cherry Valley, Ill., in 2009, igniting a fire that killed a woman sitting in her car. Three people were seriously injured, and 600 homes had to be evacuated.

The NTSB said the accident demonstrated "the need for extra protection such as head shields, tank jackets, more robust top fittings protection, and modification of bottom outlet valves on DOT-111 tank cars used to transport hazardous materials."

The accident prompted the Association of American Railroads, the industry trade group, to petition the U.S. Department of Transportation to require similar standards for tankers. When the Department of Transportation didn't act quickly, the railroad association issued its own industry standard urging that all tank cars built after October 2011 have those features.

But the vast majority of railroad cars are owned or leased by oil producers, refineries, and the ethanol industry—not by railroad companies. And those businesses chafed at the estimated $3 billion price tag, arguing that it was impossible to design a tanker to withstand every crash scenario. The solution, they said, was for the railroad companies to make their tracks safer.

"DOT has proposed tank car standards and other measures that would cost shippers billions of dollars to build new tank cars to carry crude and ethanol over old tracks," David Friedman of the American Fuel and Petrochemical Manufacturers, a refineries trade group, wrote to the Transportation Department. "That approach to risk is backwards: it is far more effective to prevent a derailment than mitigate impacts from it."

Century-Old Bridge Supports New-Era Oil Trains

While regulators have focused on the failings of DOT-111s since Lac-Mégantic, less attention has been paid to railroad infrastructure and operations.

The regulatory system's weaknesses are apparent in Tuscaloosa, Ala., where a 116-year-old bridge supports oil trains as they cross the Black Warrior River and into the city's downtown.

The steel bridge is buttressed by wooden trestles that rise about forty feet above public parks and jogging trails on either side of the river. On one bank sits the Tuscaloosa Amphitheater, where concert-goers can gaze up at trains silhouetted romantically against moonlit skies. Nearby is a construction site where condos are going up. Less than a mile downriver is a major oil refinery.

When InsideClimate News and the Weather Channel visited the bridge in May, a train of DOT-111s filled with crude oil happened to be parked overhead. At the base of the bridge, many of the pilings that support the trestle appeared to be rotted. Scores of pilings had what looked like makeshift concrete braces where the piling had cracked. Cross braces were hanging loose or lay on the ground beneath the structure. One stretch of the trestle had been blackened by fire.

The M&O Bridge and the surrounding track are the responsibility of Alabama Southern Railway, one of thirty short-line railroads owned and operated by Watco Companies, LLC, a transportation conglomerate. Watco's chief commercial officer, Ed McKechnie, said trains on that particular line carry heavy crude oil from Canada, not the explosive light crude from North Dakota. But Watco doesn't rule out moving North Dakota crude across the bridge if a customer comes along, McKechnie said.

Many rail-industry officials, academic engineers, and regulators say that even nineteenth-century bridges that appear rundown can be safe, because redundancy is built into the bridges and the defects are usually cosmetic. They note that rail bridge collapses are rare. According to FRA accident records, only fifty-eight train accidents were caused by the structural failure of railroad bridges for the twenty-seven years from 1982 through 2008. But most of the surge in oil has come since then.

For the public or even local governments, confirming that a specific bridge is safe enough to handle the new oil trains is almost impossible.

The M&O Bridge is inspected annually, McKechnie said, with the most recent inspection on June 14. But he would not disclose or summarize the results. Because railroad companies aren't required to file that information with federal regulators, there's no database to check.

In 2009, Congress ordered the FRA to draft railroad-bridge safety regulations, but the rule that emerged in 2010 is so narrow that it provides little help. Railroad operators are required to have a maintenance plan for each bridge and conduct at least one annual inspection. But they are not required to submit those plans to the FRA or to give the FRA an inventory of the bridges unless the agency requests that information.

The only direct oversight the rule called for was having the FRA, already dreadfully short of personnel and resources, conduct spot audits of the plans—not the bridges.

A Freedom of Information Act request for any documents related to safety inspections of the M&O bridge produced a January 2006 FRA inspection that found no structural problems but noted that the railroad "has no written policy on bridge inspection and/or maintenance practices."

An FRA inspection in January 2010 found several problems, including a crushed cap. A cap is a horizontal timber that plays a key role in supporting the elevated track. The railroad took the bridge out of service for four hours to replace the cap.

The inspection report said Alabama Southern is using an outside contractor to inspect its bridge but noted that "with a few a exceptions" the railroad "*is not* following the repair recommendations."

When asked to comment on the report, Watco's McKechnie said, "We continue to believe that an on-going maintenance program has kept the bridge safe and in use."

An FRA spokesman said the agency investigates every complaint about a bridge or track and invariably finds that the bridges are safe. But it's unclear how those judgments are made, because the federal government has no engineering standards for bridges.

McKechnie said Watco abides by industry standards produced by the American Railway Engineering and Maintenance-of-Way Association (AREMA). AREMA's *Manual for Railway Engineering* is available to the public for a fee, $1,370. The chapter on timber structures (purchased for $290) did not address what percentage of pilings may be rotted or otherwise defective without undermining the structural integrity of a bridge.

"It would be difficult to arrive at an allowable percentage of deteriorated piles that would cover all timber railroad bridges because of the variations in geometry, loading, and amount of deterioration among different timber structures," an AREMA representative wrote in an e-mail. "The decision as to what is safe is left to the bridge engineer."

Watco's vice president of engineering, Tony Cox, made a similar argument. He said the M&O Bridge is safe.

And what does the FRA say about the absence of federal or industry standards?

"A numerical standard for defective bridge pilings would be an insufficient standard, as every bridge is unique, and the structural integrity of every bridge must be considered in its proper context," a spokesman for the rail agency explained by e-mail. "Every bridge must be evaluated by an appropriate expert, and within the context of its construction, operational environment, and operational loading."

Ultimately, the railroad decides whether a bridge is safe.

Crossties in Decay, or Missing

Federal regulators have set safety standards for track, but whether they are adequate is another question.

In June 2014, a train carrying fuel oil derailed just west of Tuscaloosa, a few miles before it reached the M&O Bridge. The local environmentalist John Wathen, an opponent of shipping crude by rail, posted pictures of the track at the derailment site on his blog. They show crossties in varying stages of decay or completely missing.

"Rotten crossties, missing rail plates, dips and waves in the tracks," Wathen wrote on the blog.

Watco's McKechnie reviewed Wathen's photos for Inside-Climate News and the Weather Channel. He described the track as "typical Class I track," meaning it is the lowest grade of track with speed limited to 10 mph. The train that derailed was complying with that regulation, he said, attributing the accident to "a thermal displacement or a 'sun kink' caused by the rail overheating."

"While the observation of this track can lead to concerns, the track should be able to handle trains moving at 10 mph or less," he said in an e-mail. McKechnie said an inspection of the track in June found "minor deviations which were corrected immediately."

According to federal track safety standards, nineteen out of twenty-four crossties can be defective and the track still considered safe. But where do these track safety standards come from, and how do we know they're sufficient?

Holly Arthur, a spokeswoman for the industry's Association of American Railroads said the standards were enacted in 1971 and modified in 1982 and 1998 "through decisions by the Federal Railroad Administration . . . so best asked of FRA."

When an FRA spokesman was asked whether a track with nineteen out of twenty-four crossties could be safe, he replied,

"The track segment being evaluated must be considered in its totality."

The state of Alabama offered no help in determining whether the M&O Bridge or the nearby tracks where the train derailed are safe. The state DOT spokesman Tony Harris said Alabama "does not have any regulatory authority over bridges of that nature. Those are owned by the railroads themselves. Federal law requires the railroads to inspect those, and we are not vested with that duty or responsibility."

Industry Derails Regulations

After the Lac-Mégantic tragedy, senior Transportation Department officials vowed to prevent a similar accident from happening in the United States. Cynthia Quarterman, the Transportation official who oversaw the regulatory response until her resignation in October, and Joseph Szabo, the FRA head through the end of this year, assembled working groups for three issues: train securement, crew size, and hazardous materials.

Between September 2013 and April 2014, the three groups met, debated, and thrashed out their recommendations.

A drafting session of the hazardous-materials working group was held on January 27, in a large meeting room at the headquarters of the National Association of Home Builders, five blocks from the White House. About sixty people sat most of the day facing one another around a large rectangular configuration of conference tables.

FRA staffers occupied one line of tables, including Karl Alexy, head of the agency's Hazardous Materials Division and chair of the meeting. The other seats were occupied by representatives from industries that ship hazardous materials by rail, including the Association of American Railroads, American Petroleum Institute, Chlorine Institute, American Chemistry Council, Fertilizer Institute, and the Institute of Makers of Explosives.

Several railroads that run oil trains on their track also attended, including Canadian National Railway, Union Pacific, Watco, and BNSF, the largest shipper of crude. Warren Buffett's investment firm, Berkshire Hathaway, acquired BNSF for $44 billion in 2009, just as the crude-by-rail boom was taking off. Railroad-worker unions were at the session, too, including the Brotherhood of Locomotive Engineers and Trainmen.

Throughout the day, the FRA's Alexy floated safety recommendations drawn up by his staff. But none got past Michael J. Ross, the railroad association's watchful attorney. Ross interjected, objected, and parried with Alexy, dominating the discussion and delaying or diluting the recommendations.

The railroad association denied a request to speak with Ross, who was paid nearly $1.2 million in 2012 by the association and related organizations, according to the association's tax filing that year, the most recent filing available.

At one point, Alexy proposed that railroads carrying large volumes of crude oil be required to have a comprehensive spill-response plan, just as oil pipeline companies must have. Canada's Transportation Safety Board had made that one of its key recommendations after the Lac-Mégantic derailment, and the U.S. NTSB had taken the unusual step of endorsing Canada's recommendations, simultaneously announcing them from Washington.

But Ross was having none of it.

Swiveling in his chair as he swung the microphone to his lips, he said, "With all due respect to the NTSB, they completely misunderstood this regulation and this topic."

After some more back and forth, Alexy did what he would do throughout the day: He deferred to Ross.

"I agree, unless there's any objection," Alexy said.

There was none.

At one point, Alexy offered a recommendation that would have required better communication between shippers and railroads, to make sure railcars carrying heavier loads don't travel over bridges that aren't strong enough to support them. A typical oil train places roughly 15,000 tons of pressure on structures that could be as much as 150 years old.

"I'm not sure we have a problem with this in the industry," Ross said.

Alexy cited a recent incident where it had been a *big* problem— a bridge had collapsed under the weight of railcars it wasn't certified to support, resulting in a derailment. But after a few minutes of discussion, the group "parked" that recommendation, too.

An exchange between Alexy and Cynthia Hilton, executive vice president of the Institute of Makers of Explosives, reflected the tone of the meeting.

Hilton said she believed the goal that day was to produce recommendations that would give the industry guidance, not requirements that would force them to take specific actions.

"And now I'm reading that 'the shipper *must* develop and adhere to a sampling and testing program,'" she said. "That doesn't sound like a guidance document."

"You're right and I agree," Alexy assured Hilton. "This is of course open for editing, ideas, and suggestions. I circled the word 'must' . . . 'Should' is probably a little more appropriate."

In April, the hazardous materials working group produced four narrow, technical recommendations. For instance, one recommended a definition for what constitutes an oil train. Another offered a definition for what constitutes an empty rail car.

None of the staff recommendations that Ross had objected to during the drafting session made the cut. Nor did any of the NTSB recommendations, such as the one that would have required railroads to have emergency plans.

In July, California tried to fill part of the regulatory gap by imposing a 6.5-cent per barrel fee on oil shipped into the state by rail. The money will help communities develop emergency-response plans for possible spills. BNSF, Union Pacific, and the

Association of American Railroads have since filed suit against California, arguing that such matters are the province of the federal government.

Alexy declined through the railroad agency press office to be interviewed for this article. At an NTSB hearing in April, however, he responded to a questioner who asked him to characterize the results of the working group's activities.

"A lot of things that we took up initially were overcome by events," he explained.

Fred Millar, an advocate for tighter hazmat rail regulations and a longtime observer of the FRA, had another explanation: "Industry had veto power over everything."

"Who Was the Guardian of Public Safety?"

If train safety is the topic, the longtime head of the Association of American Railroads, Ed Hamberger, will be there to argue against what the industry sees as unnecessary or wrongheaded regulations. Attending these events is part of the reason the AAR and related organizations paid Hamberger almost $3 million in 2012.

At an NTSB hearing in April, Hamberger stressed the industry's safety record. He said that since 1980, the railroads had spent $550 billion on capital investments and maintenance, decreasing their overall accident rate by 79 percent.

"2011 was the safest year on record in terms of accident rate until 2012, which itself was the safest year on record until 2013," he said. "Preliminary data indicate that 2013 will be the safest year on record. With respect to hazardous materials, you've heard the number: 99.997 percent of hazardous materials go from origin to their destination without any accidental releases."

That figure, 99.997 percent, is derived from 2013 data showing that of the 2.4 million railcars carrying hazardous materials, only 78 "released their contents" before reaching their destinations, according to the railroad association's Ed Greenberg. This calculation does not factor in the magnitude of the spills, any environmental damage they may have caused, or any injuries, inconvenience, or cost to nearby residents.

When things do go sideways, Hamberger added, the railroad companies compensate communities for damages to person or property. Yet the small railroad that operated the train that derailed in Quebec declared bankruptcy almost immediately. It had only $25 million in liability insurance and was facing liabilities that might reach $2 billion. Almost a year and a half after the disaster, it remains unclear who will pay to rebuild the town, clean up the oil, and compensate the families of the forty-seven people who were killed.

Because the Lac-Mégantic accident occurred in Canada, it isn't included in the railroad association's safety statistics. But the accident was very much a "made in America" event. The railroad was based in Hermon, Maine. The oil came from North Dakota, where it was loaded onto American-made railcars and sent on its way to Canada on U.S.-owned track. Because the disaster occurred about ten miles from Maine, U.S. firefighters rushed to the scene to help fight the fires.

"It felt like an earthquake," Lac-Mégantic resident Yannick Gagne recalled in an interview. After the initial explosion rocked his house, he saw an orange flash. "Our windows were open and we felt the heat come in the house. My children started to cry."

Gagne and his family survived, but the bar he owned, the Musi-Café, burned to the ground still full of patrons enjoying live music on a festive Saturday night. No remains were found for five of the forty-seven people who died in the conflagration; the fire vaporized them.

In its final report on the disaster, the Transportation Safety Board of Canada outlined a long list of contributing factors, including a poor safety culture at the railroad, the Montreal, Maine & Atlantic.

But Wendy Tadros, who oversaw the investigation as the head of the safety board at the time, identified a deeper underlying issue: the failure of railroad regulators to keep up with the rapidly evolving safety challenges posed by North America's energy boom.

"Who was the guardian of public safety?" she lamented during a press conference releasing the report. "That is the role of the government . . . and yet this booming industry, where trains were shipping more and more oil across Canada and across the border, ran largely unchecked."

U.S. Crackdown on Oil Trains—Less Than Meets the Eye

Federal regulators don't stop oil trains from being left unattended, engines running.

The first public action U.S. rail regulators took after a fiery oil-train explosion killed forty-seven people in Canada in July 2013 seemed clear, impactful, and firm: Trains carrying hazardous materials could no longer be left unattended with their engines running unless the railroad first got approval from the Federal Railroad Administration.

Leaving a freight train unattended overnight with the engines running had been a major factor in the Lac-Mégantic, Canada, disaster, and the August 2, 2013, news release announcing the U.S. action had a no-more-business-as-usual tone. The emergency order was "a mandatory directive to the railroad industry, and failure to comply will result in enforcement actions," the press release said, adding no train shall be left unattended on the tracks with its engines running "unless specifically authorized."

But it turns out that the emergency order had a loophole big enough to drive a locomotive through.

Early on the morning of May 6, less than a year after the order was announced, James Racich, a trustee of the town of

Plainfield, Ill., noticed a train parked near a crossing in the middle of town with its engines running early. Racich didn't know about the emergency order, and he was accustomed to seeing trains left unattended on that stretch of track, enough so that it was a sore point with him. When he returned six hours later and saw the train still there—its engines still running with nobody aboard— he contacted the police. They confirmed that the train's engines were unattended and contacted the railroad, Canadian National.

"They basically told us the train was secure, was locked up, things like that," Plainfield Police Chief John Konopek said in an interview, adding "We have our hands tied. Because of federal regulation they can do that."

The half-mile long train parked in Plainfield was a mix of hazmat tankers and non-hazmat box cars, Konopek said. Its crew members had left it unattended because they had reached their maximum allowable number of hours of continuous work. By the time the replacement crew arrived, the train had been parked in downtown Plainfield, unattended with its engines running, for more than seven hours, according to Racich.

Patrick Waldron, Canadian National's director of state government relations, said in an interview that stopping the train on that section of track was part of the company's "normal operating practices and is in full compliance of the laws and regulations, including that order."

When pressed about the emergency order, he said, "I know the emergency order, but I've answered your question."

It turns out that Waldron was right because the emergency order is far weaker than advertised.

A tough-sounding FRA news release announcing the order had said that railroads could no longer leave idling trains unattended without FRA approval. Five days later, however, the FRA published the actual order in the *Federal Register* with less fanfare and tough talk. It contained fine print masking a huge loophole: The order would be satisfied when the "the railroad develops, adopts, complies with and makes available to the FRA upon request, a plan" for such stoppages. The "FRA does not intend to grant approval to any plan," the order continued. So railroads could continue leaving trains unattended without FRA approval.

According to the FRA spokesman Kevin Thompson, regulators aren't required to review the plan. The railroad simply has to keep the plan in its files.

Canadian National reported it had a plan, Thompson explained, so the company had complied with the emergency order and can continue leaving trains unattended on the tracks with their engines running.

Firestone wanted Liberia for its rubber. The notorious warlord Charles Taylor wanted Firestone to help his rise to power. At a pivotal meeting in Liberia's jungles in July 1991, the company agreed to do business with the warlord. T. Christian Miller and Jonathan Jones offer the first detailed examination of the relationship between the American tire giant and Taylor, laying bare the role of a global corporation in a brutal African conflict.

T. Christian Miller and
Jonathan Jones

16. Firestone and the Warlord

Harbel, Liberia—The killers launched from the plantation under a waning moon one night in October 1992. They surged past tin-roofed villages and jungle hideouts, down macadam roads and red-clay bush trails. More and more joined their ranks until thousands of men in long, ragged columns moved toward the distant capital.

Men in camouflage mounted rusted artillery cannon in battered pickup trucks. Thin teenagers lugged rocket-propelled-grenade launchers. Children carried AK-47s. Some held long machetes.

The killers wore ripped jeans and T-shirts, women's wigs and cheap rubber sandals. Grotesque masks made them look like demons. They were electric with drugs. They clutched talismans of feather and bone to protect them from bullets. In the predawn darkness, they surrounded Monrovia, the capital of Liberia.

They loosed their attack on the sleeping city. Artillery slammed into stores and homes. Mortars arced through thick, humid air that smelled of rot. Boy soldiers canoed across mangrove swamps. As they pressed in, the killers forced men, women, and children from their homes. They murdered civilians and soldiers. Falling shells just missed the U.S. embassy, hunkered on a high spot overlooking the Atlantic Ocean.

A new phase of Liberia's civil war had begun. It would whip savagely out of control over the next decade. More than 200,000 people would die or suffer terrible injuries, most of them civilians—limbs hacked off, eyes gouged out. Half the country's population would become refugees. Five American nuns would be slaughtered, becoming international symbols of the conflict's depravity.

Orchestrating the anarchy was Charles Taylor, a suave egomaniac obsessed with taking over Liberia, America's most faithful ally in Africa. For the attack that October morning, he had built his army of butchers and believers in part with the resources of one of America's most iconic businesses: Firestone.

Firestone ran the plantation that Taylor used to direct the October 1992 assault on Monrovia. In operation since 1926, the rubber plantation was considered to be the largest of its kind in the world, a contiguous swath of trees, mud-brown rivers, low hills, and verdant bush that at the time splayed across 220 square miles—roughly the size of Chicago.

Firestone wanted Liberia for its rubber. Taylor wanted Firestone to help his rise to power. At a pivotal meeting in Liberia's jungles in July 1991, the company agreed to do business with the warlord.

In the first detailed examination of the relationship between Firestone and Taylor, an investigation by *ProPublica* and *Frontline* lays bare the role of a global corporation in a brutal African conflict.

Firestone served as a source of food, fuel, trucks, and cash used by Taylor's ragtag rebel army, according to interviews, internal corporate documents, and declassified diplomatic cables.

The company signed a deal in 1992 to pay taxes to Taylor's rebel government. Over the next year, the company doled out more than $2.3 million in cash, checks, and food to Taylor, according to an accounting in court files. Between 1990 and 1993, the company invested $35.3 million in the plantation.

In return, Taylor's forces provided security to the plantation that allowed Firestone to produce rubber and safeguard its assets. Taylor's rebel government offered lower export taxes that gave the company a financial break on rubber shipments.

For Taylor, the relationship with Firestone was about more than money. It helped provide him with the political capital and recognition he needed as he sought to establish his credentials as Liberia's future leader.

"We needed Firestone to give us international legitimacy," said John Toussaint "J. T." Richardson, a U.S.-trained architect who became one of Taylor's top advisers. "We needed them for credibility."

While Firestone used the plantation for the business of rubber, Taylor used it for the business of war. Taylor turned storage centers and factories on Firestone's sprawling rubber farm into depots for weapons and ammunition. He housed himself and his top ministers in Firestone homes. He also used communications equipment on the plantation to broadcast messages to his supporters, propaganda to the masses, and instructions to his troops.

Secret U.S. diplomatic cables from the time captured Taylor's gratitude to Firestone. Firestone's plantation "had been the life-blood" of the territory in Liberia that he controlled, Taylor told one Firestone executive, according to a State Department cable. Taylor later said in sworn testimony that Firestone's resources had been the "most significant" source of foreign exchange in the early years of his revolt.

In written responses to questions, Firestone acknowledged the agreement with Taylor but said it had never willingly assisted Taylor's insurrection.

The company said Taylor rebels had used Firestone's trucks, food, medical supplies, fuel, and tools under the "obvious threat of violence to anyone who considered stopping them."

"Firestone had no role in the rise of Charles Taylor. It had no role in his ability to hold power in Liberia," the company said.

"At no time did Firestone have a collaborative relationship with Charles Taylor," the statement said. "The company's activities were focused on protecting its employees and property. The company had no ability to stop Taylor's forces from using the plantation for any purposes."

At the moment of the October 1992 attack that came to be known as Operation Octopus, Taylor controlled the vast majority of Liberia. He faced a weak interim government in Monrovia, backed by 7,000 largely untested soldiers from allied West African nations.

Operation Octopus effectively plunged the country into five more turbulent, terrible years of intermittent warfare. Taylor turned a civil war between his forces and the Liberian government into a bloodbath as more rebel factions joined in the fight for spoils: diamonds, timber, power. It spilled into neighboring Guinea and Sierra Leone, where rebel forces allied with Taylor hacked the limbs off civilians in a terror campaign of unchecked brutality.

In July 1997, Taylor won his war, and not on the battlefield. He was elected president, dominating with 75 percent of the vote. For many Liberians, a vote for Taylor was a vote of resignation. Many believed it was the only way to stop the killing. After Taylor became president, more factions arose, more bloodletting, more revenge. Liberia and its people suffered yet again.

In 2003, Taylor was indicted by an international tribunal for war crimes committed in Sierra Leone. He resigned the presidency. He was eventually sentenced to fifty years in prison—the first head of state to be convicted of crimes against humanity since the Nazi era.

The path to cooperation was neither direct nor easy for Firestone and its executives, according to interviews and documents. Some company officials actively resisted working with Taylor and his fighters, even in the face of real and implied threats of physical violence.

Other senior officers felt the company had no choice but to give in to Taylor's demands. They believed that working with Taylor was the only way to protect the thousands of impoverished Liberians who lived and labored on the plantation.

Firestone also received conflicting direction from the United States government. One ambassador urged the company to work with Taylor. In Washington, diplomats warned Firestone executives about the dangers of doing business with him.

But in the end, Firestone as a corporation and as a collection of men made a deliberate decision to cooperate with a man whose forces were publicly denounced as violent, vicious, and rapacious by the U.S. government and human rights groups.

The U.S. State Department had issued a report blaming Taylor's forces for killing civilians, raping women, and forcing hundreds of thousands of people to become refugees. Human Rights Watch said that Taylor's forces had engaged in a killing campaign that put a targeted ethnic group at "risk of genocide."

Today, Firestone maintains that at the time it struck its deal with Taylor, the guerrilla leader had "no well-established record" of human right violations. It said that many other companies and world leaders had treated Taylor as a legitimate political figure. Other companies operating in Liberia at the time chose to leave. But some stayed on through the violence.

"Does Firestone believe it did the right thing? Yes," Firestone said of its decisions in Liberia. "Do we, along with former U.S. presidents, the U.S. State Department, the United Nations and many leaders around the world who worked with Charles Taylor regret the war criminal he became? Yes."

The decision that Firestone faced confronts American companies operating to this day in war-torn, volatile regions in an increasingly globalized economy. All aim to make money. All must weigh, to one degree or another, their hierarchy of obligations—to their shareholders, to their foreign workers, to their host countries, and to their own sense of right and wrong.

Donald Ensminger served as the managing director of the Firestone plantation when Taylor invaded Liberia. He witnessed the violence firsthand. Taylor rebels killed and imprisoned his workers. They threatened Ensminger with death at the point of a rocket-propelled-grenade launcher.

Ensminger was let go from the company in October 1991. For the next twenty-three years, he kept silent about Firestone's choice to do a deal with a warlord. Now, he told *Frontline* and *ProPublica*, he wanted to explain.

He said that he warned Firestone that Taylor was a killer. He told the company that working with him might be a crime. He urged them to avoid deals that might legitimize the guerilla leader as the ruler of Liberia.

For him, the decision was clear. And Firestone got it wrong.

"Certainly, on behalf of our employees, the ones that were killed and suffered, it was immoral that we should now recognize the guy that caused all this," he said in an interview.

Gerald Rose, who served as the deputy chief of mission in Liberia at the time, holds an equally unsparing view of Firestone's choice.

"Do I think they have blood on their hands? Yes," Rose said. "I would not have made the decisions they made. I believe they facilitated a warlord in his insurrection and in the atrocities that he created."

Through the years, Liberia has been hesitant to examine its past. Taylor, for instance, was tried only for harm he caused in Sierra Leone, not Liberia. In 2009, the country's Truth and Reconciliation Commission recommended sanctions for scores of perpetrators. It cited Firestone for having aided Taylor in carrying out his rebellion and called for more investigation. The Liberian government never acted on those recommendations.

The stunning truth is that nobody has ever been punished in Liberia for the civil war that destroyed the nation. In fact, some of the people who helped to wreck the country are now the same people responsible for rebuilding it.

Top officials of formerly warring factions are now politicians passing laws in the legislature. They are pastors preaching from the country's pulpits. They are executives running some of the country's largest businesses.

The damage they inflicted on Liberia haunts the country even today. Liberia's shattered infrastructure and weakened health system have struggled to cope with the spread of the Ebola virus, which has killed thousands of Liberians.

In an interview with *Frontline* and *ProPublica*, Liberian president Ellen Johnson Sirleaf acknowledged that Liberia had not yet succeeded in shaking the Taylor regime or the devils of its history.

"The effect of that regime and regimes of the past are still with us today," she said. "Today we have a traumatized nation."

Efforts over many months to reach Taylor through his lawyers and family were not successful.

Johnson Sirleaf looked thoughtful when asked to describe Liberia's relationship with Firestone. A Nobel Peace Prize winner, Johnson Sirleaf said the company had benefited Liberia with jobs and revenue.

In fact, during its decades of operation, Firestone had built a nation within a nation. The company provided housing, schools, food, and health care to workers and their families. Some 80,000 Liberians lived within its borders. Firestone introduced currency, built roads, and opened up the rural interior.

At the same time, Johnson Sirleaf said, Firestone has sometimes failed to live up to its obligations to the country whose people have provided it with so much over so many years. Over the decades, the company has faced accusations that it exploited its laborers, received unfair concession deals, despoiled the environment and exacerbated corruption.

Said Johnson Sirleaf: "It is a mixed story."

I. Warlord on the Rise

Charles McArthur Ghankay Taylor was a man of many faces: bureaucrat, jail breaker, revolutionary, orator, warlord, president, war criminal.

Born in Liberia in 1948, Taylor came to the United States in 1972 to attend college. He received an economics degree from Bentley College, a private school with a campus of brick buildings and leafy trees outside Boston.

In the United States, he was one of many young, educated Liberians in the 1970s agitating for change in their home country.

Taylor saw his chance in 1980, when a Liberian army master sergeant named Samuel Doe seized control of the government. Doe's men gutted the president, William Tolbert, in the presidential mansion that overlooked the turquoise ocean. They tied thirteen government officials and political allies to wooden poles staked in the ground at a nearby beach and executed them.

Doe was twenty-eight years old and barely literate. To Taylor and other Liberians, he represented the overthrow of the old patrician order that had long ruled the country. Taylor decided to join the revolution. Taylor was appointed head of the government's procurement arm, the General Services Agency.

The urbane, educated Taylor soon fell out of favor with Doe, who surrounded himself with thuggish fellow Krahn tribesmen. Taylor fled back to the United States amid charges that he bilked the Liberian government of nearly $1 million. An ardent Cold War ally, Doe asked President Ronald Reagan's administration for his extradition. Taylor was locked up in a Massachusetts jail to await deportation.

There, the myth of Taylor began. In September 1985, Taylor broke out of the Plymouth County jail. News reports said that he sawed through bars, descended on knotted blankets, and escaped into surrounding woods.

How he accomplished the feat—if that's indeed how he escaped—has never been fully explained. At his war crimes trial, Taylor boasted that the CIA had aided the escape, a claim the agency has never confirmed or denied.

Taylor made it to Mexico and eventually Libya. There, he received instruction at a military camp established by Libyan strongman Col. Moammar Gadhafi to train African revolutionaries. In the late 1980s, Taylor and his cohorts created the National Patriotic Front of Liberia, dedicated to overthrowing Doe.

Doe had become wildly unpopular. He had massacred thousands of other, rival tribe members, surrounded himself with cronies, and driven the country into debt. In late 1989, the country was so broke that Doe convinced Firestone to provide an advance on future tax payments.

On December 24, 1989, Taylor began his revolution to overthrow Doe and ostensibly return democracy to Liberia. It was, at first, quixotic. He launched his coup d'état not from the capital but from a remote border crossing. He had a few dozen men, a paucity of weapons, and little ammunition. He was taking on a longtime ally of the United States, with little popular support and no military experience.

Few people in either the U.S. or Liberian governments saw him as a serious threat.

"He wasn't on our radar," said Herman "Hank" Cohen, who back then was the assistant secretary of state for Africa.

That soon changed. Doe badly bungled his response to Taylor, sending out troops who ruthlessly murdered civilians. Angry men and women who had suffered the brunt of Doe's oppression began taking up arms to join Taylor's nascent band.

Taylor commanded a pauper's army that grew to thousands, led by a handful of trusted lieutenants, Libyan-trained mercenaries, and professional military men.

Among the most notorious recruits were the Small Boys Unit—young children, often orphans, who swore allegiance to "Papai," as Taylor was called. To prove their loyalty, the children sometimes had to gun down their mothers and fathers. They would become among some of the most vicious killers in a war of heartless, mindless, unfathomable killing.

As the months passed and his march toward Monrovia continued, Taylor's legend and ego only grew. He presented himself as a Baptist who neither smoked nor drank. A mesmeric speaker, he would appear before adoring crowds dressed in fine white linen, spouting promises of democracy, jobs, and better days.

At other times, he wore camouflage and carried an AK-47. He would take to the radio to announce the impending capture of a nearby town, then magically do it. For many in Liberia, the spirit world remains close at hand. In such a place, Taylor became something more than a man—mystical, powerful, otherworldly.

Taylor seized much of the country's rural, tribal interior, then his forces swept down an old railroad line built by a mining company to the Atlantic coast. There, he captured the country's second-largest port, a jumble of docks and cranes in the rundown town of Buchanan. Hundreds of people were slaughtered as his soldiers settled old ethnic scores.

Elementary and middle schools emptied of children as they flocked to join Taylor. Catholic nuns reported school attendance dropping from 3,000 to 1,000 students in one town. Children too young to carry rifles were given grenades instead.

Taylor's eyes now turned west, toward Monrovia, a capital of concrete and decay overlooking the Atlantic Ocean. Between his army and his ambition lay an extraordinary treasure: the Firestone plantation. Some forty miles from the capital, the plantation had the country's most modern communications and electrical systems. It had food, gas, vehicles. Right next to it sat the principal airport, Roberts International Airport.

In the early days of June 1990, Taylor hurled his men forward.

An Old Southern Plantation

For more than six decades, the Firestone plantation had spread across the coastal plains and rolling hills of central Liberia. It was a kingdom of men, machines, and rubber trees, wedged between two tannin-stained rivers on some of the country's most fertile soil.

At the center of this kingdom was House 53, reserved for the plantation boss. It stood on a hill overlooking the rest of the plantation, a two-story antebellum-style Georgian colonial mansion of pink brick. It had a wide porch, six white Corinthian columns, and jalousie windows. Other homes for expatriates, featuring verandas and manicured gardens, were scattered nearby in a section of the plantation known as Harbel Hills. There was a nine-hole golf course, tennis courts, and a country club with a bar.

About three miles down the road was Harbel, Firestone's own company town, a portmanteau formed from the names of the business's founder Harvey S. Firestone Sr. and his wife Idabelle. It held Firestone's central office, industrial garages, and a latex-processing plant redolent of ammonia and other chemicals. The town itself was a collection of tin-roofed homes and shops, a grocery store, a bank, schools, and brick and cinder-block bungalows for midlevel Liberian managers and domestic staff.

A soccer field ran along the edge of town. On weekends, Firestone would show movies outdoors. The grounds were meticulous: close-cut grass and neat rows of rubber trees with the undergrowth cleared out. The order and precision immediately marked the plantation as different from the rest of the riotous, overgrown country.

Beyond the town were the trees, rows upon rows of trees: more than 8 million *Hevea brasilienses* planted in neat lines. Hidden in the groves and bush were dozens of work camps connected by roads that laced the farm.

These were the homes of the tappers, the Liberian workers who did the hard work of extracting the latex sap from the trees. The camps were long, low rows of residences almost like coops. Units generally consisted of a single room. The homes had wattle and daub walls and aluminum roofs. There were no windows and no kitchens. The work camps had communal pumps for water and outdoor kitchens for cooking. There was no electricity. Bathrooms were outhouses or the nearby bush.

Every day, the tappers got up to work before dawn. They cut thin slashes in the rubber trees with sharp knives, careful not to cut too deep or too often. The sap would run out into small cups—raw latex, the source of natural rubber.

Thousands of workers labored to meet their daily quotas by tapping hundreds of trees. To meet the demands or surpass them to make more money, the tappers sometimes put wives and children to work to complete their tasks.

The collected latex was poured into giant metal buckets, which each held up to seventy-five pounds of sap. They were carried two at a time by workers holding a wooden yoke across their shoulders. The latex would be weighed. The workers got a few dollars a day.

From there, the sap would be processed into hunks of block rubber or canisters of liquid latex. At the end of a good year, the daily, delicate tapping and gathering of thousands of tiny cups produced tens of thousands of tons of rubber. The raw material was shipped off to factories around the world to become car tires and rubber hoses, hospital gloves and condoms.

This was the world of the Firestone operation—described in 1990 by one company executive as resembling "an old Southern plantation."

After years of decorum and routine, it was about to become a gruesome battlefield.

The War Machine

Taylor's war machine was sighted near the Firestone factory at seven a.m. on June 5, 1990.

Ensminger, the plantation boss, woke to find Taylor's fighters on the other side of the slow-moving Farmington River—the eastern border between the Firestone farm and the rest of Liberia. Wearing their trademark red bandanas, the rebels sang and danced on the bank some 400 feet away, waving U.S dollar bills and brandishing automatic rifles.

Tough, pragmatic, and taciturn, Ensminger was not surprised by the arrival of the men. Grim stories raced ahead of Taylor's swarm.

On April 6, Ensminger had issued a "strictly confidential" memo to the forty or so U.S. and foreign-national staff who oversaw the plantation's Liberian workers.

"Due to the current unstable political situation in Liberia, we believe it is prudent to plan for the worst case scenario," he wrote. The memo instructed expats to pack emergency supplies, gas up cars, and meet at secret rally points in case of an evacuation. "The information contained in this memo—even the very existence of this memo—should not be discussed with persons not covered by it," he wrote. By May, the company had sent home expat wives and children.

To the persons not covered by the memo—the Liberian workers and their families—Ensminger projected confidence as the maelstrom drew closer.

On April 28, he met with 180 Liberian staffers who were "near panic" at Taylor's approach. Ensminger told them "they should be calm, as there was nothing to fear," a company memo said. He told Liberian managers and workers that the fighters would simply pass through the plantation on their way to attack the capital.

In an interview, Ensminger said he warned the employees that Firestone would not be able to protect them if Taylor's troops overran the plantation. He said he told them, "Our responsibility as an American company is to the expats. I told them, this is your country, you should take whatever action jointly or individually that you can take."

On the June morning when the rebels massed on the river bank and mortars thumped in the distance, Ensminger directed his staff to carry out some last-minute errands. He sent Steve Raimo, the company's accounting manager, to drive a pickup truck through the plantation to ensure that workers got their weekly pay before the rebels crossed the river.

Upbeat and optimistic, Raimo joked with Ensminger that he would hang his arm out of the window to make sure the fighters would know he was white.

"I knew that at that time that the rebels weren't out to hurt us," Raimo said. "We weren't really involved in the fray."

As the fighters began crossing the river in roughhewn canoes, they called out soothing promises. They shouted out that they had "no interest to harm workers" and were "only interested in soldiers," Ensminger wrote in a journal that he kept during the invasion.

Whether or not Ensminger believed the rebels, many Liberian workers apparently did. When the fighters finally reached Firestone's side of the river just before noon, some workers celebrated. To them, Taylor's men were freedom fighters come to overthrow Doe, Liberia's reviled dictator.

Women ululated on the main market street. They waved their hands above their heads. "Freedom fighters, freedom fighters," some shouted.

Matthew Chipley, a skinny teenager who lived with his family on the plantation, watched as the fighters entered the town, guns held high. "People were jubilating. People were happy to receive Taylor," he said. "They were in poverty, things were hard for them, and nothing good was going on."

Mary Pollee, a young mother with three children whose husband worked in the Firestone electrical generator plant, remembered that the rebels seemed concerned about people's safety. "All of you, go in your house," they shouted to villagers. "When the rebels enter, they are not killing nobody," she said.

Arthur Welwean, a college student and the son of Ensminger's cook, raced down to the river's edge to watch young boys with wigs on their heads and AK-47s in their hands spread out through the plantation. "This is gonna be good," he remembered thinking. "These guys are in town. They wanna liberate people."

Michael Mulbah Sr., a Liberian manager who had gone to college in the United States and lived on the plantation, recalled the excitement over the prospect that this motley militia might overthrow Doe. "We talked that they were our saviors," he said.

Vendettas, Violence, and Church-Robe Killers

It took only a day for the saviors to turn into devils.

The first person the rebels killed after crossing the river, according to several witnesses, was a mentally handicapped man. He was gunned down in the street. Next, the rebels began hunting down people who belonged to tribes closely associated with the ruling regime.

Kevin Estall, a British expatriate who was Firestone's agricultural operations manager, recalled seeing piles of dead bodies of Liberians laying outside the Harbel supermarket. He was told the rebels had executed the men in public because they were from a rival tribe. "They had been stitched, riddled with bullets from AK-47s straight up and down their bodies," he said. They were left in the street, their bodies swelling in the sun.

Mulbah was huddling in his bungalow when a group of Taylor's rebels demanded that he leave immediately. Several boy soldiers glared at him, their eyes red, guns dragging on the ground behind them. Mulbah fled with two pairs of pants and some shirts.

"Taylor was like an eagle," said Mulbah. "He'd come at you with his claws hidden, until he wanted to take them out."

Over the next couple of days, the rebels hunted down members of rival tribes, beating and killing them. They took Firestone trucks, fuel, and rice. They imprisoned the chief of Firestone's police force in the plantation jail.

Welwean, the cook's son, was running to hide in a small camp when he heard screaming all around him. A squad of children jumped out of the bush holding automatic weapons. They wore maroon choir robes, which they had stolen from a church on the plantation. Too big for the boys, the robes trailed on the ground, their trim ragged and dusty.

The boys believed that Welwean was a government soldier. They had him raise his pants legs since they believed that the soldiers wore boots that left marks on the wearer's calf. When they found no marks, they let Welwean pass.

"It was terrifying. They had the AK-47s. The guns are pointed straight at you," recalled Welwean, who now works as a bank examiner in the United States. "They're like, 'If you lie, we're gonna kill you.' And you are trembling, shaking."

Four days after the rebel invasion, government soldiers counterattacked, pushing the rebels back into the bush. They scoured Harbel for rebel collaborators, rounding up scores of Firestone workers.

The soldiers, members of the Armed Forces of Liberia, went on their own rampage. They beat and tortured Firestone workers who were suspected of assisting Taylor's rebels. They raped women, forcing loved ones to watch. They dumped bodies in the plantation's drainage ditches.

The plantation turned menacing and surreal: Shadows darted through the rubber trees, corpses stuck out from weed-covered ditches, artillery fire pounded like bass drums into the early hours of the night.

Neighbors turned on each other. One boy pointed NPFL soldiers to two Firestone workers from a targeted tribe. Taylor rebels slit their throats. A few days later, the dead men's families handed over the boy to government soldiers. They executed him behind the Firestone bank.

Caught in the crossfire were Chipley and his family. The soldiers accused them of being spies. As the teenager watched, the soldiers flogged his mother and father. Chipley, who worked at Firestone's processing plant, was tied up by the soldiers. Young girls that he knew were raped, he said.

Chipley and scores of plantation workers decided to follow the example of thousands of other young Liberians brutalized by Doe's soldiers: They joined Taylor's forces. They fled to rebel outposts in the northern part of the plantation and began training.

"Upon God and man, I never one day thought of holding what they called gun," Chipley said. "Because of the ill-treatment, I was forced to join."

"They were plenty that joined," he said.

The Obligation

As the battle erupted, many of the remaining expats headed for House 53. Ensconced on the hill, Ensminger and his fellow expatriates were protected from the killings below them. The men passed the time playing cards and listening to BBC reports about the war. Ensminger smoked his pipe and practiced his golf game, using a pitching wedge to place short chip shots into nearby buckets.

Still, the executives could not escape the violence. Rifle fire crackled from all around. The power was out for days. Reports streamed in of nine bodies in one camp, high casualties in another. Conflicting rumors had the rebels in control of the plantation one day, government soldiers coming to the rescue the next.

For those long used to control, confusion reigned.

"Very awkward and potentially dangerous for us, our people and our assets," Ensminger scribbled as the battle for Firestone raged. "Will there be confrontations? Who will control? How to deal with changing hands/demands?"

The last question was a daily challenge. John Vispo, Ensminger's number two and the plantation controller, had withdrawn the equivalent of $10,000 in cash from the Firestone safe before he sought shelter in House 53. It was, he figured, the best way to appease the fighters, who were often drunk, angry, and armed.

As rebel commanders streamed to the mansion with demands, Ensminger took careful notes in his journal. One commander got $500 to "insure safety [in the Harbel Hills] area." Another fighter received one hundred gallons of gas, five bags of rice, and forty dollars. Ensminger handed yet another group Firestone Truck 63A—the oldest available.

On other occasions he resisted: Tough talk prevented the theft of vehicles and a personal computer. There seemed to be no one in charge, no overall commander to contact.

"We are totally helpless!!" Ensminger scrawled after days of demands at gunpoint.

By the third day, a huge crowd of some 1,500 to 2,000 panicked Liberians headed for House 53. For decades, Firestone had provided them with food, shelter, and safety. Now, they begged for protection from the savagery.

Vispo halted the crowd as it walked up the long, broad lawn leading to House 53. There was nothing that Firestone could do, he told them. Firestone chefs cooked up a big pot of rice, which was distributed among the crowd.

"We're all in this together. We have no way to protect you or ourselves. We're as scared as you," Vispo recalled telling the people. "There's nothing we can do to protect you. It's better off if you go to your villages."

The next day, several dozen senior Liberian staffers—people who worked directly with the expats, who considered them friends and colleagues—approached a second time in hopes of rescue.

"Some of the Firestone staff said, 'Well, if the expatriates are going out to Ensminger's house and it's safe, the rebels are not going there to bother anyone,'" said Welwean, who joined the stream of refuge seekers. "There should be a sanctuary for everyone."

This time, Ensminger stood on the porch and delivered the response: There was nothing the company could do for them.

"We recognized a responsibility to our employees. But what could we do? Our position got so untenable. There was nothing I could do about 1,000 or 1,500 or 40 or 50 Liberians," Ensminger said in the interview.

The decision did not sit well with some expats. Estall refused to take shelter in Ensminger's house. He holed up in his own home nearby, taking in several Liberians who pleaded for refuge.

"They felt they had been betrayed," Estall said of Firestone's Liberian staffers. "They felt let down by Mr. Ensminger for not offering them any shelter."

The rejection stung the Liberians. Firestone employees had difficulty believing that such a powerful corporation, one with so much sway in the Liberian capital and so much money in its bank accounts, could not help in any way.

Actually it could help—but that aid would only be for the expats.

On June 13 at five-thirty in the evening, six Taylor guerillas confronted Ensminger on the front porch of House 53. The expats recognized several of the fighters as men who had worked as caddies at Firestone's golf course.

The commander pointed a rocket-propelled-grenade launcher at Ensminger and threatened to blow up the house. He demanded

$1,000. Ensminger convinced the men to leave with a truck and $200.

During the takeover, Ensminger had maintained radio contact with the embassy and Firestone headquarters in Akron, Ohio. Now, he called them again. It was time to leave.

The U.S. embassy sent military escorts to accompany the Firestone expats to safety. Just after dawn, nineteen expats in seventeen vehicles headed through Gate 15, the northwestern entrance to the plantation. U.S. special forces made sure they arrived safely in Monrovia.

The Liberian workers woke to find themselves abandoned.

Justin Knuckles, a senior Liberian manager, had taken refuge in the Firestone community center with other Liberian staff. He remembers finding a note on the door from one of the expats, apologizing for their departure. The note said they would return when the situation calmed down.

"You know when Jesus were taken and the disciples were left alone? That how we felt," Knuckles said. "Because we had a belief, as long as the Americans are on the plantation, we had a little hope. But now the Americans are gone, what gonna happen to us?"

Raimo said leaving behind the employees was "disheartening." Looking back, however, he could think of no way that Firestone could have evacuated all the employees on the plantation.

"Our hands were tied," he said. "We had no U.S. Army or Marines or whatever to come in and help us evacuate these hundreds of thousands of people who had been affiliated with Firestone, one way or another."

"It's hard to process sometimes—the inhumanity of man towards man," said Raimo, who is now a business consultant and a Christian minister. "Certainly, evil was taking reign in Liberia."

The expats headed home.

The final scrawl in Ensminger's journal: "WHAT AN ORDEAL!!"

Ensminger arrived in Akron some twenty-six hours after the evacuation. At a press conference, he recounted the story of the rebel invasion and the RPG pointed at his chest.

His biggest concern, he said, was for the workers.

"I personally . . . have an obligation to the many thousands of employees in Harbel," Ensminger told reporters.

Everybody Run Away

As Ensminger spoke to the press, Mary Pollee was trudging through thick bush to keep her shattered family alive.

A group of government soldiers had burst into Pollee's mud-walled home on the Firestone plantation just before the expats evacuated. They dragged her and her husband Joseph outdoors. They stripped him to his underwear. In front of their three children, they began beating and kicking the couple, accusing them of working with Taylor's rebels.

"When you want cry, they beat you. They say, 'You want die? You want die? You will die right now,'" Pollee said. "They hard, that day. They were not easy."

The soldiers hauled away her bleeding husband. They marched back later demanding a ransom for his return. Pollee handed over what little she had. The soldiers returned a day later. They asked for $500 more. When she told them that she did not have it, the soldiers gang-raped her. They told her they would kill her and her children.

The next day, the soldiers killed her husband behind the white-washed, cinder-block bank in Harbel. Pollee decided to flee into the surrounding jungle with her children. Just before leaving, she remembers hearing that the Firestone expats had evacuated.

It made little difference to Pollee and her children. They plodded through the bush, eating sugar cane to survive, weary, afraid, hungry. A few days into her trek, Pollee noticed that the three-year-old boy whom she had strapped to her back had stopped moving. Monko, her youngest, had died.

Pollee was crazed with grief. She held the child in front of her, stumbling through the bush. She ran into a stranger, who helped her to bury the boy in the wild.

After days in the jungle, Pollee and her remaining children reached Kakata, a rebel-held town just outside the plantation. Her ordeal was not over.

In a recent interview, Pollee sat, dignified and graceful, on her couch in her tiny, tidy home beneath a mango tree in a suburb of Monrovia.

She remains angry at Firestone. Why hadn't the company stood firm against the rebels? Why hadn't the Firestone police tried to stop the assault? Why hadn't the company asked the government soldiers to stay back?

"Nobody were there to protect the worker, nobody," she said. "They went with their children, their wives, everybody, nobody left here, and when they left that's the time the people started raising hell with us."

Still, she said she understood.

"When it come to a war," she said, "everybody run away."

II. A Century of Blood, Sweat, and Profits

To understand the ferocity of the fighting that erupted in 1990—and why Firestone and its plantation inevitably became central in it—one needs to know something of Liberia's unusual history.

The country was settled in the 1800s by freeborn American blacks and freed American slaves, the result of a back-to-Africa movement by the American Colonization Society, a philanthropic organization. It was supported by President James Monroe and the U.S. Congress.

Even after the colony declared itself independent in 1847, naming itself Liberia, or "Land of Freedom," the country duplicated many of the economic and social structures of the American South. The settlers, known as Americo-Liberians, had a complex relationship with the indigenous Africans who lived in the region. Some of the settlers built Southern-style mansions and exploited the locals' labor and land.

Firestone arrived in Liberia in the 1920s. By that time, Harvey S. Firestone Sr., the farm boy from Ohio who founded the Firestone Tire and Rubber Co., had become one of the top industrialists of the gilded age.

He dreamed of finding a rubber source beyond the grasp of the British Empire, which controlled much of the world market. In Liberia, he found a spot in the narrow band around the equator where rubber trees thrived—and a nation that was in debt and desperate for business.

After two years of negotiations, Firestone and Liberia announced one of history's great sweetheart deals. Liberia gave Firestone the right to lease up to 1 million acres—roughly 10 percent of the country's arable land. The cost? Six cents an acre. The term? Ninety-nine years.

The deal survived an early controversy in 1930, when investigators from the League of Nations found officials in the Liberian government had engaged in forcing indigenous villagers to work on private farms, including Firestone's plantation.

The investigators found no evidence that Firestone "consciously employs labor which has been forcibly impressed." Soon after the scandal, Harvey Firestone Jr., the founder's son, launched a public-relations campaign, delivering a series of radio addresses that described the company's work in Liberia.

The five-minute spots depicted a company that respected local customs, provided workers with health care, and built roads for a benighted nation—all the while benefiting American car owners.

"To the little Republic of Liberia, Firestone has brought a new day of hope and advancement," Firestone said in one broadcast.

"It has been a gratifying thought to us that by means of commercial progress we have been of service to mankind."

The 1950s were golden years for Firestone and Liberia's elite. Firestone was Liberia's largest private employer and the largest exporter in the country. Firestone's profits after taxes amounted to three times the government's total revenue for 1951, according to one study.

The company tightened its relationships with the country's ruling class in part by helping them become rubber farmers, providing free saplings and agricultural advice. When the rubber began to flow, Firestone purchased it.

Former presidents Charles King, Edwin Barclay, William V. S. Tubman, and Tolbert all owned large rubber plantations.

To preserve its plantation, Firestone worked closely with whoever ran Liberia, no matter how they came to power or what they did to hold onto it.

In office for nearly thirty years, Tubman turned into a virtual dictator, quashing dissent, imprisoning political opponents, and creating a spy network to track ordinary citizens. Firestone maintained such close ties with him that when the daughter of one plantation executive got married, she and her husband honeymooned at Tubman's summer retreat outside Monrovia.

Tolbert, Tubman's longtime vice president and successor, had the most fractious relationship with the rubber giant. As president in the mid-1970s, he renegotiated the government's contract with Firestone, insisting on raising taxes and hiring more Liberians in senior management. Firestone executives complained that the plantation's profitability began to decline.

About four weeks after Doe's bloody coup in 1980, Firestone sent Don L. Weihe, the affable executive in charge of the company's overseas rubber operations, to meet the new dictator.

"When you're the big frog in the pond, you're sort of wondering who is in charge of the pond," Weihe explained.

Doe suspended the 1976 rubber deal struck by Tolbert that had so pained Firestone executives. Until world rubber prices rebounded, he decided, the company would enjoy generous tax exemptions. "Firestone and Liberia have enjoyed a long and unique historical relationship," Doe said in a speech to Firestone's executives. "We therefore consider this relationship as a contract of survival."

Taylor ensured that Doe's role in the relationship would be limited.

III. Tough Talk in the Jungle

After chasing the Firestone managers out in June 1990, Taylor took over the colonnaded grandeur of House 53. The message was unmistakable: The company that had dominated the country for so long, that held power over its leaders and its laborers, had been vanquished.

The stately mansion was often chaotic and frenzied. Cronies and bodyguards lounged in the hallways. Sycophants waited for an audience. Battle commanders rushed in and out.

Taylor's goal was to seize Monrovia, which held half the country's population, most of its major financial and political institutions, and, most important, the executive mansion—Doe's presidential residence, a menacing, fortified structure overlooking the Atlantic Ocean.

Taylor staged his attack from the Firestone plantation. He was confident enough of his success that he announced he would occupy the mansion by early July.

His men battled to within 500 yards of the executive mansion where Doe had holed up with his men. That was as far as he would get. As the two sides traded mortar and small-arms fire, Taylor suddenly called a halt to the operation. The United States had reached out to him to plead for peace.

Cohen, the State Department's top Africa hand, talked with Taylor several times by satellite phone to negotiate a ceasefire. He even visited Taylor at a rearguard base in Ivory Coast, where he found Taylor seated on a throne, surrounded by child soldiers.

Behind him was a portrait of President John F. Kennedy and his wife, Jacqueline.

"He had visions of being a great statesman," Cohen said. "He saw himself like that. 'I'm gonna take over Liberia and make it into a new country.'"

The bid for peace failed, and Liberia faded further as a concern for the United States. Cohen said his superiors made that clear to him.

"The feeling was that we didn't want to have Liberia as our adopted child," Cohen said. "We were not going to take charge of Liberia."

Into the void stepped an alliance of West African nations led by Nigeria, the regional heavyweight. In August 1990, the alliance deployed some 7,000 peacekeepers, known as ECOMOG.

The peacekeepers succeeded in halting Taylor. But they did not save Liberia's president. Doe was captured and killed by the head of a rival rebel faction led by Prince Johnson, one of Taylor's former generals.

A notorious, vicious drunk, Johnson had himself filmed as he ordered his men to torture Doe. While he sat behind a desk with two open cans of Budweiser beer, a young woman fanning him from behind, Johnson ordered his men to strip Doe. The portly president kneeled before Johnson in his underwear, quivering, sobbing, begging. Johnson's men hacked off his ears. Blood poured down his torso. Doe's body was later found dumped outside a medical clinic.

Amos Sawyer, a Liberian intellectual, would emerge as the president of an interim government named at a meeting of leading Liberian politicians, activists, and religious leaders.

By November, an uneasy ceasefire had settled across the country. Liberians called it "no peace, no war."

Taylor, unimpressed by the peacekeepers and the new interim president, went about the business of governing.

He now controlled almost all of Liberia. In typically grandiose fashion, Taylor named his territory Greater Liberia—though it was better known by its eponymous nickname, Taylorland. He declared himself president.

As his capital, he chose the village of Gbarnga in the flatlands of northern Liberia, a scruffy regional trading center.

Taylor turned a long, low single-story house on an airy hill overlooking the village into his executive mansion. From the outside, it was modest and unpretentious. Inside was rococo furniture and walls of varnished wood.

He formed a legislative body for Taylorland, the National Patriotic Reconstruction Assembly Government, or NPRAG. He appointed a cabinet of ministers (frequently fired, sometimes beaten) and created a judicial system (hardly independent). He even hired a lobbyist in Washington, D.C.

He also built his army—eventually amassing perhaps 10,000 fighters and child soldiers armed with machine guns, mortars, and artillery cannon.

His dreams stretched wide as Liberia's sky.

"I'm not a soldier. I'm an economist. I came here believing in the very democratic principles that the United States is built on today," he told television cameras. "All I want to do is to bring back some sanity, some fair play in the country."

For a while, a group of Firestone's Liberian managers worked with Taylor to run the plantation. But they couldn't maintain the millions of rubber trees. They had no ships to transport the rubber, no sales network to sell it. The farm's hydroelectric plant supplied electricity only haphazardly.

By February 1991, the plantation was in danger of falling apart. A group of former Firestone workers met Taylor on the veranda of House 53. Their message: They wanted Firestone back.

"The employees were not benefiting," said Victor Bestman, the Liberian estates manager. Taylor's associates "sold the rubber, enriched themselves, and how they divided it nobody knows."

Taylor grew to realize that he needed Firestone. Symbolically, the company's return would amount to a bright neon sign indicating that Taylorland was open for business. Politically, its jobs and supplies of food would ensure that residents did not rise up in dissent.

"We needed Firestone to keep people busy," Richardson said.

When Firestone abandoned Liberia, it made Taylor seethe.

"There's a little war, and then you run off, and there's no food, no medicine, complete breakdown," Taylor would later tell one Firestone executive at a meeting. "That's inexcusable."

For its own part, Firestone was in no mood to kowtow to a guerrilla leader who had threatened its managers and killed its workers.

In October 1990, Ensminger sent a brusque letter addressing Taylor as "Commander-in-Chief"—not president. He requested a meeting, and a guarantee that the Firestone personnel who attended the meeting would be safe. A week later, Ensminger sent a follow-up aide memoire—a term typically used in diplomatic circles to outline discussion points.

In it, Ensminger laid out Firestone's conditions for returning to Liberia. At the top of the list: Firestone "cannot resume operations unless its employees, both Liberian and expatriate, have sufficient assurances that peace, law and order will be restored in Liberia to ensure their own safety and that of the members of their families from physical harm."

Ensminger demanded better financial terms to lower the company's tax liabilities. And he noted that Firestone would not recognize the "legitimacy" of any political or military authority so as to avoid "interfering in the internal affairs of Liberia."

"The existing situation raises questions as to whether, when and how operations could be resumed in Liberia," Ensminger wrote.

Today, Ensminger said he thought the company should not have attempted to negotiate with Taylor.

"Taylor was not a recognized government of Liberia. There was no reason or legality for negotiation with Taylor," Ensminger said in the interview. "It was only that we were trying to figure out a way to get to the plantation and resume operations."

The missive did little to improve Taylor's disposition.

Ensminger's attitude was, "'We want our plantation back. You have no business there. We want everything. Our trucks back. We want this, that, and everything else,'" said Richardson, Taylor's adviser.

Taylor was prepared to wait. If Firestone wanted its rubber plantation back, it would have to bend—and pay.

The Investment

Back in Akron, Ensminger and other managers began strategizing about how to get the plantation running again.

In 1988, the Japanese tire conglomerate Bridgestone had acquired Firestone for $2.65 billion—the largest purchase of a U.S. company by a Japanese one at the time.

Business analysts judged the deal a disaster. Bridgestone moved too slowly to make necessary cuts. The company hemorrhaged money. Between 1990 and 1992, the new U.S. subsidiary, called Bridgestone/Firestone, lost $1 billion, according to one history of the company.

On Bridgestone's balance sheet, Firestone's Liberian plantation wasn't a large item, generating about $104 million in revenue and $15.6 million in profits in 1989, the year before the civil war. But the 15 percent profit margin the plantation achieved that year was a bright spot on a corporate ledger drowning in red ink.

Top managers "were under a lot of pressure from Akron to get the plantation going," said Ken Gerhart, the Firestone manager who ran the company's soda bottling plant in Monrovia. The plantation "was very, very profitable. It was very efficient."

The company found alternative sources of rubber in Asia after the plantation's abandonment, but the latex produced in Liberia was considered to be among the finest in the world, in part because of the company's tight quality control. The plantation supplied about 40 percent of the U.S. market for latex, and 10 percent of the world market.

The value of the plantation itself—the land, the trees, the factories, buildings, vehicles, and equipment—was estimated at nearly $200 million. If Firestone pulled out for good, those assets would be unsalvageable. Even a temporary interruption posed risks: There was no assurance that Liberia would allow the company back, especially under the favorable conditions of the original deal cut in 1926.

To figure out how to deal with Taylor and return to Liberia, Firestone hired a young Liberian-born lawyer with impressive credentials. Gerald Padmore had graduated from Yale and then Harvard Law School. He had returned to Liberia to serve in President Tolbert's government. As the acting minister of finance, he sat across the table from Firestone in rubber contract negotiations.

Later, he switched to Firestone's side and began advising company leaders on whether to return to Liberia. Firestone agreed to have Padmore answer questions for the company about events in the early 1990s.

"It was a real dilemma for the company," Padmore said. There was "a lot of, I would say, soul-searching, and really tough, tough decision making that had to be done."

As Padmore saw it, there were two competing governments in Liberia, neither of which had been formally recognized by the United States. Firestone's operations straddled the lines of control. The plantation sat in Taylorland. But the company shipped its rubber and latex from Monrovia. To move from the plantation to the port, company employees had to pass through numerous roadblocks and withstand entreaties for bribes at each stop. Who made the rules? Who got the company's taxes?

Padmore said much of Firestone's determination to return to Liberia was driven by concern for its Liberian workforce. Firestone had stopped making rice shipments to the plantation in June 1990, and so men, women, and children were surviving on sugar cane and rotting bananas. During one period that fall, the company's medical director was recording ten to fifteen deaths a day, according to a sworn deposition.

The plantation and its trees were also a worry. Rubber trees must be very carefully tended and harvested to prevent them from dying. Firestone had received word that Liberians had descended on the plantation to illegally harvest latex from the company's trees. They were "slaughter tapping"—an industry term for extracting so much sap that the tree dies.

"We're hearing stories from our employees that they're distressed," Padmore recalled. "We're hearing stories that our assets are being looted or destroyed. It's a question of do we abandon Liberia, as many other major businesses had done, or will there be a future, and how do we get back on?"

Padmore said the "easy answer" for Firestone would have been to abandon the plantation. Several companies fled Liberia at the start of the war. Others had chosen to stay, according to a State Department cable.

Padmore said it was tempting for Firestone to say, "'We're out of here. It's risky. It's scary. Economically, it doesn't make any sense.'"

"In a sense, that would have been morally satisfying, that you could safely be back in the United States. But if you felt a sense of responsibility to Liberia, and, most importantly, to the workers, your teammates, really, the people you've worked with for years, who were distressed—some of them were killed—you'd say, 'Well, let's go back and see if we can help them,'" Padmore continued.

"I think those were all good decisions, because, for me, Liberia outlasts the temporary rulers it may have. It's a country. It's ordinary people whose lives are terribly important. They don't have the ability or the means, as I fortunately did, to fly off to the

United States and be safe. They've got to worry about their kids. For me, it's the right choice. Stay as long as you can," Padmore said.

Padmore acknowledged that Firestone's employees had experienced Taylor's violence. His soldiers had threatened Ensminger. Gerhart was put on a hit list, and his personal driver had the soles of his feet cut off with machetes by Taylor's men. Firestone expats witnessed Taylor's fighters savaging people in Harbel.

"We knew there had been fighting, there had been killing, and there had been some ethnic reprisal killings," Padmore said. "But at that time, from the information available to me, and, I think, to Firestone, Taylor did not appear to be conducting genocidal activities."

In the interview, Ensminger said that was "laughable."

"Firestone knew full well and was getting reports from the State Department and from the ambassador and from Liberians," he said. "They knew full well that atrocities and human rights violations were committed."

In October 1990, Human Rights Watch reported that Taylor soldiers had committed widespread killing and torture. Two-thirds of Doe's tribe, the Krahn, had fled the country. Those who remained, the report said, were "at risk of genocide."

In early 1991, the U.S. State Department released its report on human rights violations in 1990, a congressionally mandated assessment for every country in the world. For Liberia, it read like a gore novel.

All the warring factions, including government soldiers, had committed atrocities. Each time Taylor took over a new province, his forces hunted and killed hundreds of men, women, and children from the Mandingo and Krahn ethnic groups, which were seen as sympathetic to Doe. Emergency food centers set up to feed starving Liberians became grotesque snares. Those in line were forced to produce identity cards. The Krahn were killed. In one particularly nasty practice, Taylor's men set up a highway checkpoint called "No Return." More than 2,000 people were killed there.

"The overall human rights situation in Liberia in 1990 was appalling," the report read. "All combatants routinely engaged in indiscriminate killing and abuse of civilians, looting, and ethnically based executions."

"Leaders of all the armed groups did little or nothing to stop the killings and, in some cases, may have encouraged them or been directly responsible for the abuses."

Official data, painstakingly compiled years later by Liberia's Truth and Reconciliation Commission from the testimony of thousands of Liberians, attempted to quantify the human damage. By December 1990, Taylor's forces alone had committed nearly 40,000 human rights violations. The toll included more than 6,400 killings, 800 kidnappings, and 600 rapes, according to a *ProPublica* analysis of the data.

Mary Pollee said she was one victim of Taylor's fighters. From the Firestone plantation, she fled to a city held by Taylor's rebels. The fighters stole her food. They took her clothes. They threatened her with guns. And then one day, they grabbed her thirteen-year-old daughter and raped and killed her.

Pollee—her husband, a son, and a daughter now buried—went mad.

"I was like somebody going crazy," said Pollee. She began weeping at the memory in her living room, the cicadas outside whirring, the sun beating. "I was not to myself, oh."

In Ohio, Firestone executives continued to discuss what to do. Initially, they decided to wait to see if the conflict would resolve itself. But as those hopes faded, Firestone made its final decision.

The company would go back to Liberia.

"Completely justifiable," Padmore called the decision.

"Had I had a crystal ball and an ability to say that's going to happen, I would have told Firestone in January of 1992, 'Don't go back,' but we didn't know that would happen. We were hopeful that good things were going to happen."

He added: "Had [Firestone executives] not taken those decisions, I think Liberia would be much the worse for it today."

America Works for Firestone

In February 1991, Ensminger flew to Liberia to reach out to Taylor. Over the coming months, the company resumed feeding its workers. It sent shipments of rice to Taylor and to the interim government. It even hired Taylor forces to guard House 53.

Taylor ignored the entreaties.

Said Richardson: "They just wanted what's for Firestone to be for Firestone."

In April 1991, U.S. ambassador Peter Jon de Vos secured a meeting with Taylor in Gbarnga. He invited Ensminger along for the journey.

De Vos was a proponent of Firestone and Taylor reaching an accommodation. After the meeting, a cable noted that "De Vos pressed Taylor" to talk with Firestone officials.

"We are encouraging [Taylor labor minister Nyundeh] Monkonmlah and Firestone to reach accommodation since inactivity at the plantation benefits no one," one embassy official wrote in another cable.

A news broadcast from the time showed that the meeting disintegrated quickly. With cameras rolling, Taylor received De Vos in an anteroom furnished with a gilded white and gold Louis XV couch and chairs covered in plastic. Dark wood paneling rose above red carpet. Impeccable, Taylor wore a dark suit, with a white pocket square and red tie.

De Vos, dressed in a rumpled suit and bow tie, and large, square glasses, was sweating profusely. He greeted Taylor. Then, he introduced Ensminger, tan, fit, and mustachioed.

"This is Mr. Ensminger, the director general of Firestone," De Vos said.

Taylor looked puzzled. "Oh, he works for the embassy now?"

"No, America works for him," De Vos replied.

Within minutes, Taylor began to harangue Ensminger. He questioned why Firestone was using the port in Monrovia rather than the port that he controlled.

"My biggest problem with Firestone is that instead of trying to play economic games, they've been trying to play political games," Taylor told the U.S. ambassador at one point.

The camera panned to Ensminger. He sat silently. He wore a tight smile on his face.

In behind-the-scenes talks, Richardson discussed matters directly with Ensminger. Richardson recalled asking Ensminger to provide back pay to the workers. Richardson said Ensminger denied the request.

"He was a very arrogant son of whatever," Richardson said.

Ensminger told a different story. He said that he and his team had repeatedly tried and failed to meet with Taylor. The reason? Taylor's ministers demanded a bribe even to see the guerilla leader.

"They wanted money before they would talk to us," he said.

Ensminger said he refused to pay.

"Look we are a concessionaire of the country of Liberia. We've been here for many years. We've operated and made taxes and given every other means of support that's legal," he said he told the rebels. "Now you come in and try to take over the government and want us to recognize you and receive all the dues that a government should receive. If that happens, we'll be glad to work with you. But that hasn't happened."

By summer 1991, Ensminger had arrived at an impasse.

That's when Firestone executives from Akron decided to pay a visit.

IV. Deal with the Devil

In late June 1991, a top Firestone corporate executive named John Schremp traveled from Akron to Liberia.

He was a chemical engineer who wound up as director of human resources at Firestone's corporate headquarters. In February 1991, the company's new Japanese management made him head of the division overseeing the Liberia plantation. He had never been to Liberia or run a rubber farm.

The novelty of Schremp's trip was alluded to in an online biography that recounted the start of his career at Firestone: "Little did he know that 20 years later his job would take him to Liberia, where in the middle of the country's civil war, he would be whisked at machine gun-point into the jungle to meet a rebel leader."

That leader was Taylor.

Schremp and another corporate executive, Richard Stupp, first visited the plantation, traveling in a sport utility vehicle with an armed guard. They passed through checkpoints manned by West African peacekeepers whom Schremp described as "professional soldiers." Then the team passed into Taylor territory. There, the checkpoints were guarded by young boys with AK-47s.

"We were shocked," Schremp said, in a written response to questions.

On July 3, Schremp got word that Taylor wanted to meet. Richardson, Taylor's top adviser, would lead them to the talks.

The team traveled up crumbling highways and dirt roads, past soaring cotton trees and the listless, mottled bush of central Liberia before they arrived at the autocrat's capital in Gbarnga.

From there, Schremp and Stupp were taken to the sprawling retreat that had been former President Tubman's summer home. The visitors were escorted into a ballroom with parquet floors. A few minutes later, Taylor swept in. He sat in a chair that looked like a throne.

For a few moments, Taylor's ministers complained to Schremp and Stupp that Firestone had abandoned its workers. It had let down Liberia.

Taylor held up his hand, Schremp recalled. The ministers stopped talking. He declared his desire for "a new start with economic progress for all Liberians."

According to interviews, Taylor told the executives that he wanted Firestone back in business. To do so, Firestone would have to deal exclusively with Taylor's government. All taxes would be paid to Taylor. All labor problems would go through his ministers.

In effect, Firestone would treat Taylor's government as the official government of Liberia—an economic, if not diplomatic, recognition that Taylor craved to establish the legitimacy of Greater Liberia.

There was one thing that was clear: Ensminger had to go. Taylor wanted an old acquaintance to take over—Weihe, the retired Firestone plantation boss who had dealt with Liberia's politicians since the 1970s.

Two days later, Schremp indicated Firestone's willingness to accommodate Taylor. In a letter, he wrote that the company wanted Taylor's "assistance and cooperation" to clean up the plantation, resume services at the hospital, and get water and electricity running again.

"We found the discussions very enlightening and helpful," Schremp wrote in the letter. He said he was "confident" that Firestone and Taylor's rebel government "have the common goal of a better future for Liberia and its people."

"We agreed that Firestone would be given permission to restart the plantation, feed the employees and put them back to work," Schremp wrote in his written response.

The company's about-face was complete.

Before, it had resisted the guerilla leader who had killed its workers, threatened to execute its managers and ravaged the country that had long been its partner.

Now, Firestone decided to acquiesce.

"Yes, absolutely," Padmore said. "It was clear that without that, you would not be able to put a management team on the ground."

Last Stand for an Old Hand

Ensminger was upset at Firestone's newfound willingness to co-operate. He had spoken with Firestone's attorneys. They had worried about potential legal problems—including breaking U.S. laws governing companies operating overseas.

In the weeks after the July meeting, Ensminger flew back to Akron to protest the change in direction. He said he met with several senior Firestone executives. He and Schremp had a heated exchange.

"I stated the position that we had had, and we should continue to have," Ensminger said. "We should not recognize Taylor and his people as the legitimate government for the country of Liberia."

"I was very opposed to dealing with Taylor under his terms," Ensminger said.

Ensminger said Schremp called him into his office and threatened to fire him. Ensminger would not accept the dismissal letter. He said he insisted on a mutual agreement in which he would not discuss the company's actions, in exchange for a buyout package.

Schremp consented, he said. In October 1991, Ensminger left Firestone. Schremp did not respond to requests for comment on Ensminger's account.

Firestone responded to Ensminger's assertion that its decision to work with Taylor had been a mistake.

"There were many opinions within Firestone regarding what direction the company should take. Management considered all points of view and finally made the decision that they believed was best for the company and its employees in Liberia," the company said in a statement. "There were no good options."

Firestone continued with its new approach. The change in tack stirred apprehension in Monrovia and Washington.

While in Liberia, Schremp had paid a visit to Sawyer, the round-faced, genial interim president who had long opposed Taylor.

In a recent interview, Sawyer said he found Schremp "elusive" when he asked about Taylor. Sawyer said he warned Schremp about the consequences of cozying up to the warlord.

"We knew that Firestone support could fuel the war. And we didn't think that would be a good idea," Sawyer said.

U.S. diplomats watched warily. In September 1991, Firestone executives spoke with State Department officials in Washington. The diplomats warned the company about the "difficulties and dangers of doing business in Taylorland" and of "potential legal problems," according to one cable.

Firestone is "reluctant to write off huge investments in Liberia but shows increasing frustration over efforts to conduct business 'by the book,'" the cable continued.

On December 17, 1991, almost two years after Taylor's invasion, the board of directors met in Akron to discuss Taylor's demands.

Schremp delivered the presentation.

In exchange for being able to return to its operations, Firestone would work with Taylor's government. It would make a "significant" capital investment to restore plantation assets that had been damaged and looted. The company would turn Buchanan, Taylorland's biggest port, into a "viable entity." Firestone managers would also be allowed to reoccupy homes that Taylor's ministers and followers had taken over.

The board, led by Chairman and CEO Yoichiro Kaizaki, approved everything, Schremp told Taylor in a letter.

Firestone is "willing to commit the time and money to do so and respectfully request your assistance for us to move forward together," Schremp wrote. "By doing so, we both make a great contribution to Liberia."

Schremp closed his letter by wishing Taylor the peace of the Christmas season and hope for the new year.

On the very day the board in Akron voted to go into business with Taylor, his fighters were stealing Firestone vehicles, looting nearby towns, and had jailed and tortured two "hapless" villagers from Harbel, a Firestone official who visited the plantation told the U.S. embassy.

Memorandum of Understanding

On January 17, 1992, Firestone consummated its deal with Taylor.

Gale Ruff, Firestone's acting general manager at the time, headed to Taylor's capital in Gbarnga. He had been advised to bring "beverages" to celebrate the signing of a memorandum of understanding between Firestone and Taylor's self-declared government.

In Gbarnga, several of Taylor's top ministers presented Ruff with the text of the memorandum. The details had been hashed out earlier between Schremp and Taylor's representatives.

Ruff affixed his signature to the accord.

In a recent interview, Ruff said that he was fuzzy on the event's details. But he acknowledged signing the agreement on Firestone's behalf.

"I had to be a little like Sgt. Schultz. 'I know nothing,'" he said, referring to a 1960s American sitcom in which a German prison guard constantly asserts his ignorance of sensitive matters. "I was basically handed a fait accompli. They needed a warm body on the ground to sign the paper."

It was a remarkable document in the annals of corporate history.

On Taylor stationery, which bore a scorpion imprint, the agreement's preamble laid out the stakes. Taylor's government wanted to improve the Liberian economy. Firestone wanted to resume operation of its rubber plantation.

To do so, Taylor would return seized housing to Firestone's managers. He would provide security forces to protect Firestone workers.

Firestone, in turn, would pay its Liberian workers in U.S. dollars. It would rehire the employees it had abandoned.

Perhaps most important: Firestone would also make all arrangements necessary "for settlement of present and future financial obligations" to Taylor's government.

Firestone provided copies of the agreement to the U.S. embassy and to officials in Sawyer's interim government.

"Firestone conducts its business in full transparency," Firestone said in its recent statement. The memorandum "made it clear, and in public, management's determination to find a way to resume work on the farm and keep it a viable entity for Liberia as well as for Firestone and its employees."

At the time Firestone signed the document, there was still a hope for peace. But those expectations crumbled in the following months. Democratic elections called for by one peace pact in April 1992 never materialized. The horrors of the civil war continued to mount. The U.S. State Department's 1992 report of human rights violations found that 20,000 to 30,000 Liberians had died during the previous year. More than 600,000 had fled their homes.

Taylor's rebels had detained some 4,000 West Africans for months, the report said. In one county, they killed as many as 1,500 people, mostly Krahn, and destroyed entire villages. They carried out clandestine killings, raped women, looted homes, and stole cattle.

Firestone, Padmore said, was unaware of the scope of Taylor's violence.

"In 1991, I don't recall any reports of systematic and widespread human rights abuses," Padmore said. "The areas under Taylor's control seemed to be relatively peaceful at that time."

Firestone soldiered on.

On May 22, at Firestone's historic brick headquarters in Akron, the company confirmed its commitment to work with Taylor.

There, at eight-thirty a.m. in the company's second-floor conference room, Kaizaki, the CEO and board chair, met with two representatives of Taylor's NPRAG government, according to a Firestone corporate summary of the meeting.

Kaizaki had assumed leadership a year earlier, with strict orders to restore profitability to the company. He spoke little English at the time. Firestone's mostly Midwestern managers referred to him as Kaizaki-san—a traditional Japanese honorific.

Kaizaki told Taylor's men that he would be glad to return to Japan to spread the news that Liberia under Taylor was open for business—so long as Firestone's plantation was running.

In two brief phone interviews, Kaizaki said he recalled that Taylor representatives had come to Akron, but he did not remember meeting them. He did not dispute the meeting notes. He referred further questions to a Firestone spokesman.

ProPublica's questions, Kaizaki said, were "unpleasant."

Kaizaki made two promises before the events in Akron concluded: Firestone would "use every possible effort to accelerate the startup of production and the commencement of paying taxes to the NPRAG." Second, he would fulfill Taylor's request. Weihe would become the new plantation boss.

V. Money and Menace

Firestone's money started flowing to Taylor in January 1992.

That month, Firestone paid Taylor's government $69,000 in income and reconstruction taxes; $10,000 for a "social security pension scheme"; and $6,000 for a "social security income scheme," according to internal corporate records.

By the end of 1992, the records' careful rows and columns showed that Firestone had paid out more than $2.3 million in income taxes, Social Security pensions, worker-injury funds, and rent. Of that total, more than $1.3 million was paid in "cash/check" and about $1 million in contributions of rice, buildings, and equipment. The documents also showed that Firestone poured $35.3 million into rebuilding the plantation between June 1990 and February 1993. It's unclear whether that total included the tax payments. The document said the money paid for rice shipments, plantation rehabilitation, pensions and labor settlements, and $12.3 million in "miscellaneous obligations and expenses."

In the coming years, Taylor traded in smuggled diamonds and illegally harvested timber. While the exact sources of his war chest remained murky, the State Department estimated in 1996 that he could have been taking in as much as $75 million a year. In addition, he also received support from sympathetic nations, such as Libya and Burkina Faso.

But at the beginning of his insurrection, Taylor was a start-up warlord with a growing army and a need for new revenue. Taylor explained the special importance of Firestone's resources while on trial for war crimes at The Hague.

"Once we captured Harbel, we then made it very clear to the Firestone plantation company that they could no longer be permitted to exercise allegiance to the government in Monrovia," Taylor testified. "It became at that particular time our most significant principal source of foreign exchange."

At one point, Taylor said his dealings with Firestone netted $1 million to $2 million every six months. The cash was kept in a building in Gbarnga by Taylor's finance minister, since there was not yet a First National Bank of Taylorland.

As to how he used the funds, Taylor was as transparent as an Enron footnote. The money purchased "food and medicine and different things," he said.

Taylor said Firestone worried about its dealings with him.

Firestone "did not want to get involved in a violation of United States laws," Taylor testified.

To accommodate those concerns, Taylor said that he worked out a scheme with Firestone. The company provided rubber to Taylor officials, who smuggled it out of Liberia and sold it in neighboring Ivory Coast.

U.S. embassy cables from the 1990s corroborate Taylor's testimony about Firestone's worries. In 1991, U.S. embassy officials noted that Firestone was "very concerned" that Taylor was making demands that could result in the company violating the Foreign Corrupt Practices Act. The law bans American companies from paying bribes to foreign government officials. Firestone was being "remarkably cagey" about its dealings with Taylor, one cable said.

Taylor was also adamant that Firestone had never paid taxes to his rebel government.

"They did not pay taxes to the NPFL," he said in his testimony.

Padmore, however, acknowledged that Firestone had, indeed, paid taxes. Such payments were entirely legal, he explained, because Taylor was a de facto government that controlled Firestone's plantation.

Firestone "did not pay off warlords, or give money under the table," he said.

"There is nothing in the Foreign Corrupt Practices Act that says you can't pay warlords," Padmore said. The law "in essence says you cannot bribe."

ProPublica and *Frontline* unearthed previously unreported records of Firestone's payments to Taylor in a lawsuit filed in a county courthouse in Akron, Ohio.

The documents, with their green-eye-shade accounting precision, surprised both Americans and Liberians.

U.S. officials who served in Monrovia at the time said they had not heard of the payments. Ambassador William Twaddell took charge of the embassy eight months after the Firestone agreement was signed. During a recent interview in Washington, D.C., he shook his head in disbelief when he was shown the Firestone document labeled "Schedule of Payments to the NPRAG."

"It's kind of amazing that it is so broken down by columns," he said.

If Firestone became Taylor's "bankrollers as a deliberate sort of corporate decision, that's pretty disturbing," Twaddell said. "The other stuff about supplying the fuel and the communications—if that is really deliberate and voluntary, that's disturbing."

Sawyer was also taken aback. When he viewed the documents in Monrovia recently, the aging ex-president reacted angrily, saying he would recommend that the current Liberian government look anew at Firestone's role in the civil war.

"I think this is sad. I'm not only troubled by it . . . I'm angry at it," he said. "The Liberian people deserve some explanation."

"This is complicity," he said. "This is complicity."

Brenda Hollis served as one of the chief prosecutors at Taylor's war crimes trial. An expert in international law, she exhausted herself trying to untangle Taylor's finances. Even today, his sources of funds remain a mystery.

Hollis had never seen the documents, either. She scoffed at Firestone's use of the term "taxes" to describe payments to Taylor.

"You can call it taxes, but in my view they were paying him to stay in business," Hollis said. "They were dressing it up."

The Fix-It Man

Firestone fulfilled its second promise to Taylor in May 1992. Weihe came out of retirement to take over as managing director of the Firestone plantation.

A retired U.S. Air Force captain, he had wavy hair and an easy, gap-toothed grin. He liked whiskey and had a big diamond ring.

Weihe had acted as Firestone's fix-it man before. A chemist, he was not particularly experienced in operating a rubber farm.

He did, however, have a very particular set of skills that he had acquired during his long career: "I knew how to move around in the political circles," Weihe said.

In the 1970s and 1980s, he sold off the company's rubber plantations, except for the one in Liberia. Later, he bargained with Samuel Doe to get a better deal on the company's contract with Liberia. In the late 1980s, he ran the Firestone plantation in the final, turbulent years of Doe's regime.

Weihe met Taylor when the rebel leader was a newly minted bureaucrat controlling the money that sloshed through Doe's administration.

Weihe also befriended Richardson, Taylor's top adviser. Both men loved deep-sea fishing. In what could have been a scene from a Graham Greene novel, expats and Liberian anglers mixed at Firestone's fishing club, a collection of wooden docks and twenty-foot boats on a muddy creek just outside the entrance to the Firestone plantation.

"I didn't sense any racism in him," Richardson said of Weihe. "He didn't have that plantation mentality."

Although sixty-five years old and settled into retirement, Weihe welcomed the chance to return to Liberia.

"I felt a big responsibility for the plantation over there and the people there," Weihe said. Weihe was interviewed a few months before his death in 2010.

In Firestone's absence, Taylor had turned House 53 into his own personal White House, a place to retreat to as he scuttled around the country for security reasons.

A Firestone cook prepared meals for him. Firestone's repairman fixed the hot-water heater after Taylor complained that the showers were too cold. Firestone workers cut the lawn by hand.

He reveled in his power. He welcomed diplomats, UN representatives, even former president Jimmy Carter, who came to Liberia to work on a peace accord.

Still, Weihe liked what he saw—on the plantation and with Taylor.

"My first impression with Taylor was that he might be a reasonable man," Weihe said. "He certainly spoke reasonably about how Liberia should be changed, and what should be done.

"What he said made sense," Weihe said.

Taylor held up his end of the memorandum of agreement. He appointed Brig. Gen. Domingo Ramos, a mercenary from Gambia, to protect the plantation with about 300 soldiers. Matt Chipley, a Ramos commander, said Firestone paid him $425 a month and gave him free fuel and twenty-five bags of rice. Taylor also ordered Ramos to recover looted Firestone equipment, machinery, and vehicles.

Taylor and his ministers' homes in the hills were off limits. So Weihe and his crew set up a spartan dormitory in the guest house Firestone used to put up visitors.

As the first summer rains began, the expats worked to assess the damage to the plantation. At night, they gathered at communal tables for meals of rice and chicken. Afterward, they relaxed with Club Beer, the local brew. Weihe drank whiskey from a small glass.

Taylor visited the Firestone expats on several occasions. In the humid guest house, he gave long speeches on democracy and the future of Liberia.

"We called him Mr. President," remembered Brad Pettit, the plantation's controller. "I actually felt that if there was an election, he would be elected. I was impressed with the man."

Occasionally, the expats ran into roadblocks set up by rebel soldiers. They saw child soldiers roaming the grounds. Convoys of armed rebels raced past.

"Should we have waited" to resume operating? Pettit asked recently. "Probably, yes, I will agree that that's a probable, better answer. But we decided . . . that it was doable and we decided to try."

Weihe rehired thousands of Liberians to tap rubber trees, rebuild plantation buildings, and trim back jungle growth that threatened to overrun the plantation.

As decreed by Taylor for all foreign companies working in Taylorland, Firestone started paying workers half in Liberian currency and half in U.S. dollars, according to an embassy cable. As the U.S. dollars circulated, they helped provide Taylor's government with much needed liquid currency.

Weihe created a new transport system that allowed Firestone to use the port at Buchanan to export liquid latex—previously only possible through Monrovia.

Taylor returned the favor. His port charged lower fees than the interim government's levies in Monrovia. The arrangement saved Firestone money, put cash into Taylor's hands, and starved Sawyer's interim government of badly needed revenue.

It was a sweet deal for everyone involved.

"Firestone's intent was to make money. Always has and always will," Pettit said. "Why did we go back? Because we felt sorry for the people that were there? Probably not. We wanted to get the investment earning money again."

Off Limits

The languorous summer days of 1992 were filled with tension. Almost two years had passed since the cease-fire, and both Sawyer and the West African peacekeepers were running out of patience. Taylor had kidnapped more than 500 West African soldiers. He was fighting pitched battles with a rebel faction invading from neighboring Sierra Leone.

Weihe knew that Taylor's fighters were using the plantation as a staging area. They rushed off to attack peacekeeping and government forces stationed at the Schieffelin military base between Firestone and Monrovia.

"They used the plantation to, more or less, regroup, and go down to Schieffelin," Weihe said. "You could hear the cannons going off, the gunfire right on the plantation."

"You knew there was a war going on," Weihe said.

Taylor's rebels sometimes kicked Firestone workers out of their homes. In other cases, the rebels were Firestone employees—working when they weren't warring.

Welwean, the son of the general manager's cook, described a constant influx of fighters.

"There was absolute anarchy because rebels were all over the place with their guns. They were in Firestone, through Mr. Weihe, giving them lots of transportation, so most of these Firestone vehicles were owned by the rebels," Welwean said. "It was very bad."

Expats and Liberians recall planes flying overhead in the middle of the night and landing at Roberts airport, just outside the plantation entrance.

"A number of mysterious airplanes were landing at Roberts airfield bringing in God knows what," Gale Ruff remembered. "We didn't get anything off those airplanes."

Convoys of pickup trucks trundled up the main road, carrying secret cargo deeper into the shadows of the Firestone plantation.

"When the plane come, you will see vehicles coming from there covered with tarpaulin, and it seem to be weapons, you know," said Daniel D. Roberts, Weihe's secretary. "The boys that were living with us in the camp will say, 'Our weapon will come.'"

Weihe and Taylor worked to set up a communications center and radio station in another senior manager's house nearby, according to a Firestone official and a deposition from Tom Woewiyu, Taylor's defense minister.

In July 1992, Weihe gave U.S. embassy officers a tour of the resurgent plantation. He told them how Ramos had deployed around 300 soldiers to protect the operation. Another 1,000 or so rebels lived on the farm, "taking advantage of Firestone's food distribution," Weihe told the officers.

As the tour progressed, the group chatted with Ramos. He seemed laid-back, affable. They bumped into Gen. Adolphus Dolo, better known as Gen. Peanut Butter. He was infamous for recruiting child soldiers.

After the tour, embassy officials summarized the visit in a lengthy cable to Washington.

"Firestone appears to want to play ball with NPRAG and has appointed Weihe to deal more effectively with the NPFL/NPRAG over the long term," the cable said. "Impressions from the plantation visit give the feeling that Firestone management both in Akron and on the scene are determined to stay the course.

"It has a huge investment to protect and wants again to make the plantation a profitable long-term operation. Firestone seems to have concluded that to be successful they must deal with Charles Taylor now."

There was one more thing Weihe wanted the embassy to know. At some point, Weihe pulled one of the embassy officers aside. The rebels had not permitted Firestone to venture into some areas of the sprawling plantation, he said.

"Without elaborating, but giving the impression that there may be some military significance, [Weihe] also mentioned that certain parts of the plantation were off-limits," the embassy recounted in the cable to Washington.

Preparations on the Plantation

On October 8, 1992, the new U.S. ambassador to Liberia paid an official visit to the Firestone plantation.

Twaddell and his entourage traveled smoothly across the twenty-mile tarmac road from the capital to the plantation. Weihe provided a tour. There was great news.

Firestone was back in business.

For the first time since June 1990, Firestone had begun producing rubber in Liberia—600,000 pounds in August, 3.9 million pounds in September.

More than 6,500 Liberians were back at work tapping rubber trees. Buildings destroyed by looting had been repaired. The company had managed to reopen Firestone's hospital.

"It was a pretty impressive installation," Twaddell said. "We got, I think, a pretty fair snapshot of what the operation was about and how it worked."

That was only partially true. By the day of Twaddell's visit, Taylor's men had cleared the usual twenty-five roadblocks manned by teenage rebels looking for bribes. Child soldiers had vanished from sight. Taylor himself was nowhere to be seen.

Behind the scenes, though, Taylor was overseeing the final stages of preparation for Operation Octopus—an all-out push to seize Monrovia and take control of Liberia. Soldiers mounted a heavy machine gun in front of House 53 for Taylor's protection. Taylor began spending most of his days at the plantation, he testified.

On the farm, some expats said they noticed nothing different. Weihe said he had no idea that Taylor was planning an attack. John Chapman, a British expatriate who was a production manager at the rubber-processing plant, said he vaguely recalled an armed convoy passing through the plantation in the days before the operation was launched. But he didn't think much of it.

"We were concentrating on getting the factory running," he said. "We were all pleased that it was running."

During the tour, an embassy contact on the plantation "quite flagrantly told [embassy officials] that an 'Aeroflot' cargo plane had made night landings and discharged freight" at the Taylor-controlled Roberts airport in early October, a cable said.

UN reports would later attest that arms dealers from the former Soviet Union were among Taylor's chief weapons suppliers—including the notorious Viktor Bout.

Twaddell noticed that the soldiers he saw bore automatic weapons that were "shiny and new and apparently just out of the packing crate," according to the cable.

If Firestone's expats noticed nothing suspicious, their Liberian employees were more perceptive.

The monsoons of the rainy season had just given way to drier weather. The air thrummed with a kind of energy and dread. A sharp blade was scraping softly up Liberia's neck.

"You could tell they were planning to launch a full-scale war. There were weapons moving around," Welwean said. "We knew something was up."

VI. Raining Hell

At around three a.m. on October 15, Taylor unleashed his hell on Monrovia.

Howitzer cannons and 81 mm mortars set up in outlying suburbs hurled metal into the sleeping city—a narrow peninsula bordered by mangrove swamps, mudflats, creeks, and the Atlantic Ocean.

Gerhart, who lived in a house overlooking the marshes on the eastern edge of Monrovia, awoke to rocket fire sailing over the roof of his home. "We knew the battle was on," he said.

At the same time, in the fortified U.S. embassy at the other end of the capital, Twaddell woke to booms. The barrage racked the city. Mortar shells landed near the compound. "It was chaotic, very scary," Twaddell said.

Taylor had launched a mad, merciless, determined assault to seize the capital that he had failed to gain control of two years earlier. Some analysts believed that was why he had retreated to Firestone's plantation—to plot the attack, to bolster his forces, to stock his magazines.

Taylor's battle plan called for the entire weight of the NPFL and its allies to hammer Monrovia from multiple directions, enveloping it like the arms of an octopus.

Two attacks were staged from the Firestone plantation, one from the north and a second from the east. They were aimed at seizing Monrovia's suburbs and the interim government's only remaining airport. An allied rebel faction would attack from the west to destroy the base of the West African peacekeepers and seize the country's largest port.

The city would be trapped against the anvil of the Atlantic. Taylor's generals predicted it would fall in two weeks.

"We had the men. We had the will to fight," said Daniel Chea, then Taylor's defense minister.

Richardson had taken over Brad Pettit's old house. Taylor's men had captured a battle map that had belonged to the West African forces. Richardson spread it across a large table, tracking the battle as it progressed over the next several days.

The attack did not go as planned. The NPFL had stationed two aging missile launchers that could fire up to forty rockets at a time in the suburbs across from the capital. The rockets fired wildly, overshooting the city and landing in the ocean, as harmless as fireworks.

The artillery barrage also was not hitting the intended targets. The 105 mm Howitzer guns were old, their barrels locked in place by rust and disuse. The only way to change the trajectory of the shells was by moving the cannons back and forth.

The 81 mm mortars landed randomly. One even hit Richardson's family home in Monrovia.

"We were aiming pretty close. That's the best we could do," Richardson said. "People were trying to kill us. We were trying to kill them back."

Richardson tried to compensate for the indiscriminate fire by using the radio station at Firestone to warn residents where the next rounds would fall.

"I suggest you move from there, because tomorrow I'm gonna rain all hell on you guys," Richardson would tell people living in neighborhoods near military targets.

Taylor's commanders unleashed their shock troops, child soldiers who dashed across mudflats wearing cheap rubber sandals they called "Four Wheel Drive." The child soldiers were often given drugs or alcohol before battle to boost their courage, according to human rights organizations.

Appearing drugged, they ran toward West African soldiers, firing and retreating, firing and retreating. The children cut down one adult after another. The men hardened.

Innocent Nass, a military analyst and retired Nigerian officer, remembered fighting against Taylor's child soldiers at a later stage in the war. They were often the most violent, most devoted soldiers, drugged berserkers who attacked in human waves.

"You could fire and fire at them. You'd get one down, and the next one would come," Nass said. "They were more dangerous than beasts."

"You really don't see them as children in the heat of battle," Nass said.

As the rebels advanced through the suburbs, they carried out summary executions of civilians suspected of being government collaborators. They looted homes. They seized property. Some spray-painted their names across empty buildings to claim them as their own.

Some 200,000 people fled into the city to seek safety. Monrovia became a pestilent ark. People crouched in homes and died in the streets. They filled the hospitals: babies with head wounds, mothers with shattered legs, young men broken and wrapped in blood-soaked bandages.

The rebels ringed Monrovia. Chipley, the skinny kid who grew up on the Firestone plantation, was now commander of the Wild Geese brigade, considered to be one of the more professional units of Taylor's army.

Chipley marched his 1,100 men toward the suburbs of Monrovia dressed in black T-shirts bearing the emblem of a flock of geese. They were armed with RPGs, lightweight 60 mm mortars, and an antiaircraft gun.

Christopher Vambo, known as Gen. Mosquito, swept south from the Firestone plantation with more than 2,000 men. He seized a suburb called Gardnersville, which was separated from Monrovia by two miles of swamp and river. He wore camouflage battle dress, a red beret, and aviator sunglasses that dwarfed his face.

His men dressed in T-shirts and rags. They carried AK-47s and RPGs. They marched, singing, jumping. One wore a top hat and shell necklace. Another played a blue plastic recorder. One man held what appeared to be a leg bone.

West African soldiers "are trying to penetrate through," Vambo told a CNN camera crew as he pointed to a decaying, withered skeleton trapped beneath a burnt-out armored personnel carrier. "Everything will crush on them."

After several days of fighting, the perimeter around the capital had shrunk to less than two miles.

Rose, Twaddell's deputy chief of mission, began evacuating nonessential personnel from the embassy. A former army officer and helicopter pilot, Rose worried about the possibility of Taylor's success.

"The first few days were very, very touch-and-go," he said. "Taylor forces got quite close."

The Nuns

The West African forces counterattacked, their forces rapidly swelling to 12,000 soldiers. They loosed bombs from Nigerian air force Alpha jets. They drove tanks and armored personnel carriers. They shredded the rebels' swampy hideouts with big guns fired from Nigerian navy vessels.

The West African peacekeepers worked closely with anti-Taylor guerrillas and the notoriously brutal Liberian army—all of whom knew the terrain better than the foreign soldiers. The alliance began to push Taylor's fighters back.

For weeks, the battle seesawed. Taylor's men were pushed out of the capital, but the suburbs remained killing fields of whizzing bullets and rotting corpses, of child soldiers holding giant stuffed teddy bears, and poorly trained peacekeepers rampaging and looting.

Trapped in the chaos were five American nuns from the Adorers of the Blood of Christ order based in Ruma, Illinois.

Sisters Barbara Ann Muttra, Shirley Kolmer, Kathleen McGuire, Agnes Mueller, and M. Joel Kolmer (a cousin to Shirley) lived in a small convent just off the main road that runs through Gardnersville.

The convent was located on a shifting frontline between Taylor's fighters and the West African peacekeepers. Much of what happened next was pieced together by reporter Charlotte Grimes of the *St. Louis Post Dispatch* in 1993.

On October 23, the American embassy was informed that the convent had been cut off by overnight fighting. Two of the sisters were missing. They needed help. Under pressure from the U.S. embassy, West African soldiers pushed forward to rescue them. But they had to withdraw. The zone was too hot.

The sisters' bodies were found weeks later. Two were found dead in a car, a short distance from the convent. Three others were found in the convent itself. Several other bodies were found around the convent.

The deaths of the five nuns vaulted the impossible savagery of Liberia's conflict onto the international stage. Taylor was held responsible, though he protested that his men were innocent.

The State Department described the United States as "shocked and appalled" by the "cowardly act." Pope John Paul II called the nuns "martyrs" who had been "brutally murdered."

In Monrovia, hundreds of people packed the Catholic cathedral on a sunny, sweltering day for a requiem for the sisters. Archbishop Michael Francis delivered a powerful, wrenching sermon.

Embassy officials reported that he had called out Taylor for plunging the country into violent madness.

"The way to power is through the ballot box," Francis said. "But this leader has resorted to any means to achieve it."

As the throng of worshippers left the church, the choir struck up a hymn: "Ain't Gonna Study War No More."

Rose loaded the women's bodies into C-130s on the tarmac of Monrovia's municipal airport for flights back to the United States. They were buried together, on a cold winter day, in five side-by-side plots at the Ruma convent they once called home.

An inquiry by the Catholic Church and another by the Truth and Reconciliation Commission named Vambo and another NPFL soldier as the perpetrators. The FBI carried out its own investigation, but the U.S. Attorney's Office declined to prosecute.

In a recent interview, Rose said he remains upset that the sisters' killers have never been brought to justice. Two decades later, Rose is still determined to make sure that their deaths are not forgotten.

"Five American citizens were killed in an act of terror," Rose said. "We as a government and those of us who serve in government have a deep responsibility to see that justice is done."

"I have a responsibility," Rose said. "That responsibility is unfulfilled."

Sanctuary

As Taylor's wild boys tore up Monrovia, the plantation was humming.

The expats made their daily commute from the guest house to the Firestone office and factories a little more than three miles away. In October, they celebrated a new milestone: factory production had reached a record for the year: 4.7 million pounds of rubber.

The managers knew, of course, that a big attack was going on. The hospital was filled with wounded NPFL soldiers. The roads were mostly blocked.

They kept their heads down and worried about the rubber.

"I felt safer on the plantation," Weihe said. "When you've got work to do, and you know what you have to do, and you go about it, you really don't get too frightened or worked up."

A mile up the road from the plantation's guest house, Taylor's war room was humming, too. He had expected the attack to last no more than two weeks. But his rebels had failed to establish even a foothold in central Monrovia.

By November, the peacekeepers had gone on the offensive, recruiting allies from other warring groups. They were hunting Taylor now.

West African air force jets began bombing-and-strafing runs. Since they had no antiaircraft weapons, the aerial assaults chased Taylor's men from one stronghold to another. His capital, Gbarnga, was hit. So, too, was the port he controlled in Buchanan. Kakata, a town with a heavy NPFL presence just outside the Firestone rubber farm, was also struck.

Then, of course, there was the Firestone plantation. It was full of families recruited to come back and live and work by a company eager to return to business.

The Liberians on the plantation said it was hard to imagine that the West African forces would attack. The peacekeepers would not dare place the lives of so many civilians in danger.

But the plantation also held Taylor's command post. His communications equipment. Some of his soldiers. Even his weapons and ammunition.

On November 2, the peacekeepers shattered the sanctuary, and Firestone's decision to reopen its plantation in the middle of Taylor's rebel base would exact a human cost.

At about six-thirty p.m., dozens of Liberian workers had gathered at the soccer field near Harbel for a game. Men, women, and children watched from the sidelines. In the homes surrounding the field, people played checkers and Scrabble—a favorite Liberian pastime.

Suddenly, several olive-green Alpha jets streaked overhead. One loosed a bomb that exploded, flinging shrapnel, blood, and body parts everywhere. People were screaming, dying. The planes passed by on a second run. They strafed survivors.

Welwean's uncle was playing checkers with six other men. They were cut to pieces by the strafing. Julius Morlue, a Liberian who worked in Firestone's accounting section, was summoned by his daughter. He raced with her toward the field. He found his wife between two houses, blood pouring from a fatal wound to her head.

"I could not do anything," Morlue said. "I lay down side her body and cry, cry."

Roberts, Weihe's secretary, was drinking a bottle of beer in his house when the bombs dropped. His house filled with smoke. A few homes away, one of his neighbors was killed.

Mary Pollee had returned to Firestone after her journey of grief, taking up residence in the home she had once shared with her family. But with her husband dead, she said Firestone managers told her she no longer had the right to company housing. So she moved to a town adjacent to the plantation.

She was living there when she heard the bomb strike. She ran to see what had happened. She remembered stepping over the bodies of dead Firestone workers.

"Human being, these poor human being there that day, it was not easy," she said. "Body, body, body. I would not even be able to stand there again to see. I were not able."

From the guest house three miles away, the expats watched the bombing with amazement.

"I can remember all of us going out and say, 'Whoa, look at that.' And we're watching the planes dive and dropping the bombs and pulling up," Pettit said. "It was just, 'Hey, it's a show. It's not gonna bother us. They're after Taylor's machine and so we're safe.'"

In the gloaming, Weihe rushed down to the soccer field. He was sickened by what he saw: the blood, the bodies, the limbs like twisted doll arms scattered across the carefully manicured grass.

Weihe told an embassy official that forty-two people were killed—none of them combatants. Perhaps another 200 were injured. Many people were buried among the rubber trees.

Weihe appeared in a televised interview after the attack. In his gray shirt and large, wire-framed glasses, he looked angry, puzzled, exhausted.

"It's a devastating experience to witness something like this," he said. "I would find it hard to think that what we are engaged in here would have any value other than something that would be for the well-being of the world."

Nigerian general Victor Malu, the commander of the West African forces, made no apology for targeting the plantation.

"The rebels were storing supplies there. And when that happens, we'll bloody well blow it," Malu told several newspapers at the time.

Richardson denied that Taylor's use of the plantation had turned Firestone's Liberian workers into human shields.

Today he lives in central Monrovia, in a light-filled home made of native woods on the banks of the St. Paul River. Funny, erudite, a charming raconteur, he spends many evenings with friends from the NPFL days, tossing back Heinekens on the sidewalk outside a local auto-body shop.

He insists that neither he nor Taylor did anything wrong—either under Liberian or international law.

"I saw skulls. I saw dogs eating bodies. I saw bloated bodies. I saw exploding bodies. I saw women dead. I saw children dead. I saw babies dead. I saw a war. I hope to never see it again," Richardson said. "I can't apologize for war.

"Everybody has had a war."

Slaughter Tapped

Firestone decided it had had enough after the counterattack triggered by Operation Octopus. Enough bombing. Enough blood. Enough of everything.

On November 18, Weihe wrote a letter to "His Excellency" Charles Taylor. Weihe said he had consulted with Firestone's CEO Kaizaki, who was "very proud" of the work Firestone had done at its Liberian outpost. Nonetheless, Firestone had decided it was "impossible" to continue work on the plantation given the security conditions.

Weihe told Taylor that he had appointed the plantation's doctor to run daily operations. Ramos, Taylor's general, would become a member of the executive committee overseeing the plantation. William Cooper, a brother of one of Taylor's close allies, would have overall control as general manager.

Firestone later calculated that it had made $1.1 million in profits in trying to restart the plantation between 1990 and 1993.

"I wish to personally thank you for your kind understanding," Weihe wrote to Taylor. "I look forward to being able to quickly return to restart our operations."

A month later, Firestone's board of directors met again. Schremp proposed several future plans, including selling the plantation. Instead, Schremp said, "Kaizaki agreed that we should continue our efforts to restore operations at Harbel."

But for now, it was time to leave.

On the morning of November 20, Weihe loaded fourteen Firestone employees into cars and crossed Taylorland into neighboring Ivory Coast.

Once across the border, the men celebrated. They hit a local casino, boozing and gambling. Pettit won more than $1,000.

"I was unbelievably lucky," he said.

Firestone's gamble to keep its plantation active from 1990 to 1993 had failed.

Tens of thousands of Liberians were dead.
Hundreds of thousands had been driven from their homes.
Hundreds of children had been killed or turned into killers.
The nation was a ruin.

An Innocent Party

By March 1993, the West African forces had pushed Taylor's fighters off most of the plantation. That month, Sawyer took an extraordinary step. For the first time since taking office two years earlier, the president of the interim government ventured outside his shell-pocked capital into areas previously under Taylor's control.

A highlight of his tour was a stop at the Firestone plantation. There, with reporters jotting notes and senior government officials looking on, he declared that Firestone's management had colluded with Taylor in attacks that nearly toppled his government.

Firestone's plantation had served as the "command post and nerve center" for Operation Octopus, Sawyer said, according to a State Department cable.

"Firestone contributed to the war," Sawyer said in an interview. "I went to Harbel Hills. I saw the operations."

Today, Firestone calls Sawyer's suggestion that it knew of Operation Octopus or colluded with Taylor "false and slanderous."

In July 1993, Firestone answered Sawyer's charges with a lengthy letter defending the company's actions.

The letter, never previously reported, provides a candid articulation of the moral, economic, and legal calculus conducted at the highest levels of a major American corporation.

In the letter to Sawyer, Schremp wrote that Firestone had faced a difficult decision when Taylor's forces invaded the plantation in 1990.

"The best and safest course was to await a resolution of the Liberian civil crisis and the establishment of a lawful government recognized and accepted not only throughout Liberia, but among the nations of the world," he said.

Schremp acknowledged that the company had signed the memorandum of agreement with Taylor. It had paid taxes to Taylor's government. It had abided by Taylor's edicts. But, he said, the company never attempted to take sides in Liberia's conflict. It simply had no other "practical alternative."

"We have always sought only a restoration of peace and stable government in the entire country so as to end the terrible bloodshed, grief and suffering experienced by so many Liberians," he wrote.

Schremp's letter was accompanied by a ten-page legal defense. It turned upon the idea that Firestone had done nothing wrong, since Taylor's organization constituted a "de facto" government over the plantation.

Firestone cited a series of U.S. court cases which upheld this principle. Several stemmed from the American Civil War, where postbellum U.S. federal judges recognized the Confederacy as a "de facto" government which had authority to take certain actions.

Firestone compared itself to the Liberians living in Taylorland. The interim government would not hold citizens accountable for submitting to Taylor's iron fist. As a corporation, Firestone deserved the same treatment.

"Firestone, which is a corporate 'person' as a matter of law, cannot be seen to have committed an offense merely by submitting to the power and authority of the NPFL over its assets," the letter said.

Finally, the company denied Sawyer's accusation that it had willingly allowed the NPFL to use its plantation militarily.

"Firestone categorically denies at any time having permitted or encouraged the use of Firestone facilities by the NPFL for military operations," the letter said. "Firestone has an enormous investment in the plantation and wishes to preserve it rather than to expose it to destruction as a staging base for military operations."

Firestone was innocent of any wrongdoing, the memo concluded.

"Like many others, Firestone was an innocent party caught in a tragic civil conflict," the letter said. "It has sought only to protect its assets and alleviate somewhat the hardship of its employees and their families."

Nothing ever came of Sawyer's legal threats. In March 1994, his interim government was replaced by another interim government that contained representatives from Taylor's NPFL and other warring factions.

The Firestone matter was dropped. The company kept a low profile, with a skeleton crew on site to maintain the plantation. Rebel factions battled among the rubber trees. Some 600 refugees were killed in a massacre in one housing camp.

Over the next four years, Taylor participated in a series of interim governments that gave him some semblance of legitimacy. In April 1996, he launched one last ferocious attack against Monrovia. When it failed, Taylor accepted the need for elections.

A little more than a year later, he stood before adoring crowds, the legitimate ruler of a legitimate country. His dream had come to pass.

"I will not be a wicked president," he promised.

A Civil Case

Back in the United States, Firestone was engaged in its own war—albeit in a courtroom.

Firestone told U.S. embassy officials that the company had lost more than $200 million between 1990 and 1994 in Liberia. But Firestone's insurance claims had been rejected. The company's policies did not cover losses sustained in war.

In 1994, Firestone filed suit based on a bold legal theory: What had happened in Liberia was not a war. It had been a civil conflict. Thus, the insurance companies, AIG and Cigna, had unfairly denied Firestone's claims.

AIG settled the case. But Cigna fought.

Cigna lawyers subpoenaed scores of internal Firestone documents, which showed that the company repeatedly referred to the situation in Liberia as a war. They deposed Firestone managers who described the conflict as a war. They even showed that Firestone had protected itself from lawsuits by saying that the war in Liberia had prevented it from fulfilling rubber supply contracts.

From Liberia, Taylor and his cronies did their best to bolster Firestone's legal case. Taylor pressured his own Supreme Court to declare that Liberian law required payment of damages that arose from wartime looting, as Firestone was claiming.

Three months after Taylor launched his final attack to capture Monrovia in April 1996, Firestone's attorneys filed an affidavit from Woewiyu, Taylor's defense minister. He swore that the NPFL "never intended" to overthrow the government of Liberia.

Firestone's attorney's even made the argument that Cigna's refusal to pay was preventing Liberia from healing from the war that Firestone claimed had not happened.

"As you may know, the Liberian people are now living in desperate conditions by any standard," one attorney for Firestone wrote to Cigna, asking for a speedy resolution. "The economy is in a disastrous condition, and the disarmament and election processes have stalled."

Liberia's government was begging for Firestone to return. But Firestone did not have enough capital to rebuild because "we have not yet received a dime of insurance reimbursement which could be used to fund such measures," the attorney concluded.

In the end, Cigna and Firestone agreed to a settlement that limited the potential losses for each side. The companies would submit their arguments to a trial judge. If the judge decided against Firestone, Cigna would have to pay $15 million. If the judge decided for Firestone, Cigna would have to pay $45 million.

The outcome of the March 1996 agreement has never been made public. But in April, Firestone hired workers to begin clearing weeds at the plantation and to prepare for renewed production, according to cables and press accounts.

In March 1997, Schremp announced Firestone's first export of rubber from Liberia in years—370,000 gallons of latex to France, one of Taylor's early backers.

"Firestone is happy with this first step in a long process," Schremp said in a prepared statement reported in the rubber-trade press. "We support completely . . . the people of Liberia in their efforts to bring democracy and stability to Liberia."

Completely Justifiable

Since the end of the war in 2003, Firestone says it has invested more than $146.9 million in the country. It currently employs 8,000 Liberians—in some of the best-paying jobs in the rubber industry, according to the company and union officials. It educates more than 15,000 children in 27 schools on the plantation, recently adding a high school on the rubber farm. It has renovated more than 3,600 worker homes.

Its hospital is one of the best in the country. Indeed, Firestone has kept its plantation largely protected from the Ebola virus that has ravaged the rest of the country.

Firestone graduates populate the country's political, educational, and economic institutions. Firestone sends Liberian children to college each year on scholarship. Firestone's managerial ranks are now mostly filled by Liberians.

For Firestone, these accomplishments are proof that it made the right decisions in some of the country's darkest hours.

"Firestone's decision to remain in Liberia was very costly for the company," Firestone said in an official statement. "The company continues to rebuild, but along with its Liberian employees, Firestone was able to preserve an important economic asset for Liberia."

"We are proud of that," the company said.

Padmore was even more emphatic.

"It has always come back to that question of hope, hope for the future. That's why I think that the continued Firestone presence in Liberia was a good thing," Padmore said. "I only hope that this relationship will continue for many, many, many more years."

VII. A Traumatized Nation

When Ellen Johnson Sirleaf won Liberia's presidency in 2005, she campaigned on a promise to move the country forward.

Issues involving Firestone's Liberian concession provided an early test of her ability to deliver. The company had been accused of rushing a favorable new deal through the weak interim government that followed Taylor's exit in 2003.

Environmental groups complained that the company's discharge was polluting the river that Taylor's rebels had first crossed so long ago. There were complaints about child labor, substandard living conditions, and the exploitation of workers.

Johnson Sirleaf rose to the challenge by demanding a new contract between the company and the government. She reduced the number of years in the company's lease on its plantation. She improved the system that Firestone used to pay independent farmers for their rubber. She convinced the company to invest in a plan to recycle old rubber trees into building material. And she got it to improve worker housing.

For its part, Firestone adopted a zero-tolerance child-labor policy, and even union leaders acknowledge its success. The company also says it no longer discharges wastewater into the river bordering the plantation.

Johnson Sirleaf has not been inclined, however, to hold the U.S. rubber giant accountable for its long-ago support for Taylor.

We interviewed Johnson Sirleaf one rainy day in July on the top floor of Liberia's foreign ministry. A tropical rain pounded the roof and windows. She was coping with a new emergency, the Ebola outbreak. Johnson Sirleaf's health ministry was beginning to broadcast public service announcements about the disease. Soon, the crisis would overwhelm the nation.

"The results of war, the results of politicking, the results, if you may, of still trying to find a national identity, all of those have not enabled us to achieve the level of reconciliation that we want," she said. "But it's something that we'll have to continue to work on."

She was well aware that Liberia's Truth and Reconciliation Commission had recommended further investigation into Firestone as one of the companies that aided Taylor during the civil war.

But when we presented her with documents that showed that Firestone had paid taxes to Taylor, she seemed reluctant to examine them.

She had not seen them before, she said. But she already knew the company, its history, its economic, cultural, and political power. She already knew the company had survived labor strikes and lawsuits, coups and killers, renegades and reformers. She already knew that Firestone had wrapped itself around Liberia like a creeper vine around a tree.

Firestone had been part of Liberia for years. It would be part of it forever.

What was the use of looking back?

"Some of what happened in the past, we knew of. Some of this, we don't," Johnson Sirleaf said. "Quite frankly, we don't know, and sometimes we don't even want to know.

"We just want to proceed."

New York Times

The fifty state attorneys general, known as the "people's lawyers," have historically been in the forefront of holding corporate and financial wrongdoers accountable and were, for instance, leaders in investigating mortgage abuses during the run-up to the financial crisis of 2008. That's why this blockbuster investigation by Eric Lipton is all the more discouraging—and maddening. Sifting through more than 6,000 e-mails and other documents, Lipton shows the degree to which state AGs—Democrats and Republicans alike—have increasingly come under the sway of behind-the-scenes lobbying efforts to alter or kill investigations.

Eric Lipton

17. Lobbyists, Bearing Gifts, Pursue Attorneys General

When the executives who distribute 5-Hour Energy, the popular caffeinated drinks, learned that attorneys general in more than thirty states were investigating allegations of deceptive advertising—a serious financial threat to the company—they moved quickly to shut the investigations down, one state at a time.

But success did not come in court or at a negotiating table.

Instead, it came at the opulent Loews Santa Monica Beach Hotel in California, with its panoramic ocean views, where more than a dozen state attorneys general had gathered last year for cocktails, dinners, and fund raisers organized by the Democratic Attorneys General Association. A lawyer for 5-Hour Energy roamed the event, setting her sights on Attorney General Chris Koster of Missouri, whose office was one of those investigating the company.

"My client just received notification that Missouri is on this," the lawyer, Lori Kalani, told him.

Ms. Kalani's firm, Dickstein Shapiro, had courted the attorney general at dinners and conferences and with thousands of dollars in campaign contributions. Mr. Koster told Ms. Kalani that he was unaware of the investigation, and he reached for his phone and called his office. By the end of the weekend, he had ordered his staff to pull out of the inquiry, a clear victory for 5-Hour Energy.

The quick reversal, confirmed by Mr. Koster and Ms. Kalani, was part of a pattern of successful lobbying of Mr. Koster by the law firm on behalf of clients like Pfizer and AT&T—and evidence of a largely hidden dynamic at work in state attorneys general offices across the country.

Attorneys general are now the object of aggressive pursuit by lobbyists and lawyers who use campaign contributions, personal appeals at lavish corporate-sponsored conferences, and other means to push them to drop investigations, change policies, negotiate favorable settlements, or pressure federal regulators, an investigation by the *New York Times* has found.

A robust industry of lobbyists and lawyers has blossomed as attorneys general have joined to conduct multistate investigations and pushed into areas as diverse as securities fraud and Internet crimes.

But unlike the lobbying rules covering other elected officials, there are few revolving-door restrictions or disclosure requirements governing state attorneys general, who serve as "the people's lawyers" by protecting consumers and individual citizens.

A result is that the routine lobbying and deal making occur largely out of view. But the extent of the cause and effect is laid bare in the *Times*'s review of more than 6,000 e-mails obtained through open records laws in more than two dozen states, interviews with dozens of participants in cases, and attendance at several conferences where corporate representatives had easy access to attorneys general.

Often, the corporate representative is a former colleague. Four months after leaving office as chief deputy attorney general in Washington State, Brian T. Moran wrote to his replacement on behalf of a client, T-Mobile, which was pressing federal officials to prevent competitors from grabbing too much of the available wireless spectrum.

"As promised when we met the A.G. last week, I am attaching a draft letter for Bob to consider circulating to the other states," he wrote late last year, referring to the attorney general, Bob Ferguson.

A short while later, Mr. Moran wrote again to his replacement, David Horn. "Dave: Anything you can tell me about that letter?" he said.

"Working on it sir," came the answer. "Stay tuned." By January, the letter was issued by the attorney general largely as drafted by the industry lawyers.

The exchange was not unusual. E-mails obtained from more than twenty states reveal a level of lobbying by representatives of private interests that had been more typical with lawmakers than with attorneys general.

"The current and increasing level of the lobbying of attorneys general creates, at the minimum, the appearance of undue influence, and is therefore unseemly," said James E. Tierney, a former attorney general of Maine who now runs a program at Columbia University that studies state attorneys general. "It is undermining the credibility of the office of attorney general."

Private lawyers also have written drafts of legal filings that attorneys general have used almost verbatim. In some cases, they have become an adjunct to the office by providing much of the legal work, including bearing the cost of litigation, in exchange for up to 20 percent of any settlement.

Money gathered through events like the one in February 2013 at the Loews hotel is flooding the political campaigns of attorneys general and flowing to party organizations that can take unlimited corporate contributions and then funnel money to individual candidates. The Republican Attorneys General Association alone has pulled in $11.7 million since January.

It is a self-perpetuating network that includes a group of former attorneys general called SAGE, or the Society of Attorneys General Emeritus, most of whom are now on retainer to corporate clients.

Giant energy producers and service companies like Devon Energy of Oklahoma, the Southern Company of Georgia, and TransCanada have retained their own teams of attorney general specialists, including Andrew P. Miller, a former attorney general of Virginia.

For some companies, the reward seems apparent, according to the documents obtained by the *Times*. In Georgia, the attorney general, after receiving a request from a former attorney general who had become a lobbyist, disregarded written advice from the state's environmental regulators, the e-mails show. In Utah, the attorney general dismissed a case pending against Bank of America over the objections of his staff after secretly meeting with a former attorney general working as a Bank of America lobbyist.

That Bank of America case was cited in July when the two most recent former attorneys general in Utah were charged with granting official favors to donors in exchange for golf getaways, rides on private planes and a luxury houseboat.

While the Utah case is extreme, some participants say even the daily lobbying can corrode public trust.

"An attorney general is entrusted with the power to decide which lawsuits to file and how to settle them, and they have great discretion in their work," said Anthony Johnstone, a former assistant attorney general in Montana. "It's vitally important that people can trust that those judgments are not subject to undue influence because of outside forces. And from what I have seen in recent years, I am concerned and troubled that those forces have intensified."

Several current and former attorneys general say that while they are disappointed by the increased lobbying, they reject the notion that the outside representatives are powerful enough to manipulate the system.

"There is no Mr. Fix-It out there you can hire and get the job done no matter what the merits are," said Attorney General Tom Miller of Iowa, the longest-serving state attorney general in the country, at nineteen years.

Mr. Koster said he regretted the prominence of groups like DAGA and RAGA—as the Democratic and Republican attorneys general associations are known—saying the partisanship and increased emphasis on money had been damaging.

"I wish those two organizations did not exist," Mr. Koster said during an interview at his office in Kansas City, even though the Democratic group has contributed at least $1.4 million to his election campaigns, more than any other source.

But he rejected any suggestion that his office had taken actions as a result of the lobbying, instead blaming mistakes made by his staff for moves that ended up benefiting Dickstein's clients.

Some companies have come grudgingly to the influence game.

Executives from the company that distributes 5-Hour Energy, for example, have contributed more than $280,000 through related corporate entities in the last two years to political funds of attorneys general.

Company executives wrote those checks after the investigation into false claims and deceptive marketing, which initially involved thirty-three states, opened in January 2013. Requests started to come in for contributions, including a phone call this year directly from Mr. Ferguson of Washington State, whose staff was involved in the inquiry.

In a statement after the company was sued by three states in July, the company strongly denied the allegations and compared being solicited for contributions to being pressured to pay "ransom." It asked, "Is it appropriate for an attorney general to ask for money from a company they plan to sue?"

A spokesman for Mr. Ferguson first called the allegation baseless. But after being shown a copy of an invitation to a fundraising event that Mr. Ferguson held in May during a DAGA conference—where 5-Hour Energy was listed as a sponsor—his spokesman confirmed that Mr. Ferguson had made a personal appeal to the company.

Secluded Access

Breakfast was served on a patio overlooking the Pacific Ocean—a buffet of fresh baked goods, made-to-order eggs, lox, and fruit—as the Republican attorneys general, in T-shirts and shorts, assembled at Beach Village at the Del, in Coronado, Calif.

These top law enforcement officials from Alabama, South Carolina, Nebraska, Wisconsin, Indiana, and other states were joined by Ms. Kalani, of Dickstein Shapiro, and representatives from the U.S. Chamber of Commerce, Pfizer, Comcast, and Altria, among other corporate giants.

The group had gathered at the exclusive Beach Village at the Del—where rooms go for as much as $4,500 a night and a special key card is required to enter the private compound—for the most elite event for Republican attorneys general, a gathering of the Edmund Randolph Club (named for the first United States attorney general).

The club, created by the Republican Attorneys General Association, has a $125,000 entry fee—money used to fund the campaigns of attorney general candidates with as much as $1 million and to pay for the hotel bills, airfare, and meals for the attorneys general who attend the events.

As at the Democrats' event, the agenda included panels to discuss emerging legal issues. But at least as important was the opportunity for the lobbyists, corporate executives, and lawyers to nurture relationships with the attorneys general—and to lobby them in this casual and secluded setting. (A reporter from the *Times* attended this event uninvited and, once spotted, was asked to leave.)

The appeals began the moment the law-enforcement officials arrived as gift bags were handed out, including boxes of 5-Hour Energy, wine from a liquor-wholesalers group, and music CDs (Roy Orbison for the adults, the heartthrob Hunter Hayes for their children) from the recording industry.

Andy Abboud, a lobbyist for Las Vegas Sands, which donated $500,000 through its chief executive to the Republican group this year, has been urging attorneys general to join an effort to ban online poker. At breakfast, he approached Attorney General Pam Bondi of Florida.

"What are you going to be doing today?" he asked.

"Sailing," Ms. Bondi replied.

"Great, I want to go sailing, too," Mr. Abboud said, and they agreed to connect later that day.

The increased focus on state attorneys general by corporate interests has a simple explanation: to guard against legal exposure, potentially in the billions of dollars, for corporations that become targets of the state investigations.

It can be traced back two decades, when more than forty state attorneys general joined to challenge the tobacco industry, an inquiry that resulted in a historic $206 billion settlement.

Microsoft became the target of a similar multistate attack, accused of engaging in an anticompetitive scheme by bundling its Internet Explorer with the Windows operating system. Then came the pharmaceutical industry, accused of improperly marketing drugs, and, more recently, the financial services industry, in a case that resulted in a $25 billion settlement in 2012 with the nation's five largest mortgage-servicing companies.

The trend accelerated as attorneys general—particularly Democrats—began hiring outside law firms to conduct investigations and sue corporations on a contingency basis.

The widening scope of their investigations led companies to significantly bolster efforts to influence their actions. John W. Suthers, who has served as Colorado's attorney general for a decade, said he was not surprised by this campaign.

"I don't fault for one second that corporate America is pushing back on what has happened," Mr. Suthers said. "Attorneys general can do more damage in a heartbeat than legislative bodies can. I think it is a matter of self-defense, and I understand it pretty well, although I have got to admit as an old-time prosecutor, it makes me a little queasy."

Republican attorneys general were the first to create a party-based fund-raising group, fourteen years ago. An initial appeal for contributions to corporate lobbyists and lawyers said that public policy was being shaped "via the courthouse rather than the statehouse." It urged corporate lawyers "to round up your clients and come see what RAGA is all about." The U.S. Chamber of Commerce alone has contributed $2.2 million this year to the group, making it the association's biggest donor.

The Democrats at first fought the idea but two years later formed a counterpart.

Dickstein and a handful of other law firms moved to capitalize by offering lobbying as well as legal assistance to deal with attorneys general, whom Dickstein called "the new sheriffs in town."

In an effort to make allies rather than adversaries, Bernard Nash, the head of the attorney general practice at Dickstein and the self-proclaimed "godfather" of the field, tells clients that it is essential to build a personal relationship with important attorneys general, part of what his firm boasts as "connections that count."

"Through their interaction with A.G.s, these individuals will become the 'face' of the company to A.G.s, who are less likely to demagogue companies they know and respect," said a confidential memo that Dickstein sent late last year to one prospective client, Caesars Entertainment.

Executing this strategy means targeting the attorneys general "front office," a reference to the handful of important decision makers.

"Front office interest or lack of interest in an issue can come from an assessment of media reports and potential media scrutiny; advocacy group requests; political benefit or detriment; legislative inquiries; and 'pitches' made by law firms or other professionals in whom the front office has confidence," Dickstein said in the memo pitching business to executives at Caesars that asked the company to pay $35,000 a month, plus expenses, for lobbying and strategic advice, not including any legal work.

Mr. Nash and his team build relationships through dinners at exclusive spots like the Flagler Steakhouse in Palm Beach, Fla., and Brown's Beach House Restaurant in Waimea, Hawaii, during attorneys general conferences, as well as with a constant stream of campaign contributions, totaling at least $730,000 in the last five years.

Dickstein is hardly alone.

Other dinner invitations have come from former attorney general Thurbert E. Baker of Georgia, whose clients have included AT&T and the debt-buyers industry; former attorney general Patrick C. Lynch of Rhode Island, who represents payday lenders, Comcast, and makers of online video games; and former attorney general Rob McKenna of Washington State, who has been retained by Microsoft and T-Mobile.

In several cases, these former officials are clearly acting as lobbyists. Mr. Lynch, who declined several requests for comment, tells prospective clients that he can guide them "through the national network of attorneys general associations and work with them to build relationships," yet the *Times* could find no record that he had registered as a lobbyist in more than two dozen states where he has worked.

State lobbying laws generally require registration when corporations hire someone to influence legislation, but appeals targeting attorneys general are not explicitly covered, even if a company is pushing its agenda.

The documents obtained by the *Times* include dozens of e-mails that Mr. Lynch has sent to attorneys general on behalf of clients. He is also a regular at the attorney general conferences, which include social events like trap shooting, fitness training, and all-terrain-vehicle rides, in addition to cocktail parties and meals.

These conferences also include panels on topics like regulation of oil and natural gas pipelines.

Yet often a seat on these panels is, in effect, for sale. A large donation can secure the right to join a panel or provide an opportunity for a handpicked executive to make a solo presentation to a room full of attorneys general. That is what a top executive from TransCanada, the company behind the Keystone XL pipeline, did at two recent attorneys general meetings in Utah and Colorado.

For the attorneys general, there is a personal benefit, too: Their airfare, meals, and hotel bills at these elite resorts are generally covered, either by the corporate sponsors or state taxpayers.

Ms. Bondi, the Florida attorney general, for example, received nearly $25,000 worth of airfare, hotels, and meals in the past two years just from events sponsored by the Republican Attorneys General Association, state disclosure reports show. That money came indirectly from corporate donors.

She has charged Florida taxpayers nearly $14,000 since 2011 to take additional trips to meetings of the National Association of Attorneys General and the Conference of Western Attorneys General, including travel to Hawaii. Those events were also attended by dozens of lobbyists. Ms. Bondi, in a statement, said the support she had received—directly or through the Republican Attorneys General Association—had not had an impact on any of her actions as attorney general.

But Matthew L. Myers, the president of the nonprofit Campaign for Tobacco-Free Kids, who was on a panel about e-cigarettes at an event in Park City, Utah, was startled by what he saw: lobbyists from regulated industries—financial, energy, alcohol, tobacco, and pharmaceutical companies—socializing with top state law-enforcement officers.

"You play golf with somebody, you are much less likely to see them as a piranha that is trying to devour consumers, even if that is just what they are," said Mr. Myers.

Mr. Tierney, the former Maine attorney general, said that lobbyists were entitled to set up a meeting with the attorneys general in their offices. But to write a check, for as much as $125,000, to gain days' worth of private time with the attorneys general is another matter, he said.

"When you start to connect the actual access to money, and the access involves law-enforcement officials, you have clearly crossed a line," he said. "What is going on is shocking, terrible."

An Ear in Missouri

In Missouri, as in other states, the attorney general's office has provided a springboard to higher office, either to the governor's mansion or the Senate. So even before Mr. Koster was sworn in for his second term, he was being mentioned as a candidate for higher office. And that made him an ideal target for the team at Dickstein.

The Dickstein lawyers have donated to his campaigns, invited him and his chief deputy to be featured speakers at law firm events, hosted Mr. Koster at dinners, and stayed in close contact with his office in e-mails that suggest unusual familiarity.

The relationship seems to have benefited some Dickstein clients.

Pfizer, the New York–based pharmaceutical giant, had hired Dickstein to help settle a case brought by at least twenty states, which accused the company of illegally marketing two of its drugs—Zyvox and Lyrica—for unapproved uses, or making exaggerated claims about their effectiveness.

Instead of participating in the unified investigation with other states—which gives attorneys general greater negotiating power—Mr. Koster's office worked directly with Mr. Nash and Pfizer's assistant general counsel, Markus Green.

Mr. Nash negotiated with Deputy Attorney General Joseph P. Dandurand through a series of e-mails, followed by a visit to Missouri in April 2013.

But both Pfizer and Dickstein had already built a relationship with Mr. Koster. Dickstein had participated in at least four fundraising events for Mr. Koster, with its lawyers and the firm donating $13,500 to his campaigns, records show.

Several of those contributions came after Mr. Nash had invited Mr. Koster to participate in an "executive briefing" at the Park Hyatt for Dickstein's clients. That same day, Mr. Koster held a fund-raising event, taking in contributions from Mr. Nash and other lawyers involved in matters that Mr. Koster would soon be, or already was, investigating, the records show.

Pfizer had directly donated at least $20,000 to Mr. Koster since 2009—more than it gave to any other state attorney general, according to company records. That does not include the $320,000 that Pfizer donated during the same period to the Democratic Attorneys General Association, which in turn has donated to Mr. Koster's campaigns.

Mr. Koster said his office was forced to negotiate directly with Mr. Nash and Pfizer because a staff lawyer missed a deadline to participate in the multistate investigation.

"This was an accident," Mr. Koster said, adding that since he became attorney general in 2009, his office has participated in six cases against Pfizer that brought a total of $26 million to Missouri.

But the e-mails show that just as the negotiations on the 2013 case were intensifying, Mr. Koster's chief deputy received an unusual invitation: Would the attorney general be interested in flying to Chicago to be the keynote speaker at a breakfast that Pfizer was sponsoring for its political action committee?

The topic was "the importance of corporations' building productive relationships with A.G.s," according to an e-mail in March from Dickstein to Mr. Dandurand.

"As you know, these relationships are important to allow A.G.s and corporations to work together to address important public policy issues of concern to both the A.G. and the corporation," the invitation said. "The conference participants also would like to hear how these relationships can help to efficiently address A.G.s' questions or concerns before they escalate into major problems (like multistate investigations or litigation), as well as how they can carry over when A.G.s are elected to higher offices."

Mr. Dandurand worked to accommodate the request.

"Trying now to clear his calendar," Mr. Dandurand wrote back to the Dickstein lawyer, before confirming that Mr. Koster would accept the invitation.

"The folks at Pfizer are very appreciative and excited to hear from the General," J. B. Kelly, a partner at Dickstein, replied.

Five days later—and just before Mr. Koster was scheduled to give the speech—Mr. Dandurand and Mr. Nash met to discuss a settlement in the fraud investigation. They agreed that Pfizer would pay Missouri $750,000—at least $350,000 less than it would have collected if it had been part of the multistate investigation.

"Thank you for the meeting," Mr. Nash wrote to Mr. Dandurand, after the settlement meeting in Missouri. "Pfizer is pleased."

Mr. Koster said Missouri received a smaller payment from Pfizer because the state had less leverage after missing the multistate deadline. Oregon, the other state to negotiate directly with Pfizer on the Zyvox matter, secured a settlement worth $3.4 million—four times what Missouri received—even though Oregon's population is far smaller.

Pfizer was not the only Dickstein client pleased with the firm's representation before Mr. Koster's office.

AT&T was also subject to an investigation by Mr. Koster's office, something that Mr. Nash learned at the conference held at the Loews hotel. And like Ms. Kalani, Mr. Nash pleaded his case directly with Mr. Koster.

Three weeks after the conversation with Mr. Nash, Mr. Koster's office took a step that questioned the legal strategy of a multistate investigation of AT&T's billing practices, e-mail records show. Mr. Koster did not officially back out of the inquiry, and Missouri ultimately benefited from a national settlement announced this month.

But frustrating leaders of the multistate investigation, Mr. Koster decided to join a small group of attorneys general who, to the industry's pleasure, wanted to resolve the matter without subpoenas or the threat of a lawsuit, the e-mails show.

AT&T has been a major campaign contributor to Mr. Koster's political causes, donating more than $27,000 in just the last two years, half before and half after his actions regarding the investigation.

Mr. Koster said the donations had no effect on his actions, adding that he was determined to investigate the company for its deceptive billing practices. With 5-Hour Energy, he added, he pulled out of the investigation because he did not believe it was merited—adding that he personally uses the energy drink.

Yet he said he was angry that his staff had not notified him before joining investigations into these two major companies.

"Its stock price would move at the mere mention of our involvement," Mr. Koster said, referring to AT&T.

Mr. Nash's appeals were not finished.

A month after returning from the Santa Monica meeting, Mr. Koster adopted a new office policy requiring lawyers and managers in his consumer affairs division to get approval from his top aides before opening any investigations involving a publicly traded company or any company with more than ten employees.

Mr. Nash and Lisa A. Rickard, a senior executive from the U.S. Chamber of Commerce, were so pleased with the change that they asked Mr. Koster to give a talk about his new office policy at a meeting of attorneys general in Washington.

"This is going to be titled my Lisa Rickard memorial presentation," Mr. Koster said at the February 2014 meeting. "She was the one who initiated this idea."

The e-mail records also reveal the personal nature of the relationship between Mr. Koster's office and the lawyers at Dickstein.

In an August 2013 exchange, in which the attorney general's office assured Mr. Nash that it would not share potentially damaging information on a Dickstein client with another state attorney general who was investigating the company—saying the documents were considered confidential—the conversation took a sudden turn away from business.

"Let's go bowling sometime," Mr. Dandurand wrote.

"Thanks," Mr. Nash wrote back. "I'd rather eat and drink with you any time, any place."

And an Ear in Florida

The e-mail records show a similarly detailed interaction with the office of Ms. Bondi, the Florida attorney general and a fast-rising star in the Republican Party.

Mr. Nash and his partners worked to help Ms. Bondi further her political ambitions at the same time they were lobbying her office on behalf of companies under investigation by it.

Accretive Health, a Chicago-based hospital-bill-collection company, whose operations in Minnesota had been shut down by the attorney general's office there for abusive collection practices, had turned to Dickstein Shapiro to try to make sure that other states did not follow Minnesota's lead. Mr. Nash contacted Ms. Bondi's chief deputy and urged the office to take no action.

"We persuaded A.G.s not to sue Accretive Health following the filing of a lawsuit by the Minnesota A.G.," Dickstein wrote in a recent marketing brochure.

Bridgepoint Education, a for-profit online school that has been under scrutiny for what Mr. Miller, the Iowa attorney general, called "unconscionable sales practices," turned to Dickstein to set up meetings with Ms. Bondi's staff, to urge her not to join in the inquiries underway in several states. Again, her office decided not to take up the matter, citing the small number of complaints about Bridgepoint it has received.

Dickstein set up a similar meeting for Herbalife, which has been investigated by federal and state authorities for sales practices related to its nutritional shakes and other products. No investigation was opened; again, Ms. Bondi's staff said her office had received few complaints.

Perhaps the greatest victory in Florida for Dickstein relates to a lawsuit filed by Ms. Bondi's predecessor against online reservation companies, including Travelocity and Priceline, which Dickstein then represented, based on allegations that they were conspiring to improperly withhold taxes on hotel rooms booked in the state.

Local officials in Florida were confounded by the fact that the case, which was filed before Ms. Bondi was sworn in, suddenly seemed to come to a halt.

"As our state's highest-ranking law enforcement official, and as the people's attorney, you have the authority to pursue action on behalf of the citizens of Florida," Mayor Rick Kriseman of St. Petersburg, a Democrat, wrote to Ms. Bondi in 2011, while he was a state legislator, estimating that Florida was losing $100 million a year.

Behind the scenes, Dickstein had been working to get the case dropped.

"Thank you so much for chatting with me last week about the online travel site suit," said a January 2012 e-mail to Deputy Attorney General Patricia A. Conners from Christopher M. Tampio, a former lobbyist for the convenience-store industry who was hired to work in Dickstein's attorney general practice, even though he is not a lawyer or a registered lobbyist in Florida.

A year later, a second round of e-mails arrived in Ms. Bondi's office: first, one inviting Ms. Bondi or her top aide to dinner at Ristorante Tosca in Washington, and then one from a Dickstein lawyer pointing out that similar online travel cases had recently been dismissed by Florida judges.

The e-mail records provided to the *Times* show no response to Dickstein, other than a terse "thanks." But two months later, Ms. Bondi's office moved to do what the firm had sought.

"Dismissed before hearing," the state court docket shows as the case was closed in April 2013 even before it was officially taken up by the court.

A spokesman for Ms. Bondi said her office had dropped the matter after concluding, as Dickstein had argued, that state tax law was ambiguous. The office urged the State Legislature to clarify the matter. But several Florida counties have continued to pursue the matter, taking it to the State Supreme Court.

Dickstein also took unusual steps to promote Ms. Bondi's political career.

The firm's lawyers helped arrange a cover article for Ms. Bondi in a magazine called *InsideCounsel*, which is distributed to corporate lawyers, and invited her, as it did Mr. Koster, to appear at an event in Washington that included the firm's clients.

And as with Mr. Koster, the assistance included direct political contributions. Mr. Nash was a sponsor of an elaborate fund-raising event this year in Ms. Bondi's honor at the Mar-a-Lago Club in Palm Beach, owned by Donald J. Trump, which is considered one of the most opulent mansions in the United States.

Ms. Bondi, in a statement, said none of these efforts had affected her decisions.

"My office aggressively protects Floridians from unfair and deceptive business practices, and absolutely no access to me or my staff is going to have any bearing on my efforts to protect Floridians," she said.

The Revolving Door

In at least thirty-one states and in Congress, elected officials are banned from lobbying their former colleagues during a cooling-off period, which is intended to limit their ability to cash in on their contacts. Once they do start to lobby, they are required to register to disclose the work.

But even in states like Georgia, where the law prohibits state officials from registering as lobbyists or engaging in lobbying for one year after leaving office, a former attorney general made appeals almost immediately to his former office.

Mr. Baker, who left his post as the state's attorney general in January 2011, wrote repeatedly that year to the office of his successor, Sam Olens, and to Mr. Olens's chief deputy, who had served in the same role during Mr. Baker's tenure, to ask them to take actions that would benefit AT&T, which he had been hired to represent.

"Hi Thurbert," Jeff Milsteen, Georgia's chief deputy attorney general, replied to one of the e-mails that Mr. Baker sent to him in 2011 as Mr. Baker sought his successor's public support for the proposed merger between T-Mobile and AT&T. "I'll let you know as soon as I can."

The next day, Mr. Milsteen wrote back. "I've talked to Sam," he said, "and he is fine with you adding him to the letter."

A spokesman for Mr. Olens said that he saw nothing wrong with the exchanges because Mr. Baker was acting as a lawyer, not as a lobbyist, and therefore was exempt from the one-year ban—

which covers only lobbying of the legislature or the governor, not the attorney general.

But Mr. Baker declined, when asked by the *Times*, to identify a single legal filing concerning AT&T that he had been involved with. He wrote back to say that this definition of "lawyer" was too narrow.

"Lawyers are advocates," he said.

In Washington State, both Mr. McKenna, the former attorney general, and Mr. Moran, who had been his top deputy, were pressing their former colleagues within months of leaving their jobs last year, on behalf of clients including Microsoft and T-Mobile, e-mails show.

For Mr. McKenna, it was quite a turnaround. He had sued T-Mobile in September 2011 to block its proposed merger with AT&T. Now, as a corporate lawyer, Mr. McKenna was setting up meetings with his successor, Mr. Ferguson, to ask him to intervene with federal officials on T-Mobile's behalf in the inquiry over whether the company was seeking to prevent its competitors from acquiring what it thought was too large a share of the available federal wireless spectrum.

"I write today on behalf of the millions of consumers of wireless and mobile computing services," said a letter, drafted initially by T-Mobile but sent out by Mr. Ferguson in January, although it made no mention of the role played by the company or the former attorney general.

E-mail records show a similar intervention by Mr. McKenna on behalf of Washington State–based Microsoft, with outcomes that brought praise from the corporate executives. "I know that Microsoft was very pleased that you made yourself available," Mr. McKenna wrote to Mr. Ferguson last October. "Thank you again."

Mr. Baker and Mr. McKenna are both regulars at the attorneys general retreats. As former attorneys general, they are also special guests at events of the Society of Attorneys General Emeritus.

They have good company in the SAGE club: More than a dozen of the members are now lawyers and lobbyists for corporations or work at plaintiff's law firms that are seeking to secure commission-based contracts and then sue corporations on a state's behalf.

The schedule of attorney general conferences for the coming year is laid out—after a pause for the elections—with events set for the Fontainebleau resort in Miami Beach, the Four Seasons Hotel at Mandalay Bay in Las Vegas, and the Grand Wailea resort on Maui, among many others. The invitations for corporate sponsorships are already being sent.

Newsweek

An innocuous-looking pharmacy in a strip mall in Framingham, Mass., is the setting for a medical mass murder. In a gripping narrative, the longtime investigative reporter Kurt Eichenwald unwinds the tale of the New England Compounding Center, which seemed to offer promising pain-relief and other drugs to nearby clinics at low prices. But prosecutors would later allege that it fabricated records, cut corners, and ignored laws designed to keep contaminated drugs off the market—with horrific results.

18. Killer Pharmacy

Inside a Medical Mass Murder Case

I t was just another colorless trade show, one of thousands held each year in hotels across the United States. But it was there, at an Embassy Suites in Franklin, Tennessee, that the simple handoff of a business card proved to be the first link in a two-year chain of events that led to the horrific, tortuous deaths of the first victims in a mass killing that trailed from New England to Tennessee, from Michigan to North Carolina.

Health workers packed the hotel for the annual meeting of the Freestanding Ambulatory Surgery Center Association, hoping to network, listen to medical presentations, and meet industry sales-people plying their wares. Among the hundreds wandering about on the second day of the conference—September 24, 2010—was John Notarianni, regional sales manager for the New England Compounding Center (NECC), a Massachusetts pharmacy. Like any good salesman, Notarianni was glad-handing prospects while passing out business cards and advertising material. At some point, he crossed paths with Debra Schamberg, a nurse and facility director with the St. Thomas Outpatient Neurosurgery Center in nearby Nashville.

For a few minutes, Notarianni pitched his company, telling Schamberg about the pharmaceuticals NECC had available, including injectable methylprednisolone acetate, a steroid commonly used for pain management. Since her outpatient center spent much of the workday injecting steroids into hips, joints, and backs, Schamberg was intrigued. She took Notarianni's business card and pamphlets and then went on her way, thinking she may have found a great alternative to the usual pharmacies the outpatient center used.

But NECC wasn't a promising drug supplier—it was a lethal, venomous scourge. This seemingly innocuous pharmacy in a Framingham strip mall was making millions of dollars by cutting corners, fabricating records, and ignoring laws designed to keep contaminated drugs off the market. NECC perpetrated what may be one of the most murderous corporate crimes in U.S. history by pumping out deadly medicines that infected more than 800 people with fungal meningitis in 2012, 64 of whom died.

The outbreak traced to this one pharmacy set off investigations by federal and state health officials, the Justice Department, and Congress. Three months ago, a federal grand jury indicted fourteen people who worked for or were connected to NECC on 131 charges, which included assorted counts of murder, racketeering, fraud, conspiracy, and other alleged crimes.

Despite the scale of the killings and the scope of the investigations, the inside story of the events that led to the lethal outbreak and its discovery is being told for the first time here. *Newsweek*'s examination of the NECC deaths was pieced together from e-mails, order forms, investigators' notes, drug company and court records, and sworn statements of participants, as well as interviews with people connected to the case.

No More Mickey Mouse!

The murderous tale begins with that innocuous meeting between Notarianni and Schamberg, neither of whom was ever charged with wrongdoing and may well have been no more than unsuspecting pawns in a cruel and deadly multi-million-dollar scam.

Like any good salesman, Notarianni called Schamberg every few months after their encounter at the trade show, urging her to purchase the steroids and other drugs sold by his company. "I went back to my manager, and he said he really would like to offer you better to earn your business," Notarianni wrote in an e-mail on May 17, 2011. "What price would we need to give you to gain your business on the [injectable steroids]?"

Notarianni's timing could scarcely have been better. Within a few weeks, Clint Pharmaceuticals, the outpatient center's usual supplier of injectable steroids, boosted its price by $2.46 per 1-milliliter vial of the drug, to $8.95; the cost of sterile manufacturing was climbing and supply was shrinking. Schamberg pushed Clint for a better deal, but no go. So she typed an e-mail to Notarianni on June 11, 2011: "If pricing is still $6.50 [per vial], I am willing to do business with you."

Over the next few months, officials with St. Thomas Outpatient Neurosurgery Center sent orders to NECC. Mario G. Giamei Jr., Notarianni's successor as regional sales manager, took over the account, court records show. Things between NECC and the outpatient center continued to go well until around early 2012, when Giamei, who has not been charged with wrongdoing, dropped by the clinic and told Schamberg a problem had emerged—NECC needed a lot of patient names, and fast.

Unlike a drug manufacturer or wholesaler, NECC was a compounding pharmacy, licensed only to sell medications to fill individual prescriptions. In other words, it wasn't allowed to market drugs in batches to clinics and doctors—even though that was exactly what it was doing. NECC was conducting business like a manufacturer while being regulated as a pharmacy.

NECC began selling large shipments of drugs without prescriptions as early as 2009. That year, some health-care providers who wanted the convenience of having their prescription drugs in stock—which helped them speed up how quickly they could see patients—had complained about NECC's prescription requirements. On September 15, 2010, Barry Cadden, the president and head pharmacist at NECC, sent an e-mail to Robert Ronzio, the national sales manager, regarding a prospective client that was balking at the idea of assembling and providing all the prescription paperwork. Perhaps, Cadden said, NECC didn't need the prescriptions but instead could just attach names to the orders at some point—even after the medications were injected. That way, if regulators checked, they would see every dosage linked to a patient.

"We must connect the patients to the dosage forms at some point in the process to prove that we are not a [manufacturer]," Cadden wrote. "They can follow up each month with a roster of actual patients and we can back-fill."

There were two problems with that plan. First, it was illegal. Second, obtaining patient names from clinics and other medical providers after drugs had been injected was time-consuming. By the following year, some customers were just submitting the names of people on their staff, which Cadden thought was dangerous. "There are better ways to do this," he wrote in a May 2, 2011, e-mail. "Same names all the time makes no sense."

NECC's various schemes to get around the prescription requirement ran from the clever to the absurd. Some customers were exempted from sending names while others provided names that were ridiculous. Big Baby Jesus was listed as having received an injection at a facility in San Marcos, Texas; so were Donald Trump, Calvin Klein, Jimmy Carter, and Hugh Jass. A facility in Lincoln, Nebraska, placed orders for Silver Surfer, Hindsight Man, Octavius, and Burt Reynolds. And orders came in from Elkhart, Indiana, for Filet O'Fish, Squeaky Wheel, Dingo Boney, and Coco Puff.

That kind of silliness stirred up outrage back in Massachusetts. On March 20, 2012, Alla Stepanets, an NECC pharmacist, sent an e-mail to a sales representative complaining about a customer saying that "[the] facility uses bogus patient names that are just ridiculous!" The sales representative replied that "[t]hese are RIDICULOUS." But no matter—Stepanets told the sales representative the order was sent anyway.

By early 2012, St. Thomas Outpatient Neurosurgery Center had been an NECC customer for more than six months but had not yet been told of the need to provide patient names. It was then, according to court documents, that Giamei, the recently appointed regional sales manager, told Schamberg, the clinic's facility director, that the pharmacy needed to start receiving names with the outpatient center's drug orders.

That was impossible, she replied. There was no way to predict at the time of the order which patients would be receiving the drugs. That wouldn't be a problem, Giamei replied—NECC just needed a list of patient names. Schamberg consulted with the medical director, Dr. John Culclasure, and then a receptionist suggested printing out daily patient schedules and submitting those with each NECC order. That idea was put into practice right away, but still, just like at other clinics, employees at St. Thomas couldn't help but have a little fun—one of the patient names they submitted to NECC was Mickey Mouse, although no one at St. Thomas has been charged with wrongdoing.

The use of the cartoon character's name set off more anger at NECC. On May 21, 2012, Cadden, NECC's president, sent a steaming e-mail to Sharon Carter, the director of operations. Carter added to the e-mail, then printed it out and posted it in the office. "A facility can't continuously provide the same roster of names . . . . . unless they are truly treating the exact same patients over and over again!" the e-mail said, with all the ellipses. "All names must resemble 'real' names . . . . no obviously false names! (Mickey Mouse.)"

The Filthy Clean Room

That same day, as NECC executives were fuming about obviously fake names, a horror was unfolding just yards away from them in another part of the company's Framingham offices, one that ultimately would lead to the painful death of scores of patients.

Even as Cadden was typing his angry e-mail, Glenn A. Chin, a supervisory pharmacist at NECC, stepped over a dirty mat into an area known as the Clean Room. According to government charges, Chin prepared a 12.5 liter stock of the injectable steroid methylprednisolone acetate, which was labeled with the lot number 05212012@68. Proper sterilization procedures required exposing the drugs to high-pressure saturated steam at 121 degrees in an autoclave for at least 20 minutes.

Chin used the autoclave for only fifteen minutes and four seconds, almost five minutes short of the minimum time required—a shortfall that, if extended over an eight-hour day, would allow for at least two extra batches of drugs to be produced. And this was not a one-time error; charges filed by the government suggest that shortchanging the autoclave process was standard operating procedure at NECC.

There were plenty of reasons to fear that steaming the compounds for too little time was dangerous. Surface and air sampling for each of the prior twenty weeks had detected contamination in the air and on the surfaces of NECC's Clean Room—and even on the hands of Chin and other staffers. But NECC regularly and blatantly ignored the laws on decontamination, according to the government charges. Chin allegedly instructed subordinates to prioritize faster production over sterilization and ordered them to falsify documents to suggest they had cleaned areas when they had not.

There were other hazards in that Clean Room: a leaky boiler stood in a pool of stagnant water; powder hoods, which are designed to suck microscopic particles out of the room, were covered with dirt and fuzz; and the air intake came from vents that were about thirty yards from a dust-spewing recycling plant.

Still, these sloppy procedures alone did not put the public at risk. Under the law, once the manufacturing of a drug batch was completed, NECC was required to conduct a series of comprehensive tests to make sure the medication was sterile. For compounding pharmacies that follow the rules—making small quantities of drugs to fill individual prescriptions—the tests were hardly burdensome. But by illegally acting as a manufacturer and creating mass batches of drugs—while telling regulators it was mixing one order at a time—NECC had decided to simply ignore the safety check procedures. After all, how could a company comply with rules designed for testing five or six vials of drugs when it was illegally manufacturing thousands for sale all over the country?

And so Lot 05212012@68 was scarcely tested. Its safety was supposed to be verified by a process involving what is called a biological indicator; that rule was ignored. Also, although the entire batch was required by law to be tested for sterility by an independent laboratory, Chin sent only 10 milliliters of drugs in two vials for analysis. On June 5, after the lab found that the first vial tested was sterile, officials at NECC declared the entire lot ready for shipment. In other words, the batch was deemed safe for injection into humans based on the testing of just 0.0004 percent of the total. This would be the equivalent of a grocery store deciding that all of its fruit is fresh after taking a bite of a single apple—except that customers can spot spoiled fruit on their own . . . and a rotten apple won't kill you.

On June 8, NECC started filling orders for injectable steroids from Lot 05212012@68. Over the next seven weeks, 6,500 vials of injectable steroids were shipped to customers around the country. St. Thomas Outpatient Neurosurgery Center's order of 500 vials was filled on June 27, 2012. Unknown to anyone, many of those tiny bottles carried a deadly fungus.

Thirty-three days later, on July 30, Thomas Rybinski, a fifty-six-year-old autoworker from Smyrna, Tennessee, walked into Nashville's St. Thomas Hospital, a building of concrete and tinted glass that resembles a monstrous, ill-formed wedding cake. He took the elevator to the ninth floor and entered the office of St. Thomas Outpatient Neurosurgery Center. He had come for a steroid injection for chronic back pain caused by a degenerative disk disease.

In the exam room, a doctor screwed a needle onto a syringe, inserted it into a 1-milliliter vial of liquid steroid and pulled back the plunger to fill the syringe. Then he carefully slid the needle into Rybinski's back, near his spine. As the doctor slowly pushed down on the plunger, he was unknowingly injecting a microscopic fungus that had been floating unseen inside that contaminated vial.

Knowing He Would Soon Die

Dr. April Pettit was perplexed. The thirty-four-year-old internist at Vanderbilt University Medical Center in Nashville had been reviewing the medical records of Rybinski, and nothing made sense. In late August, Rybinski had come to the hospital complaining of nausea and fatigue. After running blood tests, a spinal tap and a CAT scan, the medical team diagnosed him with a community-acquired meningitis. He was loaded up with antibiotics and sent home.

A week later, Rybinski's family brought him back to Vanderbilt. His speech was incomprehensible. He was agitated and suffering headaches. Another spinal tap was followed by intravenous antibiotics, and again Rybinski seemed on the mend. But on his sixth day at the hospital, he showed signs of seizures, and the right side of his face drooped.

Pettit then had a thought—a long shot. Bacteria were the most frequent cause of meningitis, but could the problem here be a far rarer scenario of fungal meningitis? Pettit told the lab to reexamine Rybinski's spinal fluid, this time checking for fungus. The results came back positive for *Aspergillus fumigatus*, a fungus that looks like a monstrous dandelion and is usually found in decaying organic matter, like a compost heap. Yet somehow it was growing inside a Tennessee autoworker and slowly killing him.

Pettit and other doctors went to Rybinski's family, quizzing them about anything unusual he might have done in the weeks before symptoms started appearing. Someone mentioned the steroid injection at St. Thomas Outpatient Neurosurgery Center for his chronic back pain.

As the doctors worked on piecing the puzzle together, the fungus from NECC was tearing Rybinski apart. Brain tissue died as vessels that bathed the areas in blood became blocked or leaked. On his eleventh day in the hospital, Rybinski abruptly became unresponsive and started shaking his head rhythmically. He was placed on a ventilator, but his brain started to swell. Doctors cut a hole in his skull and set up a catheter to drain excess liquid. He showed signs of an aneurysm and continued to have seizures.

At that same time, in another part of the hospital, seventy-eight-year-old Eddie Lovelace was barely clinging to life. He had suffered what seemed to be a mild stroke but had been expected to recover; then his health started to deteriorate. His family gathered by his hospital bed, knowing he would soon die but not knowing why. His ninety-eight-year-old mother telephoned him to say her goodbyes, telling her son that he was her "dear, sweet boy."

On September 17, 2012—less than a month after his last steroid injection at St. Thomas Outpatient Neurosurgery Center—Eddie Lovelace died. Unknown to his doctors, he had been killed by fungal meningitis. He was the first victim of NECC's heinous crimes, a link that wouldn't be discovered for weeks.

The next day, unaware that a patient at Vanderbilt had just died from the same infection she had discovered in Rybinski, Pettit was still scrambling to deal with his rapidly deteriorating condition. She e-mailed the Tennessee Department of Health on September 18 with a copy of the lab results showing the fungal infection. State officials immediately asked for more information. Then they called St. Thomas Hospital—where the Outpatient Neurosurgery Center is based—and discovered doctors there were treating two other patients suffering from meningitis. Both patients had also received steroid injections.

As health officials in Tennessee scrambled, Giamei, the NECC regional sales manager, dropped by the St. Thomas outpatient center on September 24. According to court records, Schamberg, the facility director, and Culclasure, the medical director, spoke to him about the meningitis outbreak. "This could not possibly be coming from us," Giamei stated confidently, adding that NECC complied with all sterility procedures and had a state-of-the-art facility. Perhaps they should come for a visit to Framingham, he suggested, just to see the quality of the company.

By the next day, September 25, state officials working alongside the U.S. Centers for Disease Control and Prevention (CDC) had identified eight patients with meningitis, all of whom had received steroid shots at the outpatient center. Health officials called NECC to inform it of the investigation and to identify the lot numbers of the steroids linked to the deaths, but NECC executives said there had been no other complaints about these drugs. Within twenty-four hours, state health agents in Massachusetts raided NECC. They were horrified by what they saw. While a few employees were desperately scrubbing the Clean Rooms with bleach, the filthiness of the place could not be covered up. Every lot of NECC steroids suspected of being contaminated was recalled that day.

But it was too late. The next morning, September 27, officials at the CDC received the worst news possible—the outbreak was not limited to Tennessee. State health officials in North Carolina called to report that a patient at High Point Regional Hospital was suffering from meningitis with the same symptoms as the Tennessee patients. The patient, Elwina Shaw, had received a steroid injection a few weeks before at the High Point Surgery Center, a NECC customer.

The day after health officials reported her condition, Shaw suffered a stroke. And less than a day later, Thomas Rybinski, the autoworker whose case first alerted health authorities to the emerging crisis, died at Vanderbilt Hospital.

Dressed and Ready to Go to Jail

The NECC meningitis outbreak sickened and killed patients in twenty states. The worst hit was Michigan, with 264 cases and 19 deaths. Tennessee had the next worst toll, with 153 cases that left 16 people dead. Hundreds of lawsuits were filed—against NECC, its executives, their related companies, the outpatient centers, and the hospitals. NECC filed for bankruptcy in December 2012, and the court issued two rulings enjoining the executives and owners from moving their money. Almost immediately after the first order was handed down, Carla Conigliaro, the majority shareholder of NECC, and her husband, Douglas Conigliaro, transferred $33.3 million to banks in a series of eighteen transactions in violation of the court's instructions, according to the government indictment.

By the fall of 2014, NECC's once-respected executives and pharmacists knew they faced criminal prosecution for a wide range of serious offenses. On September 4, Glenn Chin, the supervising pharmacist, was arrested at Boston's Logan Airport as he prepared to board a flight with his family for Hong Kong. Then, on December 17, federal agents launched a series of predawn raids, arresting fourteen NECC executives, owners, and staffers. Cadden, the company's president, was dressed and waiting when law enforcement officials reached his door; he was expecting them and had climbed out of bed at four a.m. so he would be ready to go when they knocked on his door.

In U.S. District Court in Boston, all fourteen defendants pleaded not guilty to a wide assortment of crimes, including racketeering, fraud, conspiracy, violating federal drug laws, and financial crimes. Only Cadden and Chin have been charged with murder. They face a maximum sentence of life in prison if convicted on all counts.

Milwaukee Journal Sentinel

It sounds harmless: a yellow flavoring agent used in coffee and popcorn. But the industrial liquid, known as diacetyl, has been linked to permanent lung damage in exposed workers. And now it's being used to provide sweet flavors to electronic cigarettes, which are directly inhaled by consumers, including a growing number of adolescents. According to a federal study, e-cigarette use among middle- and high-school students tripled from 2013 to 2014. Scientists at the CDC have shown the danger of inhaling diacetyl, but the government has failed to regulate exposure. Raquel Rutledge tells the story in the *Milwaukee Journal Sentinel* with an understandable sense of urgency.

Raquel Rutledge

19. Gasping for Action

The yellow liquid used to flavor candy, chips, coffee, and e-cigarettes smells and tastes like butter. It's hard to tell from looking at it that it can obliterate your lungs if you breathe it in.

Emanuel Diaz de Leon didn't know it as he poured jugs of the concentration into giant vats at a coffee roasting plant in Tyler, Texas.

Neither did his coworkers, who spent twelve-hour days roasting and grinding the coated beans that would later be sold in grocery stores and restaurants nationwide as hazelnut flavored coffee.

The workers never guessed it even when they noticed they were short of breath, when what they thought were colds and allergies worsened then never went away.

Doctors assumed they had asthma and bronchitis.

It would take a year to learn the truth: Something in that yellow liquid had destroyed their lungs, permanently.

The suspected culprit: diacetyl.

It was the same chemical linked to hundreds of injuries—and at least five deaths—to men and women who worked at popcorn factories and flavoring companies in Wisconsin, Missouri, Illinois, and other states in the last fifteen years.

Many scientists and pulmonologists have known about diacetyl's dangers. Flavoring manufacturers and members of the

National Coffee Association have held executive-level meetings discussing its risks.

And federal regulators tasked with overseeing worker safety in the United States have been well aware of the lung destruction tied to diacetyl.

They have known about it for years.

But the federal government failed to regulate exposure to the chemical.

Every day, men and women across the country clock into jobs roasting and grinding coffee and mixing flavors to satisfy cravings for everything from butterscotch candy to cheese-flavored chips—and unknowingly inhale toxic and potentially fatal fumes.

And now, diacetyl has quietly seeped into other products, this time being inhaled straight into the lungs of a growing number of consumers as they smoke or "vape" e-cigarettes.

As many as 70 percent of sweet-flavored e-cigs contain diacetyl, according to a September 2014 study by the Society for Research on Nicotine and Tobacco.

E-cigarettes are exploding in popularity as the industry markets them as a safer alternative to conventional cigarettes and attracts teens and young adults with flavors such as cherry blast, bubble gum, and chocolate cheesecake.

While the U.S. Food and Drug Administration has given the green light for diacetyl to be eaten in trace amounts, scientists with another branch of the government have deemed inhalation of the chemical to be toxic.

Inhaling the chemical can quickly destroy the lungs, according to more than a dozen studies by scientists, including those from the National Institute of Occupational Health and Safety, or NIOSH, a research arm of the U.S. Centers for Disease Control and Prevention. Some of those studies have assessed the health of people working with diacetyl; others have been conducted on lab animals.

"Diacetyl causes an enormous amount of damage," said Kay Kreiss, a scientist with the agency and one of the lead researchers on the chemical's health risks. As to whether those who smoke e-cigarettes should be concerned, Kreiss had a one-word answer: "Absolutely."

．　　　　．　　　　．

Diacetyl (pronounced die-AS-i-til), also known as butanedione, is found naturally in low concentrations in foods such as butter and beer and is a byproduct of fermentation. It is artificially produced in factories across the country. Cheese makers, bakeries, candy and snack manufacturers all use it to add a buttery flavor to their products. E-cigarette companies add it to their "e-juice" cartridges to enhance vanilla, maple, coconut, and other flavors.

Coffee roasters sometimes add it to flavor coffee. High concentrations of diacetyl also form naturally during coffee roasting.

Whether natural or synthetic, the chemical can destroy the respiratory system when inhaled, according to Takayuki Shibamoto, a professor in the Department of Environmental Toxicology at the University of California, Davis.

"They are exactly the same," Shibamoto said.

What matters most, he said, is the amount and concentration of exposure.

Yet after more than a decade of studies detailing diacetyl's danger, the U.S. Occupational Health and Safety Administration, or OSHA, has failed to issue regulations specifying what a safe level of exposure might be.

．　　　　．　　　　．

Emanuel Diaz de Leon was born in Chicago. He had been living in San Luis Potosi, Mexico, running his family's grocery store business in 2009 when he got tired of drug cartel members extorting money and threatening violence.

He and his wife, Maria Elena, an English teacher at the time, returned to the United States. They moved with their three young children to Tyler, about a hundred miles east of Dallas. Maria Elena's brother lived there.

The family settled in a modest three-bedroom ranch on the southeast side of Tyler, where signs bill the town as "The Rose Capital of the World." Diaz de Leon was thirty-nine at the time. Healthy and active, he immediately set out to find work.

It didn't take long.

Within weeks he was hired at Distant Lands Coffee, an international specialty coffee company headquartered in Renton, Wash. The company employs more than 150 full-time workers in the United States and has farms in Colombia and Costa Rica.

A businessman with a college degree, Diaz de Leon didn't balk at the manual labor. He took pride in loading and unloading giant sacks of coffee from trucks, cleaning floors, and taking out the trash.

In May 2010, he was promoted. He would work in the flavor room earning about ten dollars per hour. His wife remembers his excitement.

"His goal was to show them how capable he was, how he could do more," said Maria Elena. "He did it. He was so happy."

Within eighteen months, Diaz de Leon's lungs were shot. His soccer days were over. He would never again snorkel in the ocean or even sink chest deep into a swimming pool. Walking a flight of stairs will forever be a struggle. A bad cold or respiratory infection could easily kill him. Doctors expect he "will die years before his normally expected lifespan."

"It never crossed my mind that it would be dangerous," Diaz de Leon said of his job.

•   •   •

Diacetyl attacks, inflames, and virtually obliterates the bronchioles, the lung's tiniest airways. As the body tries to heal, scar tissue builds up and further restricts the airways. The disease is called *bronchiolitis obliterans*; the damage, irreversible.

Rats exposed to diacetyl at levels similar to those in popcorn factories suffered major lung injuries, according to a 2001 study by federal scientists. Half died within six hours. Numerous additional animal studies between 2004 and 2012 documented significant damage caused by the chemical.

The *Milwaukee Journal Sentinel* first wrote about diacetyl in 2006 when a young Wisconsin man became ill working in a flavoring factory in Milwaukee and a forty-one-year-old flavor worker near Chicago was diagnosed with *bronchiolitis obliterans*. He had lost 76 percent of his lung capacity.

That year, public health officials from forty-two institutions, including Harvard, Yale, and the Massachusetts Institute of Technology, signed a letter urging the U.S. Department of Labor to adopt a standard limiting workplace exposure to diacetyl. An occupational epidemic was on the horizon, they feared.

Three years earlier, in 2003, NIOSH had advised 4,000 plants nationwide to limit workers' exposure to flavorings such as diacetyl. While the agency does research on occupational safety issues, it has no authority to issue regulations.

That responsibility falls to OSHA, which is part of the Department of Labor. Regulators there first began making the connection between diacetyl and respiratory illness in the early 2000s.

But cases of *bronchiolitis obliterans* had surfaced in food-processing workers years earlier. Two young, previously healthy workers at an Indiana baking company were diagnosed in 1985. The workers, who didn't smoke, had been working at the plant less than a year when their symptoms arose. Diacetyl was among the ingredients used at the bakery

In the 1990s, a handful of employees at a Cincinnati-based flavoring company, Tastemaker, were identified with the illness.

Roy McKay, a pulmonary toxicologist, was hired by Tastemaker after one of the workers, a twenty-nine-year-old woman, died from the disease. McKay's job was to help assess worker health at the plant and improve a respiratory-protection plan for the company, which was later bought by Swiss flavoring giant Givaudan.

In a 2006 court deposition involving injured workers, McKay testified that he faced significant problems trying to help the workers. Company managers restricted his actions, he said.

"I was limited [as] to the type of language and wording I can use to describe the potential respiratory hazard that may exist," McKay said, according to the transcript of his testimony. "I was reminded never to say the word '*bronchiolitis obliterans*' to any of the workers.

"Every day it was like 'God, we could do so much more.' It was frustrating."

Transcripts from depositions of other doctors and consultants hired by the company show Tastemaker required them to sign confidentiality agreements forbidding them to publicly discuss the cases—even at industry conferences—without prior approval.

In the years that followed, clusters of cases continued to surface. In July 2006, the International Brotherhood of Teamsters and the United Food and Commercial Workers International Union petitioned OSHA to adopt a Temporary Emergency Standard for exposure to diacetyl.

"We will not let food processing workers continue to be the canary in the coal mine while waiting for industry to regulate itself," Jackie Nowell, safety and health director of the food workers union, said in a news release at the time.

It took OSHA more than a year to announce it would deny the petition.

In January 2009, three years later, the agency published a notice that it would make a rule on occupational exposure to diacetyl.

Such a ruling could prevent as many as 4,000 cases of diacetyl-related lung disease every year, a draft of the proposal suggested. Agency officials said each case of the disease could cost as much as $1.5 million—considering the illness often leads to permanent disability and sometimes death. The total estimated cost savings if the rule went into effect: $2.3 billion each year.

In March that same year, the National Coffee Association held its annual convention in Boca Raton, Fla. Among the items on the agenda: "Diacetyl—worker safety concern."

A slide presentation told attendees that diacetyl is "formed when coffee is roasted" and that "naturally occurring is not exempt!" from OSHA's proposed rule.

The slides listed Candace Doepker, of J. M. Smucker Co., as the speaker. Doepker did not return phone or e-mail messages for this story.

The presentation said the coffee association's scientific advisory group was helping "ensure companies are aware of issue and considering any risk for workers as well as impact of legislation on company."

Even as Doepker was sounding the alarm, OSHA was backing away. The agency had dropped the matter just days before the coffeemakers convention. There would be no regulation.

The agency had faced objections from small businesses in the dairy, baking, brewing, and wine-making industries. The companies argued that they didn't use enough diacetyl to justify the extra oversight and added costs to improve ventilation, monitor the air, and make other safety improvements.

The American Bakers Association maintained that officials had not established the need for sweeping new rules.

"This data is inadequate to impose the burdensome requirements of an OSHA standard on the entire food manufacturing industry," wrote Theresa Cogswell, president of BakerCogs Inc., and Rasma Zvaners, of the bakers association, in a letter to OSHA officials.

Instead, OSHA issued a Safety and Health Information Bulletin the following year, suggesting ways manufacturers could reduce exposure to the chemical. Such bulletins are advisory in nature.

OSHA also said it would continue to study the issue.

In 2011, the agency created programs designed to draw attention to the dangers of diacetyl by doing more frequent inspections of facilities that used the chemical and beefing up assistance to manufacturers trying to improve worker safety.

At the same time, NIOSH scientists were trying to establish a recommended limit to exposure. That agency held a hearing to get public input on its proposal to limit worker diacetyl exposure to no more than five parts per billion in the air during an eight-hour shift.

More than three years later, the agency has yet to finalize the recommendation.

If eventually approved, that recommendation could be forwarded to OSHA to be used as a basis for a regulation requiring companies to adhere to the rule. OSHA officials said they are "keeping tabs" on NIOSH's research.

"It's just the way OSHA operates and the way rule making is done," said Azita Mashayekhi, an industrial hygienist with the International Brotherhood of Teamsters, which represents 60,000 food-processing workers nationwide and in Canada. "It's cumbersome and difficult to get it done."

"We are frustrated," she said. "We are concerned. We cannot wait for OSHA to do its thing."

But David Michaels, assistant secretary of labor for OSHA, says setting a specific exposure limit for diacetyl isn't the answer. He said companies will simply use substitute chemicals that could be equally or more dangerous—some already are doing so—and the regulatory process would have to start over.

"It's regulatory Whack-A-Mole," Michaels said. "This chemical by chemical approach doesn't work."

Michaels was among the most outspoken advocates of getting diacetyl regulated in 2006 when illnesses began showing up in popcorn workers—before he took the job with OSHA.

At the time, he was a professor of environmental and occupational health at George Washington University and was among the dozens of public health officials to sign the letter calling on the agency to take action.

To address the issue, Michaels has set up a work group—industry and union representatives, safety experts, and others—to create a plan to overhaul OSHA's system for regulating exposure to chemicals in the workplace. The group is taking comments from the public until April 8.

"We need a different system," Michaels said, noting the current one often depends on "proof that people are getting sick, and that's not adequate.

"Diacetyl is a good example of that."

·   ·   ·

James Stocks thought it odd when Emanuel Diaz de Leon showed up in his medical clinic huffing and puffing in December 2011. Diaz de Leon was forty-one, active, and a nonsmoker.

"It just didn't make sense," said Stocks, a pulmonologist at the University of Texas Health Science Center at Tyler. "His chest X-rays and lung function were like that of a seventy-year-old or a fifty-year-old who smoked two packs a day."

Stocks asked Diaz de Leon where he worked and what he did for a living. The answer made him curious. Stocks knew a bit about flavors and had read medical journals and media reports about injuries popcorn workers had sustained from a flavoring chemical. But he hadn't heard of anyone becoming ill working in a coffee-roasting plant.

He asked Diaz de Leon to bring him the company's material-safety data sheets, which list the potential hazards of the ingredients that he worked with every day.

"The moment I saw the word *diacetyl*, I knew," Stocks said.

Stocks said it was fortunate the safety data sheets listed the chemical. Sometimes companies write "proprietary" in an attempt to protect secret recipes.

"They shouldn't be able to hide behind that," he said. "They're supposed to make it easy to identify risk, not to protect flavor profiles like a patent."

Other obstacles could have thwarted the discovery as well. *Bronchiolitis obliterans* is an unusual disease. It's not the first thing doctors think of when a patient has a bad cough or shortness of breath. More common diagnoses are asthma or chronic obstructive pulmonary disease.

"When you hear hoofbeats you usually think horse, not zebra," Stocks said. "If he told me he had been smoking since age ten, I wouldn't have asked for the (safety data sheets).... There may well be a number of people out there doctors aren't catching."

Within months of seeing Diaz de Leon, Stocks identified four other workers at the coffee plant with the same life-threatening illness.

"I'm not sure we should have to wait for people to become as deathly ill as these patients are before we can ban a chemical," Stocks said.

Part V

Financial Follies

Wall Street Journal

The fast-growing world of private equity—the business and buying and selling whole companies for profit—is full of promising young financiers with fancy credentials and loads of ambition. So when the dashing, twenty-something Alexander Chatfield Burns, claiming a Yale degree and pedigree dating to the *Mayflower*, started something called Southport Lane Management and began buying a string of insurance companies, it all seemed plausible enough—even when his firm bought a Caravaggio as an investment. Then he checked himself into Bellevue.

Mark Maremont and
Leslie Scism

20. Young Financier's Insurance Empire Collapses

Alexander Chatfield Burns cut a dashing figure in young New York financial circles.

Still in his midtwenties, he controlled a private-equity firm that owned several insurance companies. He called late-night meetings at a penthouse cigar club and donated the wine for a Guggenheim Museum event from a vineyard he later bought.

Then one day about a year ago, Mr. Burns checked into a mental-health ward at New York's Bellevue Hospital, leaving behind an affidavit describing an unusual series of asset transfers. Soon after, he resigned from his company, Southport Lane Management LLC.

Now, insurance investigators are sifting through the rubble. Delaware regulators say Southport under Mr. Burns siphoned off millions of dollars of mainstream insurance holdings, replacing them with assets that were "illiquid, grossly over-valued or hard to value, worthless, and in some cases non-existent," as the state's insurance commissioner put it in a filing in Delaware Chancery Court.

Among unusual assets that ended up on insurance-company books, which traditionally hold conservative bonds and stocks, were rights to a purported Caravaggio masterpiece.

In all, Mr. Burns, now twenty-eight years old, amassed a business including two U.S. insurance companies, two offshore reinsurers, a brokerage firm, and a web of dealings with other insurers that left him in charge of investing hundreds of millions of dollars in additional assets.

Regulators seized control of the two main insurance companies last April. One in Delaware now is being liquidated while one in Louisiana has been sold. Insurance-company losses total nearly $250 million, based on write-downs taken, while insurers still hold tens of millions of dollars in other questionable assets, according to insurance regulatory filings and court documents.

Louisiana insurance commissioner James Donelon, whose department opened a fraud investigation, said Mr. Burns "apparently is convincing and good at snookering regulators."

Nine months after Mr. Burns's departure, Southport alleged in Delaware Superior Court that he had moved $35 million from regulated insurers to his personal investment vehicle. The company—which is still operating, mainly to help regulators find and recover assets—withdrew the complaint over jurisdictional concerns but said it planned to pursue the claim.

Mr. Burns, in statements sent through his lawyer, called that suit's allegations baseless. He blamed "highly unexpected" events at the insurance companies that he said forced a restructuring of holdings. He said that Southport complied with all relevant laws and that he doesn't face any litigation. Mr. Burns hasn't been accused of wrongdoing in any criminal or civil proceeding.

Aside from his regular compensation, "at no time did I ever, nor will I ever, receive any personal financial benefit from any Southport transaction," Mr. Burns said.

"Unfortunately," he added, "Southport's restructuring, compounded by the timing of my departure, has left ill will among my former colleagues and distortions and exaggerations about my personality and integrity are inevitable." It isn't clear how long Mr. Burns stayed at Bellevue; he later moved to South Carolina.

Southport's acquisitions were part of a wave of new money flowing into the insurance industry after the financial crisis. Private-equity and hedge funds were attracted to the stable business, with its big pools of money available for investment until claims are paid.

The raft of new entrants has raised concerns about the ability of the patchwork of state regulators who oversee the industry to screen out unsuitable owners. "Regulators can't be asleep at the wheel," said Etti Baranoff, who teaches insurance at Virginia Commonwealth University. "Too many non–insurance experts are trying to find their way into this complex business."

Mr. Burns, growing up in Westport, Conn., was a financial prodigy. When he was about thirteen, his mother told Robert N. Gordon, a friend and head of Twenty-First Securities Corp., that her son had determined that a famed options-pricing model "was wrong" and "he had a better idea," Mr. Gordon recalls. The model, called Black-Scholes, had won its authors a Nobel Prize. Mr. Burns's mother, a former Citigroup Inc. executive, declined to comment.

In 2010, at age twenty-three, Mr. Burns launched Southport Lane with several associates, taking majority ownership. It moved into offices on Madison Avenue, decorated with vintage stock certificates, and grew to about twenty-five people.

Many were experienced finance and insurance managers, attracted in part by Mr. Burns's plan to buy small property-and-casualty insurers and invest their surplus assets for better returns.

Associates describe Mr. Burns as sometimes socially awkward but gifted with numbers and at structuring complex transactions. "He wanted to be a superrich guy," said Jeffrey Leach, a former Southport president. "His goal was to build this into a multi-billion-dollar insurance operation."

Mr. Leach and others said they now don't know what to believe about claims Mr. Burns made about his background.

He said he had attended Yale and often wore Yale apparel, and he traced his Chatfield ancestry to the *Mayflower*, according to former associates.

Yale said it has no record he attended. Chatfield is the last name of his stepfather, who married his mother when Mr. Burns was thirteen.

His résumé said Mr. Burns "began his career" at Twenty-First Securities. That firm said he never was an employee, although Mr. Gordon said he "did hang around the trading room a bit when he was a kid."

The résumé also said Mr. Burns had been a "partner and head of structured products at Belstar Group." Belstar said he was a contract employee for four months, with "partner" on his business card, and "we terminated the relationship."

Questions about Yale and his employment were among those on a list sent to Mr. Burns that he didn't address.

For its first insurance acquisition, Southport bought a struggling workers' compensation and general-liability insurer called Dallas National Insurance.

Southport renamed it Freestone Insurance Co. and switched its base to Delaware. From the same seller, Southport acquired a reinsurance company, a firm that assumes risk from others.

There were red flags. Southport paid nothing up front for Freestone but agreed to inject $50 million into it. After the deal closed in March 2013, the insurer's books showed an added $50 million in "Beaconsfield Funding ABS Trust 2011."

The name suggested a fairly standard 2011-vintage security, but entities by that name had been established just four days before the deal closed, Delaware corporate records show. The Beaconsfield securities don't appear in federal regulatory filings.

Freestone's former owner, who kept an economic interest in it, questioned Beaconsfield's value but hasn't received a satisfactory answer about it, according to the former owner's Dallas attorney, Michael Gardner.

Southport then bought an insurance company in Louisiana, paying $25 million up front. It turned out this money came not from Southport but from Freestone and related entities, through "a complex financial structure," according to Louisiana court filings Southport made after Mr. Burns's departure.

In other words, Mr. Burns gained control of the first insurer by putting up an opaque security whose value was quickly questioned, then allegedly used some of this first insurer's resources to buy a second insurance company.

The insurance units agreed to let a Southport subsidiary controlled by Mr. Burns take responsibility for managing their assets.

In New York, associates of Mr. Burns say, he often visited the Grand Havana Room, a members-only cigar club. He purchased tables at charity events, where he was photographed with young women on his arm. On the wall of his Greenwich Village apartment was an Andy Warhol print of Teddy Roosevelt, according to Andrea Johnson, who attended some of the functions with him.

"He liked the better restaurants, the best wines, the best cigars," said Jim McNichols, a former Southport insurance executive.

In 2013, Mr. Burns finished an undergraduate degree at Columbia University's school for returning and nontraditional students and was lauded by the university for donating $50,000 for veterans' education.

Before Southport's first insurance-company purchase had closed, he arranged for a Southport entity to buy a painting, purportedly by Caravaggio, titled *David in the Act of Picking up Goliath's Severed Head*, according to Delaware court filings. The painting, nearly identical to a Caravaggio in Madrid's Prado museum, would later play a role in the asset swaps.

The filings show Southport agreed to pay $40 million but put down just $1.5 million, with the rest due more than five years later.

Though it was deemed a likely Caravaggio by a now-deceased Italian art expert, three auction houses have said in the past it was probably a copy painted long ago, according to filings in a Florida court case involving a trust that had owned the painting.

Southport had some impressive names on its insurers' boards, including four former state insurance commissioners. Bill Richardson, the former New Mexico governor and U.S. energy secretary, became chairman of Southport's Freestone Insurance.

A spokeswoman for Mr. Richardson said he was "unaware of these diversions" of assets during his six months on the board and participated in a meeting at which directors decided to notify regulators of Freestone's problems.

Mr. Burns had ties to Gov. Nikki Haley of South Carolina, home to two insurers for which a Southport company managed certain assets. Mr. Burns hosted a campaign fundraising lunch for Ms. Haley at Southport's New York offices in 2013 that her office says raised $26,500. Most came from Mr. Burns and Southport entities, campaign-finance records show.

A spokesman for Ms. Haley said she and Mr. Burns didn't discuss state business at the fund-raiser, and he never sought help with insurance matters during the several times they met.

Mr. Burns said, "None of my contributions have ever been improper nor have any been made with any ulterior motive."

Not long after Southport gained control of its two main insurers, regulatory filings show, it began selling millions of dollars of their conventional stock and bond investments. These were replaced with investments that appeared to be mainstream but that, according to court testimony in Delaware, often turned out to be anything but.

Freestone's then-CEO, H. Marcus Carter Jr., confronted Mr. Burns about the shifting asset mix in January 2014, according to Michael Pickens, a former Arkansas insurance commissioner who served on Freestone's board. Mr. Burns gave assurances all would be well, said a person familiar with the matter.

On January 31, 2014, the start of Super Bowl weekend, Mr. Burns left Southport offices and shortly thereafter checked himself into Bellevue. Days later, Ms. Johnson said, he texted her, saying, "I'm at the hospital. I had a nervous breakdown. Everything's fine." She said she visited him there.

"We were all just absolutely shocked," said Jamie Sahara, then a Southport reinsurance executive. "How did he completely disappear on us?"

Mr. Burns left behind a notarized affidavit, reviewed by the *Wall Street Journal*, taking sole responsibility for a frenzy of asset swaps at the Delaware and Louisiana insurance companies about three weeks earlier.

In the affidavit, he cited a client's complaint that a Southport-managed portfolio contained investments for which there was no active market. Mr. Burns ordered the "illiquid portfolio" placed in the accounts of Southport's insurance companies, he wrote.

Mr. Pickens, the Freestone director, said board members were stunned when their CEO briefed them about unusual investments they now held.

As for Mr. Burns's hospitalization, Mr. Pickens said he thought "it was probably a ruse to keep his butt out of jail." Mr. Burns didn't respond to questions about his hospitalization.

Directors of Freestone and another insurer hired a law firm to investigate and alerted regulators.

A report by valuation adviser Duff and Phelps—commissioned by the law firm and placed into Delaware court records last month after legal intervention by the *Journal*—provides the most comprehensive public record of what happened.

Some money was used for private-equity investing, Duff and Phelps said. It said it couldn't readily account for much of the rest.

A $25 million preferred-stock investment in an offshore insurer was "worthless," the report said, in part because ownership was never transferred to Freestone.

Documents showed that $100 million from Freestone and other Southport-controlled insurers had been invested in a telecom startup, but there was no sign that much cash changed hands, Duff and Phelps said. "Where the hundred million dollars went, we don't know," the report's author, Jerome M. Arcy, testified in Delaware Chancery Court. Mr. Arcy has left the firm and declined to comment.

As for the purported Caravaggio, Duff and Phelps said $128 million, part of it Freestone's money, had been funneled into entities that owned rights to the painting. The entities would have value only if the artwork was sold for more than the $38.5 million still owed to the seller.

Freestone wrote down its assets by about $136 million after receiving the Duff and Phelps report, becoming insolvent. That still left it with $70 million in hard-to-value holdings on its books. Delaware moved last July to liquidate the company.

"We're still determining where the money went," said James J. Black III, an attorney for Freestone's receiver. He said receivers in Delaware and elsewhere are pursuing Mr. Burns "for his conduct," without elaborating.

Mr. Burns blamed Freestone's insolvency on losses dating to before his firm acquired the company that weren't discovered until later.

One of the South Carolina insurers for which a Southport company managed trust money booked a $113 million loss from it in last year's third quarter. Two other insurers that Southport either owned or managed money for also had about $40 million face value of illiquid assets.

Mr. Burns moved to an apartment in a renovated historic building in downtown Charleston, S.C. Last fall he purchased land at Brays Island Plantation, an exclusive golf, equestrian, and bird-hunting resort about sixty miles away.

Bloomberg

Investing in penny stocks is a mug's game. The tiny, thinly traded companies are susceptible to manipulation and fraud. But Josh Sason, a twenty-seven-year-old aspiring rock musician turned financier, has come upon a can't-miss strategy: lending money to desperate companies on terms that guarantee him a profit. Most companies will never be able to pay the money back, but when the collateral is shares in the company at below-market prices, that doesn't matter. Zeke Faux's profile shines a light on a kind of predatory corporate lending known as "death-spiral financing."

Zeke Faux

21. This Twenty-Seven-Year-Old Made Millions Riding the Death Spirals of Penny Stocks

Two thousand people cheered as Joshua Sason walked up to a boxing ring at an arena in Providence late last year. He trailed the actor Miles Teller, and the crowd was made up of extras—they were shooting a boxing movie, directed by the guy who made *Boiler Room*. Sason got to make a cameo in the fighter's entourage because he's producing the movie with Martin Scorsese and put up the budget. He's twenty-seven years old.

After the December shoot, Sason took a Christmas vacation in Malaysia with his lingerie-model girlfriend, Rachel Marie Thomas. He checked on the renovation of his Tribeca penthouse. And he hit a recording studio in London to help mix an album by an Israeli actress and singer he's signed for his company, Magna, which he describes as a global investment firm.

Six years ago, Sason was living in his parents' house on Long Island, doing clerical work for a debt-collection law firm, and dreaming of becoming a pop star. Then a family friend showed him a trick that seems to have earned him millions in the stock market. He won't say exactly what he does or how much he's made, but regulatory filings by dozens of companies show that Magna has invested more than $200 million since 2012.

Sason, who has full sleeves of tattoos he covers with tailored three-piece suits, calls himself a self-taught value investor. He has about thirty employees in trading, venture capital, music, and film. "I'm not going to give away the details of how we do what we do," he says in a January interview at his sixteenth-floor office in Manhattan's financial district. "We create businesses, and we invest."

Actually, it's a little more complicated than that. What Sason discovered is a way to get shares in desperate and broke companies at big discounts by lending them money. Magna has done deals with at least eighty companies. Of those, the stocks of seventy-one have gone down since the investment. He can still turn a profit because the terms of the deals allow him to turn debt into equity at a fixed discount. No matter where the stock is trading, he gets it for less.

Magna functions as a pawnshop for penny stocks—shares of obscure ventures that change hands far from the rules of the New York Stock Exchange. His customers have included a would-be Chilean copper miner, an inventor of thought-controlled phones, and at least two executives later busted for fraud. They come to Sason to trade a lot of their stock for a little bit of money. Often they're aware the deal is likely to be bad for their shareholders.

If the share price goes lower before Magna can unload its investment, the companies have to give up even more stock, all but eliminating the risk for Sason. Critics call it "death-spiral financing" because it drives stocks into the ground. Others in the field say they sometimes make double, triple, or even ten times their investment in just a few months.

The business is legal, but the loopholes in securities law it exploits are too sketchy for most of the Ivy League types at banks and hedge funds. At least six other lenders of last resort to penny-stock companies have been sued by the Securities and Exchange

Commission for breaking the rules around dumping shares or other violations. One was arrested by the FBI. It's worked out better for Sason, who hasn't had any issues with the authorities. He's using death-spiral profits to diversify Magna and turn himself into an entertainment mogul.

·   ·   ·

The son of an Israeli immigrant who works as a contractor, Sason grew up in Plainview, a middle-class Long Island suburb about an hour east of Manhattan, in a beige ranch-style house near the Seaford–Oyster Bay Expressway. When he was ten or eleven he started a rock band called The Descent with some neighborhood kids. They did Blink-182 covers, and he sang and played drums, guitar, and keyboards.

Sason built a recording studio in his parents' basement and started writing music for the band. The Descent got pretty good. Around sophomore year, someone got their music in front of Trevor Pryce, a 260-pound defensive end for the Denver Broncos who invested in music as a sideline. He flew to Long Island to sign them to his record label—but first he had to sit down with their concerned parents. "I was in the living room with five Jewish families surrounding me asking me about calculus," he says. "It was hilarious." Pryce gave Sason and his bandmates $5,000 each, and they started to dress the part of rock stars at school, according to Chris Antonelli, a band member. "We called it Rock Star Fridays," Antonelli says. "I'd wear my grandmother's mink coat and sunglasses, and Josh would wear a boa."

The Descent played showcases for executives from major labels, but the other kids Sason and Antonelli recruited weren't very good. "They botched it beyond belief," Pryce says.

"It was a big letdown," Antonelli says. "There was a lot of anticipation that we were going to be the Next Big Thing, and it didn't happen."

Sason enrolled at nearby Hofstra University and lived at home. A second band, Vibes, was less successful, playing its biggest shows at Temple Beth Am in Merrick, N.Y. Bandmate Michael Morgan says Sason was eager for another shot at the big time. "When you're signed to a record label and you're in high school, your perception of success has to change," Morgan says. "You're like, 'OK, that's possible. What else? What's next?'"

Sason got a job making deliveries in his black Mustang for an Asian restaurant then did filing for the debt-collection firm. Morgan says they worked out together every day at a Jewish community center—where kids now play basketball in the Joshua A. Sason Gymnasium, renamed in 2013 after a donation.

In an entrepreneurship class at Hofstra, where he was a member of the class of 2009, Sason came up with a plan to import sand from Israel and sell it as a collectible called "Sand from the Holy Land." He liked the 2006 Oprah-endorsed documentary *The Secret*, based on a self-help book about the power of positive thinking. Another friend says Sason still talks about his belief in the book's "law of attraction"—how you can achieve anything you want by imagining that it will come true.

The way Sason tells his story, that's pretty much what happened to him. He says he was on vacation with his family in Puerto Rico when he read *The Intelligent Investor*, the 1949 book by Benjamin Graham that Warren Buffett cites as an inspiration. "It was pretty much a life-changing moment for me," Sason says. "I read it once. The second time I read it, I went through and highlighted it. The highlights became a guideline for me to write my own interpretation."

Sason says he doubled his bar mitzvah money on blue-chip stocks in 2009. "I realized I had maybe a little bit of a knack for how investing works," he says. He borrowed his mother's retirement savings, took a "low six-figure" loan from a friend of the family, and started Magna from his bedroom. The business grew,

Sason says, as word spread about how Magna could finance small companies.

"It was a gradual and progressive growth," he said in the January interview. "There wasn't anything in particular that I would recall from back in the day, to be honest with you."

.   .   .

I still couldn't understand how a wannabe musician from Long Island had become a millionaire investor virtually overnight. I'd found a 2012 lawsuit in which a financier named Yossef Kahlon accused Sason of copying his business model, but the only thing Sason would say about him is that they hadn't spoken in years.

There's little else online about Kahlon, and his number is unlisted. His address is on the lawsuit, though, so I drive to his house in Great Neck, N.Y., a wealthy town on Long Island's north shore. A white Range Rover is parked in the semicircular driveway outside the brick colonial mansion, which was listed for sale last year for $6.3 million. Dance music thumps from inside. A slim man with gelled black hair and gray stubble answers the door and says Kahlon isn't home.

An e-mail arrives the next day. "My name is Yossi Kahlon," it says. "I heard you are looking for me." We arrange to meet at a steakhouse in Manhattan, and at the appointed time, the man with the gelled black hair walks up. It was Kahlon after all. "Nice to meet you again," he says. Then he pulls out a wad of tens and hundreds to pay for a Tanqueray and tonic and tells the story of how he met and mentored Josh Sason.

Kahlon, forty-eight, is an Israeli immigrant, too. After arriving in Queens in 1989 and driving for a taxi service, he built a small fortune by getting in early on arcade games and financing car dealerships. He hired Sason's father to work on his house and soon befriended the family, inviting them over for holidays. One

Passover, when Josh won the traditional game of hide-the-matzoh, which usually comes with a prize of $1 or $10, Kahlon says he gave the kid $1,000.

Around 2009, Kahlon heard the Sasons were having financial issues. He told the elder Sason he could help. "I said, 'Bring your son here, I'll teach him to make money,'" says Kahlon, who by then was in the penny-stock business.

The market for penny stocks can be traced back to the scrum of brokers who used to trade shares that weren't welcome on the New York Stock Exchange. A 1920 article in *Munsey's* magazine called them "a close-packed mass of creatures apparently human" and described the auctioning of shares in a puppy.

Penny stocks exist so that, say, an oil wildcatter with a hunch he's about to drill a gusher can raise the money he needs without the hassle of listing on an exchange. They feed a desire for a hot tip that could double or triple. It's a disreputable corner of the market. Many listings are bogus. Most are, at best, just a guy with an idea, and often that idea is to raise some money so he can pay himself a fat salary. Other listings are real businesses that have been dropped from the big exchanges because they're on the verge of failure.

Kahlon paid brokers to scour the market for penny stocks with high trading volume, then call the companies to see if they wanted to issue new stock. These struggling companies can't sell new shares to the public the usual way, by enlisting a proper investment bank, because it's too expensive and the offerings too tiny. But they can sell to private investors such as Kahlon. They gave him steep discounts, and he'd sell the shares into the public market right away, often doubling his money as everyone else's shares were diluted. There are laws against doing this, but Kahlon thought he spotted an exception in Texas. He incorporated his company there, while operating from New York.

Kahlon says he showed Sason how to trade like him—and then cut off contact so that no one could accuse them of conspiring. "I'll teach you the business, but the minute you open, we can't talk anymore," he said to Sason. "I don't have any friends in this business." Texas corporate records show Sason incorporated Magna Group in the state in 2010, using the same mail drop as Kahlon.

Once Magna got going, Sason's younger brother, Ari, dropped out of the University at Buffalo and started working with him in their parents' home. They pulled a sewing machine table out of the garage and set it up in Sason's bedroom for Ari. They quickly made enough money to move to a suite at 5 Hanover Square in Manhattan and hired a team of "finders" to identify targets.

"They had at least two guys pretty much cold-calling corporations they would look up on the Internet," says John Perez, who worked for Magna for a few months in 2012 as a trading assistant. "The other two guys worked on the deals." One of Sason's salesmen, Ari Morris, made up the alias "Michael Goldberg" to use for himself on the phone. Magna's website listed Goldberg as "director of structured investments" in 2012. Clients say he sounded nice.

Magna wasn't the only group calling. Executives of penny companies say that when their stock has a high trading volume, they get bombarded by young salesmen and washed-up bankers asking if they need cash—and often they say yes.

That activity caught the attention of the SEC. In the summer of 2012, the agency filed separate lawsuits against Kahlon and another penny-stock financier, saying their clever Texas loophole in fact wasn't. The SEC said Kahlon made $7.7 million buying penny stocks at deep discounts and dumping them on the public. Kahlon says he did nothing wrong; the case is still pending.

Kahlon closed down his fund. He hoped his former student would help with legal costs. Sason didn't, and Kahlon says he felt slighted—not given enough credit or respect for bringing Sason in on the game. Kahlon sued Sason, alleging that he damaged a relationship with a broker; a judge dismissed the case.

When I ask Sason about Kahlon's story, he says it isn't true. "Nobody showed me the business," he writes in an e-mail. While his family friend's success inspired him to look into penny stocks, he says Magna's deals aren't like Kahlon's, the shared mail drop was a coincidence, and he never got a $1,000 Passover prize.

None of the SEC actions mentioned Magna, and Sason has never been in trouble with the agency. Almost all of the regulatory filings by Magna's clients show deals that are more intricately constructed than Kahlon's.

•　　　•　　　•

Paul Riss's deal with Magna in July 2011 was typical. The New York entrepreneur's company, Pervasip, was developing a communications app to compete with Skype, but it was down to its last $100,000, barely enough to last a month at the rate the company was losing money. When Magna's "Michael Goldberg" called offering cash, he didn't even ask to look at the app, Riss says. "All they care about is the liquidity of the stock," he says. "They want to see how many dollars are trading a month."

On the surface, the $75,000 loan Magna offered seemed all right. It was in the form of an "8 percent convertible promissory note," meaning it asked for an 8 percent return and gave Sason the right to convert it into stock. The fine print explained that if Pervasip didn't pay back the money within six months, the lender could convert at a 45 percent discount to the market price. So, no matter where Pervasip's stock was trading, the company had to give Magna shares that were worth more than $136,000—an 82 percent return in just six months. Essentially, Magna locked in a fixed return.

The lower the shares went, the more Pervasip had to give up so Magna could get its money. The only risk Magna took is that no one would buy Pervasip's stock at any price. "Unfortunately, that's about the only money available," Riss says.

Pervasip didn't repay, and gave the discounted shares to Magna in January 2012. Riss says he doesn't have records that show just how much Magna made. After bouncing up to three cents for a bit, Pervasip now trades for nine-thousandths of a penny. Riss says he still gets calls from lenders like Magna offering more money.

An analysis of eighty public filings shows that a company that does a deal with Magna sees its shares plummet 55 percent over the next year, on average. Most never recover and wind up trading for thousandths of a penny or less. Sason says that's not Magna's fault.

"I want to help the company, I really do," he says. "We never, ever make an investment where we knew our activity in the marketplace would potentially decrease the value of the company. There would be no benefit for us."

Sason bought his penthouse in Tribeca for $4.2 million in January 2013. At some point he upgraded from the Mustang to a $200,000 two-door Mercedes-Benz, his high school buddy Antonelli says. He started hanging out at Lavo, a bottle-service club in midtown Manhattan popular with celebrities. "He's there like Thursday, Friday, Saturday, Sunday," says Antonelli, "holding court with all the beautiful waitresses."

Magna's biggest score came in 2013, when it helped a Greek shipping company called Newlead avoid bankruptcy. The shipper, which once owned fifteen tankers and container ships, was down to four vessels. It had enough cash to cover about a month of operating losses.

The deal had a twist. Instead of giving Newlead a loan, Magna paid some of Newlead's lenders for the right to collect its old debts. After Magna sued Newlead to collect, the two companies quickly filed a settlement where Newlead agreed to give Magna discounted stock that it could sell right away. A New York state judge signed off on the arrangement.

Sason said in an affidavit filed in the case that Magna, together with an unnamed partner, paid off $45 million of debt and received stock that it sold for $62 million—a $17 million profit before expenses.

The financing technique is legal as long as the debts that are being paid off are real and the financier doesn't kick any of the money from the stock sale back to the company, according to Mark Lefkowitz, another penny-stock financier who pleaded guilty in 2012 to breaking those rules. "The bottom line is, it's supposed to be used for bona fide conversions of debt to equity," says Lefkowitz, who's cooperating with the FBI. He cut an interview off quickly, saying he was due to be sentenced soon and needed to check with his FBI handler before talking.

The financing may have saved Newlead as a company—it avoided bankruptcy and bought new tankers—but it ruined it as a stock. The company has been so thoroughly pillaged that if you'd bought $3 million of shares in March 2013, just before Magna invested, you'd be left with a dime. Adjusted for reverse splits, the shares trade for 20 billionths of a penny—$0.0000000002. Newlead did not respond to a request for comment.

It's hard to say exactly how much Magna has profited since 2010. Sason says Magna has done $200 million of deals, confirming calculations from clients' regulatory filings, though some were with partners. He says the majority of the company's equity is his, with the rest owned by his employees.

Rivals in the business say that penny-stock financiers typically demand at least a 50 percent return, a figure supported by SEC findings. Sason says he can count the deals that backfired "on one hand." By any reasonable estimate, his returns would top almost any hedge fund. "The returns are healthy," he says. "We're not getting into any business or any strategy not to be profitable."

Since the Newlead score, Magna has been diversifying. Sason started a "ventures" division, which invested in PledgeMusic, a London-based website that lets musicians sell albums they're working on in advance, and Mainz, a sort of high-end receptionist-outsourcing company. He hired a former executive at Madonna's record label to help him run his entertainment division.

Sason got into filmmaking through Chad Verdi, who started producing movies in 2011 after financing penny-stock companies that failed at nuclear-waste cleanup and military chemical detection. Verdi was producing straight-to-video-on-demand movies when he met Sason. After Sason invested in a romantic comedy, Verdi took him to meet Martin Scorsese at his office in New York's theater district. The director mentioned a documentary he was making about the *New York Review of Books*. "We ended up putting some finishing funds into that, and we were executive producers on that project," Sason says.

Then Verdi approached Sason about funding a biopic—the story of Vinny Pazienza, a boxer from Rhode Island who came back to win three titles after breaking his neck in a car crash. Scorsese had come on as a producer for the film, called *Bleed for This*. Also on board was *Boiler Room* director Ben Younger. *Boiler Room* is a classic about penny-stock swindles, but Younger didn't see any connection.

"We were looking for financing," says Younger, "and Joshua came in and saved the day." Younger says it wasn't Sason's idea to make a cameo in the movie. "He's an artist, so he's respectful of other artists' process." Younger and Verdi say the budget for *Bleed for This* is $6 million; Sason says it's lower but won't give a number.

Sason is preparing to move Magna to 40 Wall St., a tower down the block from the New York Stock Exchange, where he signed a lease for two full floors. He says trading stocks is now just one-twelfth of Magna's business.

"I'm really trying to build a company and build an organization that's here for the next 1,000 years," Sason says. "I want to build something powerful and something meaningful and lasting."

Bloomberg

Over the years, Congress has tried to close the loophole that allows companies to shift their headquarters overseas to avoid paying taxes, a maneuver known as corporate "inversion." President Obama has called the practice "unpatriotic," but never underestimate the ingenuity of American tax lawyers. In a story that won Bloomberg News its first Pulitzer Prize, Zachary Mider explores the pioneers—if that's the right word—of the practice in a fascinating tale involving a defense contractor, a Chopin-playing tax expert, a furious Admiral Hyman Rickover, and a hilarious operetta made to celebrate the tax scheme.

22. The Greatest Tax Story Ever Told

The only operetta ever written about Subpart F of the Internal Revenue Code made its debut on a rainy Sunday evening in May 1990, in a Fifth Avenue apartment overlooking Central Park. In bow ties and spring blazers, partners of the law firm of Davis Polk & Wardwell dined on lobster prepared by a Milanese chef. Then everyone gathered around a piano, and a pair of professional opera singers, joined by the few Davis Polk men who could carry a tune, performed what sounded like a collaboration of Gilbert and Sullivan and Ernst and Young.

The thirteen-minute operetta, *Charlie's Lament*, told how the party's host, John Carroll Jr., invented a whole category of corporate tax avoidance and successfully defended it in a fight with the Internal Revenue Service. The lawyers sang:

The Feds may be screaming,
But we all are beaming
'Cause we'll never pay taxes,
We'll never pay taxes,
Never pay taxes again!

The first corporate "inversion," as Carroll's maneuver came to be known, was obscure then and is all but forgotten now. Yet at least forty-five companies have followed the lead of Carroll's client, New Orleans–based construction company McDermott International, and shifted their legal addresses to low-tax foreign nations. Total corporate savings so far: at least $9.8 billion—money that otherwise would have gone to the U.S. government.

This year, inversions have received more attention than ever as well-known companies such as Burger King and Pfizer announced plans to change their addresses. (Pfizer didn't follow through.) In July, President Obama called the practice an "unpatriotic tax loophole" and urged Congress to put a stop to it. In September, the Department of the Treasury tightened regulations to discourage the deals. "My attitude is, I don't care if it's legal," Obama said in July. "It's wrong."

If history is any guide, the stiffer regulations won't stop the exodus. Ever since the McDermott deal, inversions have been the subject of legions of congressional hearings, bills, and regulations, yet companies continue to find ways to circumvent them and escape the U.S. tax system.

> John Patrick Carroll,
> You're the man for me.
> You have a firm that is first-rate.
> You have the skill to solve
> this tax quandary
> (Although you come in
> to work very late).

·   ·   ·

Around the Manhattan offices of Davis Polk, Carroll was known as a wit and a curmudgeon. To keep fellow lawyers on their toes, he slipped nonsense words, such as "phlaminimony," into legal documents. He always seemed to do his best work in the middle of the night. His office was a mess. He didn't own a television set.

If someone asked how he was doing, he'd reply, "They haven't caught me yet."

A Brooklyn native who served in the marine corps in China during World War II, Carroll attended Cornell University and Harvard Law School. He worked at the IRS before joining Davis Polk in 1957, when the firm still required its men—there were no women partners as yet—to wear hats. A committed liberal, he was one of the few members of his firm to oppose the war in Vietnam. He once considered leaving the practice to work for antiwar candidate George McGovern's 1972 presidential campaign. "He would stop by my office and say, 'Let's go commit lunch.' He had all sorts of wonderfully fictional phrases for noncriminal crimes, like 'mopery in the second degree,'" says M. Carr Ferguson, a colleague. "I simply adored him."

Carroll proved to be a brilliant pioneer in corporate law. He helped open the North Sea to oil exploration and invented a financial instrument known as the currency swap, now a $2-trillion-a-day market. Carroll was modest about that achievement. When a book credited him with inventing the swaps, he penned a tongue-in-cheek letter explaining that, although he attended the London brainstorming sessions where the idea was hatched, he was merely "a foreigner who attended most meetings principally for beer and free lunch." He named five others who he said deserved more credit.

Around 1980, Carroll got a call from a client: Charles Kraus, the tax director at McDermott, a construction and engineering giant with a thriving business in building offshore oil rigs. Throughout the 1970s, high oil prices, helped by the Arab oil embargo and the revolution in Iran, had kept its tugboat crews and welders busy from Indonesia to Saudi Arabia. McDermott was the biggest company in Louisiana's booming oil-services industry. It occupied half of a downtown skyscraper and, at its peak, employed more than 40,000 people around the world.

My name's Charlie. Here's my problem:
Our subsidiary
Pays too much in bloody taxes.
It's dying fiscally.

As Kraus explained to Carroll, McDermott's profits had created a big tax problem. Most of the income had been earned
abroad, and the parent company in New Orleans couldn't touch
it without first paying U.S. taxes on it—at a rate of as much as 46
percent. The earnings were piling up in Treasury bonds offshore.
When they came back, the total bill would be about $220
million.

John, be a hero; cut our
tax down to zero,
Because if your plan's not inspired,
Next month we may all be fired!

After months of kicking around ideas, Kraus and Carroll hit
upon an elegant but untested solution: Simply flip the company
structure, so its main foreign subsidiary, incorporated in Panama,
becomes the parent. Just like that, all those offshore profits would
slip out from under the U.S. corporate tax system. Carroll nick-
named it the Panama Scoot. There was something screwy about
the plan, like a daughter legally adopting her own mother, and
the details were staggeringly complicated, involving share swaps,
dividends, and debt guarantees. But Kraus and Carroll were convinced it would work.

Kraus, now eighty-five, is a slight man who relishes the arcana
of tax accounting. He once dreamt of becoming a concert pianist,
and he used to spend his free time rehearsing Chopin's polonaises
on his baby grand piano. During an interview in his pink-brick
home in the Louisiana woods, he recalls using a different name
for the novel deal he helped put together. "We called it the Flip

Flop," he says, laughing, his hands folded behind his head. "There was a loophole in the law, and we capitalized on it legitimately."

Kraus's boss, John Lynott, McDermott's chief financial officer at the time, says he sometimes puzzled over Carroll's motivations. "It was always an enigma to me," Lynott says. "We knew this guy was a Democrat, and yet he would take on the government in a New York minute over a tax issue. There was nothing liberal about his thinking as far as the tax code was concerned."

> John's really flipped this time.
> He's surely lost his mind.
> If we should do it,
> I know we shall rue it.
> We'll pay interest, penalties and fines.

The McDermott team knew the deal would face resistance. Shareholders needed to approve the transaction, requiring a public announcement and a filing with the Securities and Exchange Commission, which would inevitably forward the papers to the IRS.

Then there was the U.S. Navy. McDermott was a major supplier of nuclear fuel and boilers for the fleet. When Admiral Hyman Rickover, the father of the nuclear navy, caught wind of the plan, he was alarmed enough to summon Lynott and another executive to Washington. Lynott says he and his colleague spent half a day waiting outside Rickover's office until they realized the admiral was snubbing them and had left the building. They flew back to New Orleans on their private jet without meeting Rickover. Eventually, the navy set aside its concerns about Panama, Lynott says. "They were reassured there was nothing there but a post office box," he says. "We weren't moving anything."

McDermott disclosed the plan publicly on October 28, 1982. The next day, the *New Orleans Times-Picayune* quoted the company's chairman, who assured the community that "no changes in the operations and management of the company are planned, and the principal executive offices will remain in New Orleans." Shareholders had no objection, and by December, the address change was official. Kraus hung a skull and crossbones in his office, a nod to Panama's piratical past.

Once the deal was announced, McDermott rushed to complete it as quickly as possible, according to Carr Ferguson, who was a federal tax prosecutor before he joined Davis Polk. They were hoping to reduce the chance the Treasury Department would learn about it and ask Congress to block it. As it was, no one heard from the Treasury until the following January, when Ferguson got a call from a top tax official he knew there.

"Carr, you can't do this," Ferguson remembers the official saying.

"That was my first impression," Ferguson replied, "but we worked at it pretty carefully, and we think we can."

"You're going to have to prove that in court to me."

Move down to Panama!
Think of our painful chagrin:
The Feds will be cheerful,
and we will be tearful
'Cause we'll all end up in the pen!

The IRS fought the case for seven years, giving up in 1989 only after a federal appeals court upheld a U.S Tax Court decision in the company's favor.

In 1984, Congress passed a law specifically designed to prevent more McDermott-type arrangements. But don't bet against the imagination of tax lawyers. A decade later, a company in El Paso that made curling irons and hair dryers found a way to create a foreign parent in Bermuda without triggering the McDermott rule. More laws and regulations followed, in 1994, 2004, and 2009, but the deals just kept coming, each permutation more complicated than the last. Somewhere along the way, tax lawyers started calling them inversions because they turn a company's corporate structure upside down.

.   .   .

However helpful the Panama Scoot was for avoiding taxes, the new address couldn't protect McDermott from getting clobbered by an oil slump. Lower energy prices and an economic downturn led to a series of losses during the 1980s, Kraus says. Later, the unit that supplied the navy's nuclear fuel was engulfed by asbestos claims. After Hurricane Katrina in 2005, McDermott moved its corporate headquarters to Houston. It closed its remaining office in downtown New Orleans last year.

In a way, Admiral Rickover's beef with McDermott got a second life in 2007, when Congress passed a law banning federal contracts for inverted companies. Eventually, McDermott was forced to spin off the unit that worked with the navy to avoid losing all its contracts.

Kraus says he hasn't thought much about inversions since his retirement in 1989, nor has he followed the debate in Washington this year. He remains proud of his work. When a congressional committee in the 1980s complained that the McDermott deal made a "mockery" of the tax code, Kraus says, he half-jokingly called it "the crowning achievement of my career."

"The law is an unintelligible monstrosity, and it's Congress's fault," says Kraus, who still has a small Lucite trophy commemorating the Panama deal. He uses it as a paperweight.

A few months after Carroll's victory over the IRS, he and his wife, Luceil, threw the party at their apartment. A video survives of the moment when, to his surprise, his colleagues began performing *Charlie's Lament*, named for Kraus. A musically inclined lawyer in the tax department, William Weigel, wrote the libretto and recruited a professional tenor and soprano through his church choir. Carroll listened from an armchair, and at the finale he clapped and rose. Somebody called for a speech.

"I wrap myself in the American flag," he said. "And I say, without the slightest fear of successful contradiction—blah, blah, blah, blah!"

Carroll retired later that year. He didn't play a role in the copycat deals that eventually followed McDermott, nor did he seek any recognition. In a tax journal in 2007, a law professor referred to the McDermott deal's creator as "a brilliant tax lawyer (I don't know who)."

One of Carroll's two sons, Brian, recalls that his father, toward the end of his career, reflected on his role in making the tax system even more convoluted. "Look, I did all these crazy things," Carroll told him. "I would really like to see the tax code completely scrapped. The whole business of trying to define income and deductions is pure madness. And I've got no one to thank except myself for creating that."

Carroll died in 2009 at the age of eighty-four. Following his wishes, in lieu of a funeral there were parties with food and wine, including one for his many friends at Davis Polk's Manhattan headquarters. Amid the talk and laughter came the familiar strains, playing over and over again on a TV in the next room:

The Feds may be screaming
But we all are beaming
'Cause we'll never pay taxes no,
Never pay taxes,
Never pay taxes again!

Reuters

First he lobbied against requiring banks to disclose more about the asset-backed securities that helped trigger the Great Recession. Then the attorney Keith Higgins was picked to head the division of the Securities and Exchange Commission charged with writing the rule. The doors at the SEC revolve with predictable results—risky mortgage-backed securities remain hidden off the books at banks, hedge funds, and private-equity groups. "What's playing out is exactly what we were worried about," said Sheila Bair, the former chairwoman of the Federal Deposit Insurance Corp. What possibly could go wrong?

23. How Wall Street Captured Washington's Effort to Rein in Banks

New York—In the aftermath of the 2008 financial crisis, Keith Higgins was certain: Banks weren't to blame.

Higgins, a top attorney at prominent law firm Ropes and Gray LLP, was chairman of an American Bar Association committee on securities regulation. As such, he lobbied strenuously against a rule U.S. regulators were drafting that would require banks to disclose a lot more about asset-backed securities like those that had just torpedoed the economy.

In letters to the Securities and Exchange Commission, Higgins argued that divulging more details about the mortgages and other financial products that go into such securities would only confuse investors. And it was investors, with "insufficient understanding and . . . commitment" to their investments, who had been the real cause of the crisis, he argued in a July 2008 letter.

Then, in May 2013, as the SEC was still hashing out the rule, Higgins was tapped to lead the very 500-person SEC division that was writing it.

When the final version of Reg AB II came out last year, disclosure rules advocated by many within the agency had been stripped out. Of particular concern: Banks could continue to sell asset-backed securities to institutional investors on the private market with no new disclosure requirements.

Reg AB II was one of many rules Congress ordered up in the 2010 Dodd-Frank Wall Street Reform Act to fill regulatory holes in the market for asset-backed securities. An unprecedented expansion of this multi-trillion-dollar market, in which banks repackage mortgages and other assets into complex securities and sell them to investors, lay at the heart of the financial crisis.

But as the evolution of Reg AB II suggests, banks and their advocates have managed to preserve many of the industry's precrisis practices by focusing lobbying efforts on obscure corners of the regulatory world, far from the glare of congressional debate or public scrutiny. Many of these agencies are staffed by appointees from the industry they regulate and return to it when their stints are over.

"The banks have done an end run around all the disclosure efforts," said Thomas Adams, a securitization lawyer at Paykin Krieg and Adams LLP.

Four of the six lawyers now in the leadership of the American Bar Association committee that Higgins chaired have worked for the SEC's Division of Corporation Finance. And between 1993 and 2006, the proportion of financial-services veterans on the Financial Accounting Standards Board (FASB) went from 0 to 25 percent, according to a 2012 Harvard Business School study.

Higgins declined to comment.

SEC chief of staff Lona Nallengara said the selection of Higgins to run the division was a reflection of his status as "a respected securities practitioner with thirty years' experience."

Nallengara, who was acting director of the Division of Corporation Finance for seven months before Higgins took over, said the decision to remove disclosure requirements for private offerings from Reg AB II was made before Higgins arrived. "Keith had no influence on that decision," he said.

Like the SEC when it was weighing rules on asset-backed securities, FASB, the private group that sets accounting standards for public companies, came under political pressure to tighten rules blamed for exacerbating the financial crisis. Critics said FASB had made it too easy for banks to stash mountains of securitized loans in off-balance-sheet vehicles based in the Cayman Islands, hiding their exposure to risks that eventually swamped them and the global economy.

Here, too, banks pushed back hard. And here, too, their protests reached sympathetic ears. Ultimately, FASB's rules barely dented the size of banks' off-book holdings.

The practical effect of these lobbying efforts has been obvious.

Thanks to the private-market loophole in the SEC's Reg AB II, banks are selling a greater share of securitized debt than ever on private markets—largely off the radar of regulators and watchdogs.

Residential mortgage-backed securities tendered on the private market jumped to 78 percent of all new offerings last year from 46 percent in 2013 and just 10 percent in 2007, according to data obtained by Thomson Reuters. The privately sold share for commercial mortgage-backed securities jumped to 83 percent from 37 percent in 2013.

The markets for asset-backed securities today are a fraction of what they were in the run-up to the crisis. But they are showing strong signs of revival. What bothers some current and former regulators and industry watchers is that much of the regulatory framework that enabled the crisis remains in place.

"What's playing out is exactly what we were worried about," said Sheila Bair, former chairwoman of the Federal Deposit Insurance Corp. "Most everything is going into these private markets where regulations require little visibility of what's happening."

With their access to off-balance-sheet entities largely preserved, the banks continue to hold vast sums of securitized loans offshore and off their books. Together, JPMorgan Chase and Co., Bank of America Corp., Citigroup, Wells Fargo and Co., Goldman Sachs Group Inc., and Morgan Stanley hold nearly $3.3 trillion of securitized loans in off-balance-sheet entities.

"I still think there is significantly more risk there than is being reflected on banks' balance sheets," Bair said.

It isn't just the banks. As hedge funds and private equity funds have ramped up high-risk lending in recent years, their use of off-balance-sheet vehicles has ballooned. For example, KKR and Co. LP's reported exposure to loss from off-balance-sheet entities has risen tenfold since 2010. A KKR spokesperson said less than half of the firm's off-balance-sheet entities are composed of corporate loans originated by KKR and securitized into collateralized loan obligations but declined to provide numbers or other information.

Robert W. Stewart, a spokesman for the Financial Accounting Foundation (FAF), which oversees FASB, said the new rules "resulted in a dramatic increase" of the holdings financial firms and companies in other industries keep on their books. "These standards eliminated long-standing exceptions for securitizations, and that reduced the opportunity for workarounds," he said.

Holding the Bag

Even before the crisis, FASB struggled for years with how banks should account for off-balance-sheet entities and the assets held in them.

Every additional dollar in assets on a bank's balance sheet requires holding more idle cash in capital reserves to cover those assets if they drop in value. The increase in reserves means less revenue and earning power and smaller employee bonuses.

Off-balance-sheet vehicles free banks to make more loans and build assets without having to add to capital reserves. These assets include all sorts of things: Treasury securities, home and commercial real estate mortgages, auto loans, even "junk" loans used to finance leveraged buyouts. Banks bundle the assets into securities, sell the securities to investors, and then park the assets in separately incorporated off-balance-sheet vehicles.

In theory, if one of these vehicles fails because the underlying assets sour—as, for example, when large numbers of homeowners default on their mortgages—the bank does not have to bail it out.

In practice, they often do—to preserve their reputations in a lucrative market, and because specific asset-backed securities often carry implicit or explicit guarantees that leave banks legally liable to make investors whole.

"Repeatedly, constantly, when the new off-balance-sheet entity got into financial difficulty, the bank bailed out the entity that they supposedly didn't have any more connection with," said Halsey Bullen, who was with FASB from 1983 to 2006, much of that time managing financial instruments projects.

FASB sought to address the issue several times before the crisis—to no avail. It tightened rules on special purpose entities, the off-balance-sheet vehicles that played a big role in the collapse of Enron Corp in 2001. But banks simply started using alternatives called qualifying special purpose entities (QSPEs).

Again, in 2005, as banks were stuffing huge amounts of securitized subprime mortgages into QSPEs, FASB chairman Robert Herz began to push for change. Earlier in his career, Herz turned down a shot to be U.S. chief executive officer of the accounting giant PriceWaterhouse Coopers, where he was a partner, rather than give up his campaign to remake accounting standards. Now, he wanted to toughen the rules and require banks to put more loans back on their balance sheets.

"Clearly there were lots of things that had been given off-balance-sheet treatment that should not have been designated as such," said Herz. "All the big Wall Street firms were doing it."

Herz was opposed, former FASB officials said, by former JP Morgan vice president Leslie Seidman—a FASB member known to some of her critics as "Loophole Leslie" for her advocacy of bank-friendly accounting rules.

Herz's effort fizzled out. "I started to realize that some people on the board didn't want to get anywhere," said Don Young, a FASB board member at the time.

Seidman said she objected to the initial proposals because they would have made the rules more complex and created more exceptions.

Then, in 2008, the U.S. housing bubble burst, and with it, the market for mortgage-backed securities.

Citigroup announced that it was on the hook for more than $100 billion in loans it had placed in off-balance-sheet vehicles. All told, the biggest U.S. banks wound up bringing back onto their books more than $300 billion of guarantees for off-balance-sheet loans and bonds, according to a report by RiskMetrics Group Inc. The banks paid out billions more in lawsuits to investors demanding that they take responsibility for off-balance-sheet loans.

Under pressure from Congress, FASB again took up the issue. Banks bombarded the board with comment letters and tasked full-time staff to sway it as it started drafting new rules.

Force banks to report too much lending on their balance sheets, Citigroup, Bank of America, and other banks argued, and credit available to ordinary Americans would shrink. Make them disclose too much information about what was going off-balance-sheet, and it would just confuse investors.

In September 2008, Young, the FASB member, told a congressional hearing: "There was unending lobbying of the FASB" to preserve banks' right to continue stashing loans off their balance sheets.

Even so, FASB's draft rules did away with QSPEs. That left something known as a variable-interest entity, which carried a tougher standard banks had to meet to secure off-balance-sheet treatment. But then, as the lobbying continued, FASB relaxed the rules for VIEs, essentially closing one loophole while opening another.

"The changes were all in the direction of watering it down," said Marcus Stanley, director of Americans for Financial Reform, a consumer group in Washington, D.C.

There are concrete measures of the banks' lobbying success. When FASB published the first draft of the rules in 2008, Citigroup warned in its annual report that it expected to increase its risk-weighted assets by $100 billion as a result of having to bring loans onto its books.

A year later, after FASB issued its final draft of the new rules, Citigroup brought just $24 billion in risk-weighted assets back onto its books. At the time, it had $557.5 billion in off-balance-sheet loans.

The new rules took effect on January 1, 2010. The top six U.S. banks brought about $400 billion of loans back onto their books, a 2010 Deloitte Study found, a fraction of the $4 trillion of loans—mostly mortgages—those banks then held off their balance sheets.

That August, Herz walked out of a FASB meeting and resigned. He said at the time that he wanted to spend more time with his family. Several people close to him said FAF, the overseer of FASB, forced out Herz amid growing backlash against his tough stances on some accounting rules important to banks.

Stewart, the FAF spokesman, declined to comment on the circumstances surrounding Herz's departure.

The six-person committee overseeing the selection process for Herz's successor included a former chief investment officer of the Swiss bank UBS AG; the managing partner of Brown Brothers Harriman and Co., one of the largest private banks in the United States; a former American Express vice president; and a lawyer from Brown and Associates, a law firm that caters to financial industry clients.

They chose Seidman, the first former bank executive—rather than auditor—to hold the top spot.

Bank stocks rose on the news.

Seidman's term at FASB ended in 2013. She is now a director at the ratings company Moody's Corp. and on the board of governors of the Financial Industry Regulatory Authority, Wall Street's self-regulatory group.

Private Matters

A few months after FASB published the final version of its new accounting rules, the SEC released a draft of Reg AB II.

The rule represented regulators' effort to address a big factor in the financial crisis: lack of information about the mortgages, leveraged loans, and other securitized assets that banks had been stuffing into off-balance-sheet entities.

Among other things, Dodd-Frank ordered the SEC to "adopt regulations . . . requiring each issuer of an asset-backed security to disclose, for each tranche or class of security, information regarding the assets backing that security."

An early draft of the rule would have required, for example, that a seller of mortgage-backed securities provide "loan tape" to regulators and investors. That's an industry term for a breakdown of all the mortgages in a security, including each borrower's credit history, the loan-to-value ratio of each mortgage, and other measures of risk.

The first draft of the rule applied the stricter requirements to securities sold on both the public and the private markets. SEC rules have long distinguished between investments meant for ordinary mom-and-pop investors and those for wealthy, sophisticated institutional investors.

The mass-market investments are registered with the SEC and require extensive disclosure before they can be offered to the public. The private investments typically aren't registered with the SEC, carry scant disclosure requirements, and are sold to "accredited investors" considered savvy enough to know what they are buying.

That distinction fell apart during the financial crisis, when it became clear that supposedly sophisticated investors were holding vast stores of toxic mortgage-backed securities. "The disaster was way worse in unregistered private markets during the crisis," said a senior industry regulator. "Not addressing that market did not seem to be addressing the crisis."

SEC staff overwhelmingly supported the rule, according to people inside the agency. So, too, did two important SEC constituencies: investors, who believed the rule would make it easier to assess the quality of the securities, and ratings agencies, whose failure to accurately rate such securities landed them in hot water in 2008.

The banks, however, opposed the early draft. In dozens of comment letters to the SEC, they argued that the additional disclosures would saddle them with an unnecessary and costly burden that would cripple the securitization industry and in turn dry up credit for millions of Americans.

Banks were helped by a particularly vocal and effective advocate: the American Bar Association. The ABA's Committee on the Federal Regulation of Securities—that's the committee with four former SEC employees—wrote ninety-four comment letters to the SEC and other regulators after the crisis, making it one of the most prolific commenters on SEC rules. Nearly all of the comments parroted letters from banks and financial industry lobbyists.

Higgins, chair of the committee when the SEC started drafting Reg AB II, personally signed forty-six of the letters. He also was one of Ropes and Gray's top securities lawyers, advising clients such as Hasbro Inc. and Reebok International Ltd.

Time and again, he argued that investors had only themselves to blame for their losses in the financial crisis. "These problems have been compounded in the structured finance markets not by insufficient information, but by insufficient understanding of the information that is already available to investors," he wrote in one letter. "Rather than needing more information, these investors need both the commitment and the tools to analyze and distill the information that is already available."

The ABA's lobbying carried particular weight with the SEC because of the banks' growing reliance on the courts to fight reforms they opposed. In the year that followed 2010 passage of Dodd-Frank, the SEC churned out an average of 5.5 new rule proposals a month, one of the fastest rule-making clips in SEC history. Rules governing swaps, whistleblowers, and reporting of executive compensation were among dozens of proposals the agency issued.

Then, on July 22, 2011, the U.S. Circuit Court of Appeals in Washington, D.C., struck down an unrelated SEC rule mandated by Dodd-Frank that would have made it easier for shareholders to replace company directors. The court said SEC staff hadn't done a sufficient cost-benefit analysis of the new rule.

The ruling, which was sharply critical of the SEC's rule-making process, "intimidated the agency," said Barbara Roper, director of investor protection for the Consumer Federation of America and a member of the SEC's Investor Advisory Committee.

SEC rule making ground to a halt. Since the court decision, the SEC has published less than one new draft rule a month.

In May 2013, one month after Mary Jo White was sworn in as SEC chairwoman, she tapped Higgins to be director of the agency's Division of Corporation Finance, in charge of writing the rule he had lobbied against. Some inside the SEC were shocked.

Higgins was close to White's husband, John White, a partner at Cravath, Swaine, and Moore LLP who had himself chaired the SEC division when Higgins was head of the ABA committee, according to people who know both men.

John White and Mary Jo White declined to comment.

On August 27 last year, fifty-two months after the original draft proposal of Reg AB II was floated, the SEC adopted the final version. The 683-page rule detailed a raft of new disclosure requirements for asset-backed securities—but only for those registered with the SEC for general offer to the public. For the same securities sold on the private market, disclosure requirements remained scant.

SEC chair White said the new rules would ensure that investors "have full information, the tools, and the time to understand potential investments and the nature and extent of associated risks."

In the end, 2014 saw a bigger share than ever of asset-backed securities being sold on private markets, with little disclosure or regulatory oversight.

Bloomberg

One thing that Julisaa Arce remembers from growing up poor in Taxco, about a hundred miles southwest of Mexico City, is watching a Spanish-language version of *Dennis the Menace* that featured a recreational vehicle. "So when I was a little kid in Mexico my aspiration in life was to live in a mobile home like the Americans," she says. She did a bit better than that. Max Abelson documents how an undocumented Mexican immigrant went from selling funnel cakes to derivatives and became a young star at Goldman Sachs, the country's preeminent investment bank.

Max Abelson

24. How an Undocumented Immigrant from Mexico Became a Star at Goldman Sachs

Sitting at her desk at Goldman Sachs, Julissa Arce is doing her best to keep it together. It's September 2007. Her father is dying in Taxco de Alarcón, a small and hilly city in Mexico, and she has just hung up after a call from her sister with bad news. Arce stands and leaves the row where she and her colleagues create derivatives and market them to rich people. She walks down the hall, opens the bathroom door, and locks herself in a stall.

"Do not be anxious about anything," she says under her breath, repeating Philippians 4:6. "Do not be anxious about anything." Then she straightens, washes her face, and returns to work. Her banker colleagues can't understand why she won't get on a plane to see her father. Arce tells them that her family will keep her posted and she might be leaving tomorrow. There is no crying on the private wealth management floor.

The overachievers at Goldman Sachs aren't all the same. Some have been valedictorians or navy SEALs or the sons or grandsons of the company's bankers. Some will stop at nothing to amass a fortune; others are patient. And at least one was an undocumented immigrant. Arce, who turns thirty-two in March, owed her bright career on Wall Street to fake papers bought for a few hundred dollars in a stranger's living room in Texas. Over seven years at Goldman Sachs, she rose from intern to analyst, associate, then vice president, later becoming a director at Merrill Lynch. When her father died in Taxco hours after the 2007 phone call, she didn't leave to see her family because with her bogus papers she couldn't have come back.

•　　　•　　　•

Arce was eleven when she moved to San Antonio from Mexico. Despite arriving with little English, she joined the basketball, softball, cross-country, and dance teams; the student council; a Renaissance club; and two honors societies within a few years. She's still intense. She likes *The Seven Habits of Highly Effective People* and *How to Win Friends and Influence People* and is eager to explain, without irony, why they're illuminating. She does CrossFit and can hold 150 pounds behind her head. "You have to have a very A-type personality," she says about weightlifting, sipping a beer in Ulysses, a bar three blocks south of Wall Street. "This workout—*it's* not going to win. *I'm* going to win."

She didn't have to adjust to Goldman Sachs's culture of undisguised ambition because she embodied it. A few weeks into her first summer there, as an intern in 2004, before her senior year of college, she arranged to have coffee with a managing director whose team she admired. She told him she had learned a lot and was ready for something faster. "I want to play basketball and go up and down the court," she told him. When she followed up with a handwritten thank-you card at the end of the summer, the managing director told her to expect good news.

A sharp kind of dread sank in after Goldman offered her a full-time position. She was afraid of what could happen when one of the world's most sophisticated companies examined her fake green card and Social Security number, took her fingerprints, and ran a background check. She had a recurring dream about being caught: She was sitting in an investment bank office. No one had to tell her she was being deported or threaten her; she just knew what was to come next. Then she'd wake up.

But Goldman never did discover her secret. It was 2005 and a good time to become one of the 23,000 employees of Wall Street's most profitable securities firm. "I was like, sky's the limit," she says. "I'm in."

·   ·   ·

Taxco is about one hundred miles southwest of Mexico City. Arce remembers houses all painted white, tourists who flocked there for the silver work, and a dubbed version of *Dennis the Menace* called *Daniel el Travieso*. In one episode a flatbed truck moves the mean neighbor's house, and in another he drives an RV. "So when I was a little kid in Mexico my aspiration in life was to live in a mobile home like the Americans," she says. "Then when I got here I was like, 'Oh!'"

Her parents left Taxco regularly to sell jewelry in Texas. They got her a tourist visa so she could join them, and on one trip the family simply stayed. They moved into an apartment in San Antonio and then a house one block from the interstate. She went to a local Catholic school and took to math right away, eventually placing in the honors track. She remembers a classmate raising his hand to ask how a Mexican could possibly keep up.

Arce was fourteen when her visa expired. "I knew what that meant," she says. "I became undocumented." Desperate to stay in the country she had come to love, she pitched her parents on a plan to have her friend Tiffani's family adopt her. The Arces didn't go for that, or her half-hearted suggestion at age sixteen that they pay a gay U.S. citizen who worked with the family to marry her.

She also wanted to be rich. "I just had this idea in my head that if I can work my way into this wealth and status, then it won't matter that I'm undocumented," she says. "I thought if I had a bunch of money I would be accepted."

In her senior year of high school, Arce sent out college applications with the Social Security box blank—and got rejections. Just as she was graduating in 2001, a new law made it possible for undocumented Texas students to attend public universities at in-state rates. Five weeks later the director for admissions at the University of Texas at Austin wrote to say her application had been reviewed and she'd been accepted.

She majored in finance. The equations "made sense to me," she says. "There was always a right answer. There wasn't anything ambiguous about it. There was so much ambiguity in my life that I really appreciated that." Antonia Bernal, a leader of the Hispanic Business Student Association that Arce joined, describes her at the time as vibrant and driven. Arce hadn't seen many Hispanic men wearing business suits before joining the club, and she still does a Hollywood swoon when she describes them. Meetings with successful women were just as important. "I could be ambitious and go-getter without seeming greedy and aggressive," she says. "There are all these amazing jobs, and there's all this money to be made." When the group handed out awards one April, it named her its Future Millionaire.

Arce's parents moved back to Mexico in 2001, and she took over a food cart business they left behind. Every Friday she rode a Greyhound bus eighty miles to San Antonio's Market Square to sell funnel cakes with strawberries, whipped cream, and cinnamon. Every Sunday she returned to Austin with money for rent and school.

When the cart lost its spot, Arce couldn't land a new job with her expired tourist visa. And she couldn't stay in college without a job. Getting a fake green card turned out to be unexpectedly simple. She confessed her need to a suite-mate, who connected her to her boyfriend, who introduced her to a woman, who asked her to come to her home. It was a mundane transaction, Arce says, in an average apartment with an average living room. She handed over the money, had her picture taken, and about two weeks later had the forged documents.

They worked. Arce used them to land customer service work on nights and weekends for a debit-card company in Austin and interned for a Major League Soccer team. Then she saw a presentation about summer positions at New York banks. The pay could be $10,000.

"Oh my," she remembers thinking. "That is where I need to go, and that is where I need to be."

·   ·   ·

The most influential document at Goldman Sachs may be a list of ten business commandments written by co-head John Whitehead, who died this year at ninety-two. "Important people like to deal with other important people. Are you one?" no. 8 asks. "Don't waste your time going after business we don't really want," says no. 1. By putting the Goldman thirst for competence, connection, rank, and respect into words, Whitehead set the strike zone for hitters at the bank, including ones born long after he retired in 1984.

The chances of joining them, with 350 summer analysts chosen by the investment banking unit from 17,000 applicants in 2013, are worse than the odds of getting into Harvard University. For those who do make the cut, the competition—for assignments, pay, power—only intensifies. Women do this battle knowing that nine of the company's ten executive officers are men.

Arce got a 2004 internship through a nonprofit called Sponsors for Educational Opportunity, which places Hispanic and black students into summer roles at banks. She liked it at Goldman, where she helped put together presentations for existing clients and searched for new ones among the names of yacht owners. She was asked to return to the firm full-time after graduation in 2005. In New York her career got off to an extraordinary start when she was invited to join a new team that built derivatives for the private wealth division's clients. These were financial products that might, for example, include options whose value would rise 3 percent for every percentage point that an index gained, up to a cap. Arce became a rookie analyst reporting directly to a managing director, making it to the office by seven a.m. to beat her boss, eating a peanut butter and jelly sandwich for breakfast.

If there's something valued more deeply at Goldman than separating the irrelevant from what matters or anticipating issues before they erupt, it might be the dogged pursuit of opportunity. An early performance review praised Arce for all three. She talked to bosses months in advance about what she had to do to make their year-end decision to pay or promote her as easy as possible. She was so forceful that a boss once told her to laugh less loudly, advice she still doesn't follow when discussing ex-boyfriends or her cats, Pancho and Nikko. Her uniform was so consistent that colleagues donned sweater vests and scarves for a photo tribute.

She was also willing to do what others wouldn't. One week, when she was calling colleagues to get a price for a deal, teammates listened as she began raising her voice to a senior colleague she thought was making a bad offer. Then she started yelling. In the end, a boss sided with Arce.

"Julissa is the type of person that a Wall Street firm wants," says a former coworker, Jodi Salsberg. "Somebody who is incredibly driven and hardworking and fiercely loyal to the firm." Clients started asking for her, according to another former colleague, Bryan David Hughes. She looked after younger colleagues, too. "There are a lot of smart people, and the expectation is you should get it the first time," says Hughes, thirty. "Julissa was the person I could go to and say, 'OK, Julissa, explain it to me for the tenth time.'"

Arce and her friends liked to sit back at Ulysses and watch Goldman guys attempting to flirt with women. If a banker came up to her and name-dropped the firm, she would ask what exactly he did there and try to stay polite when he answered that she wouldn't really understand. If he asked about her, she would cordially explain that she structured derivatives at Goldman Sachs for its richest clients.

.   .   .

Perhaps the biggest reason Arce's secret went undiscovered was that no one was looking. At this altitude, people assume that their friends belong. Mark Campbell, who had been hired at the same time, says he knew Arce was from Mexico, and it never occurred to him to question her citizenship. "It seemed to me that she had it all figured out," he says. "You just sort of assume everything is fine."

He explains his reasoning with a story about working construction in college, before joining the bank. When someone showed up at a site in a suit one day, workers bolted, thinking he was from the government. "Those were the people who were undocumented immigrants that I knew," says Campbell, who now works for Morgan Stanley. "I think of people who are here to work in service-related jobs and work their way up for the next generation—but not here to become masters of the universe."

Some days, Arce was tormented. "I don't feel alright," she wrote in a July 2008 diary entry. "I feel the stress in my stomach, in every muscle." At Goldman international experience was crucial, and she knew that her fake papers wouldn't withstand a border crossing. After a clash with a colleague based in London, he suggested it might be good for her to spend some time at the

UK office. Yes, she told him, that makes sense. She stalled. When her own boss was transferred to London, Arce was afraid that the company would ask her to join him—and at the same time furious that she couldn't pursue the opportunity.

In 2008 the global financial system was on the verge of collapse, Goldman's clients were jittery, and the firm was losing money. When Arce opened her mail one day that July, she found a letter from the IRS asking about her tax filings. An operations manager for a unit called Input Correction wanted "more information to process the return accurately." She put it in her closet and tried to forget about it.

"It was terrifying," she says. More letters arrived; she shelved them, too. "You sort of have to force yourself to live in this alternate reality, just pretending like it doesn't really exist."

Arce's anxiety would spike when a colleague looked at her weirdly, or if she was suddenly called into an office. "This is it," she always thought. One day, distracted, she made a mistake on a Japanese trade for a client. She thought her career might end.

Other times she was too busy to worry. She thought it was taking too long to get promoted to associate, and as soon as that came through, she went to work on becoming a vice president. And she started dating someone she had met in college. She liked that he was strong and good at pool, and she felt safe around him, she says.

After her father died in 2007, she thought about taking some of her things on a flight to Mexico and not coming back. Her boyfriend told her he thought getting married might be a solution. "I hope this is not a proposal," she remembers telling him. "Because if it is, it kind of sucks."

It was a proposal, and she said yes. "In retrospect," she says, "I don't think we were ready. But I did love him." Her college friend Bernal, who hosted the small wedding in her building's yard and was a witness and photographer, remembers the ceremony as short and happy.

By 2011, Arce was making $300,000 to $400,000—she won't give the exact amount—and had been promoted to vice president. She replaced her fake green card with a real one from the U.S. government after the wedding. She was legal, elite, and rich. She was also unhappy. The only thing stranger than going from selling funnel cakes in Texas to equity derivatives in New York was how vacant she felt.

Three-and-a-half years after quietly chanting her anxiety prayer in a locked bathroom stall, she took a piece of paper that listed her bonus into the ladies' room. "I made it to this place that I always thought would get me everything I wanted," she says. "But I remember leaving and going to the bathroom with my little letter that said how much money I was being paid and just feeling so empty."

She started a blog whose first posts counted down her last days at Goldman Sachs. "I am nervous in an excited kind of way. In the way that I imagine a QB is nervous in a rivalry game," she wrote. "I feel responsible to the universe to go and live my dream," she posted the next day. Less than a week later she was gone, writing: "Now is time to go ask more questions and hopefully find more answers."

Arce visited her family in Taxco, flew to Europe on a Mexican passport, and paddled down North Carolina's Roanoke River. She thought she could start a website for arranging impromptu vacations, then a business to get community funding for small ventures; both fell through. She and her husband, who moved away for a job, separated. "Life is all about adapting to change, moving when things are shaken up," she wrote on her blog.

In 2012 a coffee with a friend working at Bank of America's Merrill Lynch turned into a job opportunity, and she took it. The role wasn't what she'd thought—mostly project management and compliance strategy. When her boss stopped looking her in the eye, she says, she knew what was going to happen. She was let go last May.

She may have gone back to banking if she hadn't seen a 2013 movie called *Documented*. It follows Jose Antonio Vargas, who was part of a *Washington Post* team that won a Pulitzer Prize in 2008 and came out as an undocumented immigrant in a 2011 *New York Times* essay. "My life on film—I was just so inspired by it," she says. "I basically stalked him."

. . .

Arce is moving to California this March as the development director of Define American, a nonprofit founded by Vargas. The group pushes for rights for undocumented immigrants with projects including a campaign to have newspapers drop the term "illegal immigrant" in favor of "undocumented."

The group faces a backlash against rights for immigrants. Former Texas governor Rick Perry, who signed the bill that allowed Arce to attend college, told a Republican forum in Iowa this year that "if Washington refuses to secure the border, Texas will." Texas senator Ted Cruz asked his fellow Republicans to "show me where you stood up and fought" an executive action on immigration President Obama announced late last year. (In an awkward coincidence, Heidi Nelson Cruz, the senator's wife, worked in the same Goldman Sachs unit, private wealth management, as Arce.)

Making hundreds of thousands of dollars on Wall Street didn't protect Arce from fear. "There is still the stigma that what we did is shameful," she says. "I'm tired of being ashamed for pursuing my dream, for climbing up the ladder, and for having success."

When asked for comment on Arce's story, Goldman Sachs sent a statement from chief executive officer Lloyd Blankfein: "Wouldn't it be great if we could give a home to more of the talented young people who come to this country for an education and want to apply their energy and skills to supporting our economy?" Goldman now verifies information from job applicants against government records, according to two people at the firm who asked not to be identified discussing its vetting process.

In August, Arce arrived at a courthouse in Lower Manhattan to become a U.S. citizen. She struggled to speak and had to take a breath before reciting the Oath of Allegiance. Her passport came in the mail in September.

She got tattoos after quitting Goldman, including a line linking moles on her left arm. "I guess I just always felt everything happens for a reason, and I just have to connect the dots," she says. "And the one here says Redeemed." She crooks her arm up by her head. "I always sleep like this, so when I wake up every morning it's the first thing I see. It reminds me that no matter what happens, no matter how I feel, I have been redeemed."

Contributors

MAX ABELSON writes about Wall Street's money and power for Bloomberg News, where his work sometimes appears in *Bloomberg Businessweek*. He was a *New York Observer* reporter until 2010, and before that a *Yale Daily News* arts editor.

STEPHANIE BAKER, a graduate of the London School of Economics and Political Science, is a senior writer at Bloomberg who has written about race horses, hedge-fund managers, tax evasion, and Russian billionaires. She joined Bloomberg in 1998, having worked as a reporter for the *Moscow Times* and a correspondent for Radio Free Europe/Radio Liberty.

ADRIAN CHEN is a freelance journalist and a contributing editor for *The New Inquiry* who has written extensively about Internet culture. Chen joined *Gawker* in November 2009 as a night shift editor, graduating from an internship position at *Slate*.

KURT EICHENWALD is a contributing editor with *Vanity Fair* and author of four books, one of which, *The Informant*, was made into *The Informant!*, a motion picture.

ZEKE FAUX is a Wall Street reporter for Bloomberg News in New York and a contributor to Bloomberg's *Businessweek* magazine. He is a graduate of Cornell University and previously wrote about minor-league baseball for the *Brooklyn Paper*. He lives in Brooklyn with his wife.

FRANKLIN FOER is a fellow at the New America Foundation. He edited *The New Republic* for eight years.

JONATHAN JONES is an investigative journalist based in San Francisco, focusing on issues pertaining to business and human rights.

In 2013, he cowrote "Life and Death in Assisted Living," an in-depth investigation into the assisted-living industry, with A. C. Thompson of *ProPublica*.

SEBASTIAN JONES is a 2014–15 Investigative Journalism Fellow at Harvard University's Edmond J. Safra Center for Ethics. Previously, he was a 2014 Alicia Patterson Foundation Fellow and has worked for *The Nation*, *ProPublica*, and *Washington Monthly*. His articles have appeared in a variety of outlets including the *Washington Post* and *USA Today*.

CHARLES LEVINSON was named Reuters' investigative editor in September 2014. Before joining Reuters, he was at the *Wall Street Journal*, where he covered white-collar crime. Previously, he spent ten years in the Middle East covering the Iraq war, Israel's wars in Lebanon and Gaza, the ups and downs of the peace process, and the sweep of the Arab Spring in Tunisia, Egypt, Libya, Syria, and Bahrain.

ERIC LIPTON is two-time winner of the Pulitzer Prize and an investigative reporter in the Washington Bureau of the *New York Times*, where he writes about corporate agendas and lobbying, covering industries including financial services, energy, telecommunications, and pharmaceutical. He previously worked at he *Washington Post* and the *Hartford Courant*, where he won a Pulitzer for a series of stories he cowrote on the scientists and engineers responsible for the flaw in the main mirror of Hubble Space Telescope.

ALEXIS C. MADRIGAL is the editor in chief of Fusion, an ABC-Univision joint venture. He's also a visiting scholar at UC Berkeley's Center for Science, Technology, Medicine, and Society, and the author of *Powering the Dream*.

MARK MAREMONT is a senior editor with the *Wall Street Journal*, specializing in investigative articles. He was part of a *Journal* team that won a 2007 Pulitzer Prize and is a three-time winner of the Gerald Loeb Award for business writing.

FRANCESCA MARI is an associate editor at *Texas Monthly*. Her essays, reporting, and criticism have appeared in *New Republic*, the *New York Times*, *The Paris Review*, *Dissent*, and elsewhere.

MARGIE MASON has been covering news in Asia for the Associated Press for more than twelve years, including a decade as regional medical writer. She was posted in Vietnam and is currently based in Indonesia.

ROBIN MCDOWELL has been covering Southeast Asia for the Associated Press for nearly two decades, with postings in Cambodia, Thailand, and Indonesia. She is currently based in Myanmar.

MARTHA MENDOZA has been covering domestic and international news for the Associated Press for two decade, as a national and investigative reporter. She is currently based in the Silicon Valley.

ZACHARY MIDER is a reporter for Bloomberg News in New York, where he has covered topics including campaign finance, tax avoidance, and mergers and acquisitions. He lives in New Jersey with his wife and three children.

HUGO MILLER covers legal news across Switzerland, France, and other countries from Geneva and also reports on asset freezing, money laundering, and other financial crimes. He joined Bloomberg in 2003, reporting in both North America and Europe, working in Bloomberg's Toronto bureau until moving to Geneva last year.

T. Christian Miller is an award-winning investigative reporter, author, and war correspondent working for *ProPublica*.

Gretchen Morgenson, who won the Pulitzer Prize in 2002 for her "trenchant and insightful" coverage of Wall Street, is assistant business and financial editor and a columnist at the *New York Times*. She has covered the world financial markets for the *Times* since May 1998.

Sarah Maslin Nir was born in Manhattan and graduated from Columbia University and the Columbia Graduate School of Journalism, is a staff reporter for the *New York Times*, covering Queens. Before joining the *Times* in August 2011, she had lived in London and had freelanced in both London and New York for national and international newspapers, including the *New York Times*.

Mary Pilon is the author of *The Monopolists: Obsession, Fury, and the Scandal Behind the World's Favorite Board Game* (Bloomsbury 2015).

Jessica Pressler is a features writer at *New York* magazine who balances out the sometimes mind-bending nature of writing about The Business World by extracting skin, makeup, and life advice from the Hollywood celebrities she profiles for *Elle*, *GQ*, and *Allure*. She lives in Brooklyn.

Catherine Rampell writes a semiweekly, nationally syndicated opinion column for the *Washington Post*. Catherine previously worked at the *New York Times* as an economics reporter, theater critic, the founding editor of the award-winning Economix blog, and guest columnist for the *New York Times Magazine*'s "It's the Economy" column.

Investigative reporter **Raquel Rutledge** has won two Pulitzer Prizes for local reporting and also has won the Goldsmith Prize for Investigative Reporting, the Worth Bingham Prize for Investigative Journalism, and a George Polk Award. She worked for the *Waukesha Freeman* and the *Colorado Springs Gazette* before joining the *Journal Sentinel* in 2004.

LESLIE SCISM is a news editor at the *Wall Street Journal*. She joined the paper in 1993, following several years at the *Philadelphia Daily News* and the *Bucks County Courier Times*. She has a MBA from Columbia Business School and a BA in journalism from UNC-CH.

MARCUS STERN shared a Pulitzer Prize for National Reporting for an investigation that led to the bribery conviction of Congressman Randy "Duke" Cunningham, a Republican from San Diego County, California. He worked for Copley News Service for nearly twenty-five years and has worked at *ProPublica*.

CLAIRE SUDDATH is a writer for Bloomberg's *Businessweek* magazine. Before that she worked for four years as a writer for *Time*, covering music, culture, and national news stories. She's a graduate of Vanderbilt University and the Columbia University Graduate School of Journalism. She lives in Brooklyn.

RANDALL SULLIVAN is a former newspaper columnist and magazine journalist who has won a number of national awards (including the Robert F. Kennedy Journalism Award and the William Randolph Hearst Feature Writing Award). He is also an author who has written three books nominated for the Pulitzer Prize and a screen writer. He is a contributing editor at *Rolling Stone* a regular contributor to *Wired*.

JORDAN WEISSMANN is *Slate*'s senior business and economics correspondent.

Permissions

the Investigative Fund at the Nation Institute. Reprinted by permission of Marcus Stern and Sebastian Jones.

"Firestone and the Warlord," by T. Christian Miller and Jonathan Jones. Published by *ProPublica*, November 18, 2014. © Pro-Publica. Reprinted by permission. www.propublica.org

"Lobbyists, Bearing Gifts, Pursue Attorneys General," by Eric Lipton, from the *New York Times*, October 20, 2014. © 2014 The New York Times. All rights reserved. Used by permission and protected by the Copyright Laws of the United States. The printing, copying, redistribution, or retransmission of this Content without express written permission is prohibited.

"Killer Pharmacy: Inside a Medical Mass Murder Case," by Kurt Eichenwald. From *Newsweek*, April 16, 2015. © 2015 IBT Media. All rights reserved. Used by permission and protected by the Copyright Laws of the United States. The printing, copying, redistribution, or retransmission of this Content without express written permission is prohibited.

"Gasping for Action," Watchdog Report by Rachel Rutledge. From the *Milwaukee Journal Sentinel*, June 20, 2015. © Copyright 2015, Journal Sentinel, Inc. All Rights Reserved.

"Young Financier's Insurance Empire Collapses," by Mark Maremont and Leslie Scism. From the *Wall Street Journal*, March 20, 2015. Copyright © 2015 Dow Jones & Company, Inc. All Rights Reserved.

"This Twenty-Seven-Year-Old Made Millions Riding the Death Spirals of Penny Stocks," by Zeke Faux. Originally published by Bloomberg *BusinessWeek*, March 12, 2015. Used with permission by Bloomberg. © 2015. All rights reserved.

"The Greatest Tax Story Ever Told," by Zachary Mider. Originally published by Bloomberg.com, December 18, 2014. Used with permission by Bloomberg. © 2014. All rights reserved.

"How Wall Street Captured Washington's Effort to Rein in Banks," by Charles Levinson, from reuters.com, April 9, 2015.